EXPERIENCE MONTANA

A TOURIST'S GUIDE TO MONTANA: BIG SKY COUNTRY AND THE LAST BEST PLACE

LM TAYLOR

CONTENTS

Part III
SOUTHWEST MONTANA—A TAPESTRY OF HERITAGE

Part IV

SOUTHEAST MONTANA—
EXPLORING THE PLAINS

INTRODUCTION

Montana is known as the "Treasure State," the "Last Best Place," or "Big Sky Country" for a reason. Its majestic attractions, scattered with cultural and historical gems, invite adventurous discovery. The first word that comes to mind when someone says Montana, is "space": grandiose landscapes where the great plains and imposing mountains meet, making the traveler believe that anything is possible.

It's *the* place to visit if you are a nature lover or wildlife explorer. The open spaces will delight families, sports adventurers, as well as any geological and archaeological treasure hunter. History buffs will delight in nostalgia from yesteryear. Even art lovers will be stunned and inspired. You can lose yourself in the abundance of 7,000-year-old glaciers, lakes, hot springs, mountains, prairies, and forests while meeting bison and bears, spotting golden eagles, or following trout as they glide through abundant streams.

Here, you can experience all four seasons in one day with the state's extreme weather conditions of temperatures rising and falling to 100 degrees in one day! (Montana holds the record for the largest temperature change in history in 1972, when the range changed 103 degrees in 24 hours—from -54 to 49 degrees Fahrenheit).

Did you know that mining and agriculture are the two most important revenue-generating industries in Montana? It's a prominent livestock farming state. Its motto *"Oro y Plata,"* meaning gold and silver, is based on the historical sources of its gold and silver deposits discovered in 1852. According to the Editorial Staff of The Fact File:

Coal lies underneath about thirty-five percent of Montana, part of what may be the largest coal basin on earth. If all of Montana's coal reserves were mined and the mines continued production at their current rate, the coal would run out in about 3,000 years. (2019, para 27)

It's the U.S. state with the third lowest population density per square mile, around six to seven people per square mile, behind only Alaska and Wyoming. This frontier county, where the countryside comprises vast landscapes of uninhabited natural splendor, even has more cows than humans!

Glacier National Park is a UNESCO World Heritage Site. The spectacular mountain scenery is interspersed with 26 glaciers and landforms, 200 lakes, prairies, forests, alpine landscapes, and rivers that feed the abundant ecosystem of its fauna and flora. Combined with Waterton Lakes National Park in Canada, Glacier Park became the first International Peace Park in 1932. Parts of Yellowstone National Park (another UNESCO site) also spread into parts of Montana.

Prepare to be swept away on an exhilarating journey through Montana's untamed diverse landscapes. Adventure, self-discovery, and the raw spirit of the wild converge in generous space to ignite your wanderlust. Montana's endless big-sky landscapes will leave you longing for your own epic adventure.

This book's unique blend of vivid descriptions, thrilling adventures, deep exploration of the transformative power of nature, and precise and personal tips on how to travel hassle-free and explore Montana thoroughly will allow you to immerse yourself in Montana's untamed beauty and connect with your untamed spirit on a profound level.

BOOK ITINERARY

I'll offer information on each region's attractions, hidden gems, and insider tips. Ultimately, I want to enhance your experience in Montana by discovering local hidden gems and comfortably exploring the region—rich with authentic cultural and historic features. I'll incorporate sites that are meaningful for various family dynamics and couples, budget-friendly, extended travel, short visits, off the beaten track, and also popular tourist attractions. Let's create memories together.

I love to discover sites that satisfy my yearning for freedom, grant escape from a monotonous routine, support a sense of adventure, and enhance self-discovery and personal growth through travel experiences. I generally find these moments in unique, lesser-known destinations, hidden gems, and authentic experiences rather than generic tourist attractions. For that reason, I will focus mostly on interests in outdoor activities such as hiking, camping, wildlife watching, photography, stargazing, adventure sports, and exploring nature.

However, to keep my appreciation for local culture, history, and cuisine alive as well, I'll take you with me to some popular sites where we can find these among the crowds. Ultimately, I believe that meaningful traveling is a combination of the known paths as well as the unknown ones. The known paths often lead us to the more remote and isolated stretches, especially when we are willing to get lost!

With that in mind, remember that Montana is a place of diversity. Not only in landscape but also with weather and wildlife threats! You have to come prepared for all seasons, drastic, unexpected temperature changes, unforeseen encounters with dangerous animals, sudden gusts of snow and rain—and all of these in one day, any time of the year (well, almost)! Always have your ten survival tools with you, especially when your itinerary includes remote terrain. Here is a handy site for the items: www.rei.com/learn/expert-advice/ten-essentials.html

Montana means lots of driving in between destinations. I wouldn't venture out here and depend on public transport, especially if you plan to travel to remote destinations. Montana is vast and remote and most places are not well-supported with public transport systems. It's best to have a car, RV, or rental car if you intend to fly in. In winter, you will need snow tires. I also suggest keeping informed about road closures and weather changes to avoid frustrations. Use www.511mt.net for traffic updates throughout Montana. The website also offers an app to download while traveling through the state, providing useful information about road conditions, closures, construction, and traffic backups. Obtain the necessary information before venturing out, remain mindful of drastic weather conditions that may cause impassable road closures, and be sure to enjoy the journey.

I don't intend to plan your trip, as I am sure that your first visit to Big Sky country will entice you to return. I plan to inform you about some authentic places to visit and their true essence so that you can build a list of all your future Montana visits. I'll recommend a few accommodation sites that won't ruin your budget. Alternatively, *Booking.com, VRBO, Airbnb,* and *Expedia* are good sites to find lodgings. One exception to the rule is Dude Ranches: more on that in later chapters. I firmly believe in responsible traveling, respecting communities and their environment, and being mindful of a minimal ecological footprint.

WELCOME TO MAGICAL MONTANA

"The name Montana is based on the Spanish word for mountain (*montaña*). Western Montana is forested and mountainous (part of the Rocky Mountains), but the eastern section is a high barren plain" (State Symbols USA, n.d.). Montana got its name when the area was subdivided from Nebraska in 1864. "She" found her state independence in 1889. Montana is the largest landlocked state in the US. It borders the Canadian states of British Columbia, Alberta, and Saskatchewan and the U.S. states of North Dakota, South Dakota, Wyoming, and Idaho. The defining aspect of Montana is its powerful contrasting geographic features. Rolling grassland plains with scattered hills and rugged Rocky mountain outliers flow into valley regions. The area roars space and grandeur based on the vast expanse between inhabited areas.

Its nickname, Treasure State, is based on its immense mineral wealth. At 147,040 mi^2, Montana is the fourth largest U.S. state and is mostly famous for the Rocky Mountains. This majestic range of mountainous terrain includes about 100 other smaller mountain ranges in the western part of Montana. The highest elevation in the northern end of Yellowstone National Park is at Granite Peak (12,800 ft) in the center of Montana. The Missouri River (America's longest river of nearly 2,485 miles) finds its source in Montana.

The capital city is Helena, and the largest city is Billings. Most parts have scattered human habitation and are known as the Great Plains flowing with yellow grasslands. The state is oriented toward outdoor activities and long-distance socializing, and the basis of escape for suburban outdoor activities are mountaineering, fishing, and adventure sports.

Gray wolves were reintroduced in the 1990s, and bison numbers have increased to a more sustainable count since their threatened extinction in the late 1890s. Apart from the bison and wolves, the immense diversity of animals includes mostly grizzly and black bears, moose, elk, deer, coyotes, and bald eagles. Wildlife remains a primary attraction for tourists.

History Overview

Montana hails much of its development to the discovery of minerals and gold in the 19th century. Euro-Americans were lured by gold-strike stories and as they encroached on indigenous land, inevitable conflict ensued. Most inhabitants trace their roots back to Europe, but Montana has a vast Native American population with seven Indian Reservations, which make up about one-tenth of the population. The tribal nations played a distinctive role in the forming of Montana's history and today, their invaluable part is seen in their rich heritage that spreads across the vast Montana landscape.

The Native American Plains People (famous tribes include the Cheyenne, the Crow, the Blackfoot, the Flathead, and the Kalispell) confirmed their tribes' presence after the 17th century when they were discovered in early 1740 by French explorers François and Louis-Joseph Verendrye. The Lewis and Clark expedition (called the Corps of Discovery) was the first non-Native American exploration in the area that secured land around 1804–06. Shortly after, the fur trade followed, and forts and trading posts were set up to trade with the Native Americans. Catholic missionaries followed a few years later and established a mission close to present-day Stevensville. This was probably the first Montana settlement. In 1889, it became the state of Montana.

By 1820, most of the area had a range of Native American tribes, each with their unique culture, language, and history.

Major Indian wars took place between 1867 and 1877, including the famous battle of The Little Bighorn (1867), also known as Custer's Last Stand. In this battle, the Sioux and Cheyenne defeated Custer and his men in southeast Montana. This site is now a national monument.

Much of the state's early history is based on the area's natural resources, which attracted people from all over. These were mostly concerned with mining industries: copper, coal, gold, lead, silver, zinc, and oil. After the 1860s, gold prospectors flocked to Montana to secure their mineral wealth with land, initiating the gold rush. At this time, the pressure for American settlers increased after the establishment of Bannack, leading to furious fighting with the Native Americans who tried to protect their hunting grounds.

Cattle ranches flourished in the western parts after 1860 with its famous open-range cattle operations on the plains. In 1872, Yellowstone Park was established as the first U.S. national park. In 1880, the Native American tribes were forced to settle in reservations. After the copper boom began in Butte (1883), one of the largest former mining conglomerates in the world by 1915, the Anaconda Company, controlled the state for most of the century.

The post-war era (1945–2000) changed Montana forever. The state moved away from an economy reliant on the extraction of natural resources to a service-based economy. After 1970, the tourism industry became the second largest source of income for the state, while agriculture remained the primary, stable, reliable source of economic strength.

Cultural Overview

An inheritance of the pioneering spirit and Native American heritage remains today: ranches and horses still play a big role. The Wild West, sparked by the gold rush with outlaws, con men, prostitutes, and prospectors were all taking part in the wealth and adventure. Montana's natural splendor—its wildness and cowboy culture—were all enabled by the area's remoteness.

Today, art galleries and museums display these customs and cultures with painting, sculpture, ceramics, and photography while regular events, craft fairs, and festivals celebrate them. Colorful and skilled beaded Native American arts and crafts with intricate designs that adorn household and clothing items are displayed in tribal communities. In addition to this, you may also find leather, woodwork, and weaving articles that represent the diverse cultural heritage.

Bison (or buffalo as the inhabitants call them) are a big part of the cultural spirit. After their near extinction, their importance as part of religious practices and a cultural spirit was revived with deliberate attempts to reestablish their numbers in national parks, ranches, the public domain, and through private conservation efforts. Now these imposing beasts are protected and honored animals again, as their history represents their immense contribution to man's subsistence: providing food, clothing, and weapons for many Native American tribes. Through collective effort, their honor was restored.

Pishkun, also known as the buffalo jump, was a traditional hunting practice practiced by Native American tribes. The method allowed the hunters to kill large numbers of buffalo, but today, there are established protected pickup hunting sites that offer guided tours to explain these hunting methods and their gathering styles.

East Meets West

Dramatic geographical differences between the east and west sides define the state of Montana. The continental divide splits Montana into two diverse sections. Although mountains are a prominent part of Montana, about 60% of its landscape profile consists of grasslands famously known as the great plains or prairies. These flat rolling landscapes (mostly farmland) make up the vast eastern area of Montana.

In the northwest, where Glacier National Park is situated, endangered species (such as wolverines and the Canadian lynx) can be found. Here, the tundra, forests, and prairies combine to create spectacular scenery of the unique ecosystem.

Closer to the central part and moving toward the west, the transition terrain becomes more mountainous, gradually merging away from the grasslands. A variety of mountain ranges appear from here, with increased elevation and higher precipitation and snow. More forests appear, made up of fir and pine trees, such as the Bears Paw Mountains, Big Snowy, Highwood, and Crazy Mountains.

At the southern and central sections, the sheer sandstone cliffs of the Rimrocks appear. In addition to this, rich archaeological evidence confirms the first Montana human presence as far back as 7,000 years. From here, the Rocky Mountains take over and cover the other third of the southwestern parts of Montana. Mountain ranges of the Rockies include the Absaroka, Beartooth, Elkhart, Bitterroot, Big Belt, and Gallatin ranges and the valleys between these mountains contain most of the state's bigger cities, including the capital, Helena. The western area has more lush forests with cascading waterfalls, housing bears and mountain lions, among other mammals.

Because of this vast ecological differences in the state, the climate is shaped by its terrain causing the huge temperature ranges from east to west and also producing the chinook as a result of adiabatic heating from the Rockies. This rare weather phenomenon causes rapid heating as the wind descends westerly from the mountain ranges.

One of the largest oil-producing geological formations in the US stretches into this area from Montana's eastern neighboring states (North and South Dakota), known as the Bakken Formation—covering an area of about 750 square miles. Also, the badlands of Makoshika on the eastern side form dry and rugged eroded formations. The famous Montana artist Charles M. Russell's paintings were inspired by the northern parts close to the badlands, known as the Missouri Breaks. These rugged formations are close to the Missouri River, the largest river in Montana which is about 2,341 miles in length.

The population is mostly made up of northern European descent whose forefathers settled in Montana—adding to its multiculturalism atmosphere and contributing to its diverse linguistic heritage and cuisine. Cultural differences between the east and west is furthermore built on its rugged pioneer history. These differences align with the state's geographical landscapes. Eastern sectors encourage agricultural interests or jobs in the oil industry, while the western areas predominantly cater to tourism, outdoorsy types, and nature adventurers. Eateries have a similar different ambiance: In the east, the atmosphere is more relaxed and family oriented while the western areas include more sophisticated restaurants.

The unique Montana lingo of "cowboy up" is just one of the phrases that are simply unique to Big Sky Country. Native American culture makes up about six percent of Montana's population and all seven Indian cultural tribes reside in reservations where they can continue their traditions. Apart from Native American traditions, western cultures are also supported, such as rodeo gatherings.

Amazing records are held in the state. Perhaps the most famous of these are the largest steer weighing 3,980 pounds, more T-Rex specimens than anywhere in the world, and the largest snowflake. Legends from Montana include Gary Cooper, Sitting Bull, and David Lynch. One defining element that unites the east and west and a variety of cultures is certainly the love for nature. With so much space and only about one million inhabitants, no wonder that nature comes first. Montana has a presence that calls for adventure.

Significance

Montana is known for its natural beauty of forests, vast spaces, expansive peaked mountain ranges, and alpine lakes:

More than 300 peaks exceeding 9,600 feet grace the landscape (James, 2023). And of course, its unique Native American heritage and frontier history immediately comes to mind. But there is much more when thinking of Montana: It's famous for the precious blue gemstone, sapphire, and Montana remains one of the leading producers in the world. Flathead cherries and huckleberries—the latter is the official state fruit—are both used in their famous pies. There are more bookstores per capita than in other U.S. states. Abundant wildlife and rich mineral sources can be found. But mostly, Montana is known for its low inhabitants-to-area ratio, as the third least-densely populated frontier county where cattle outnumber the people.

Landscape

Diverse landscape is synonymous with Montana and we will explore that in this book. Apart from alpine meadows and forests or glaciated lakes nestled between mountainous terrain and abundant streams, the Montana traveler can also choose to enjoy alternative wide open valleys rolling away in yellow prairie fields to a distant horizon.

The Treasure State

Outdoor recreation equals the name Montana. A core 27% of the state (mostly in the western half) is forested. This area contains magnificent national parks, glacier parks with ancient ice, charming towns, deserted gold-rush-day ghost towns, pine forests, snow-capped peaks, and spectacular skylines. It calls for white water rafting, kayaking, world-class skiing, trails off the beaten track, hiking and mountain biking, and the Yellowstone River is a premier fly fishing destination. The Big Sky Resort hails the absolute luxury of alpine bliss with winds ripping through you while you feel like you are on top of the world among the jagged peaks.

Climate

The climate is characterized by abrupt weather changes. The warm winter wind, the chinook, often interrupts the biting cold climate of the plains. Elevational zones closer to the Rockies introduce varied climates ranging between arid and cooler wet weather. The higher elevation zones have vast temperature ranges.

The area has hot summers and cold winters with little annual rain, often prone to drought interrupted by occasional heavy flood rains. Almost 200 days of the year show frost and freezing as Montana is notorious for its freezing cold temperatures below zero degrees during January.

As the elevation increases, the climate becomes wetter and cooler with heavy snowfalls. The extreme and unpredictable weather produces short summers with cold nights, associated with windy, drastic, and unexpected weather changes. All weather conditions are neatly packed in one place!

When to Visit

All year round offers something different: Montana's seasonal changes and each one's treasure trove of sights and experiences enhance a wilderness in tune with nature's rhythms. Any season will keep any adventurer occupied. Peak tourist seasons are both winter (December to February) and summer (July to August), mostly due to a plethora of hiking, water, and skiing activities. But fall and spring draw differently oriented travelers when these shoulder seasons provide quieter journeys as fewer tourists arrive and many local businesses focus on renovations. These seasons turn traveling into a similar experience as the frontier days.

Summer draws mostly families. As the snow melts, the bears come out of hibernation. Abundant wildflowers and festivals delight visitors and many seasonal workers visit the popular resorts. The downside of summer visits is the heat, haziness, regular wildfires, and inflated prices.

Winter draws snowboarding and skiing enthusiasts, and epic wildlife spotting in the northern parts of Yellowstone in the Lamar Valley. The downside of winter is that roads are tricky to navigate, temperatures are dangerously low (be prepared for emergencies), you'll have very little sunshine, and some businesses are closed for the season. March weather can be quite unpredictable.

Traveling from September to November is the best time to avoid crowds and these months include pristine mild weather. You'll encounter fewer tourists, and in October, the leaves display their fall paradise colors, making it a photographer's paradise. There may be some more rain, though.

Budget travelers should aim for spring visits from April to June. (Locals call it the "mud season" because the snow starts to melt.) This is also a good time to visit if you are a 4x4 enthusiast but the downside may be hazardous roads and hazy vistas. However, you will find alternative activities like art galleries and farmers' markets or historical sites to visit and definitely fewer crowds.

National Parks

Montana is rich in national parks that will delight any itinerary. These include parks of historical and cultural significance, as well as many forests, and natural wonders.

- **Glacier National Park:** This park remains the top-rated Montana park with abundant rivers, forests, peaks, lakes, wildlife, and birdlife to enjoy.
- **Yellowstone National Park:** The section that winds into southeastern Montana gives easy access to the park's main geological attractions. In winter, the northern entrance at Gardiner is the only access entrance that remains open.
- **Gallatin National Forest:** A forested and mountainous area filled with hiking and biking opportunities.
- **Waterton-Glacier International Peace Park:** A product of good neighborly relations as it borders Canada. This park has a vast variety of sights and scenic drives.
- **Nez Perce National Historical Park:** Here you'll find 38 important places commemorating the ruggedness and riches of tribal life.

Missouri River

The Missouri is a tributary of the Mississippi River and the 15th-longest river in the world. It starts in the Rockies at

Three Forks, flows through 10 U.S. states as well as two Canadian provinces, and was formed 115,000 years ago. The river feeds a network of fauna and flora that attracts any nature enthusiast with its 150 species of fish and 300 species of birdlife, playing a vital role in the ecosystem. It's mostly famous for its world-class fishing activities with its abundant fishing and hunting spots, which keep campers and outdoor enthusiasts happy and provide ample opportunity for recreational boating. It rightly earns its nickname of "sportsman's paradise" with numerous scenic places alongside the river. The river's flat surface offers a smooth and relaxing canoe sightseeing ambiance.

The river was a place of historic Native American spiritual practices and burials. Lewis and Clark's expedition was the first to explore the river in its entirety after 1804. It has seen the works of commercial traffic, steamboat expeditions, and trading routes and connected the mining villages as the major gateway to open the west to the rest of the US. The Missouri River later became a valuable source of irrigation to the croplands of the area and today remains a major source of tourism, recreation, and hydroelectricity. Adjacent recreational sites from the river are the following:

- **Bowdoin National Wildlife Reserve:** Excellent birdwatching after a migratory bird refuge in 1936 was established, which incorporates wetlands and prairies
- **Missouri Headwaters State Park:** Offering campsites and tipi rentals

- **Giant Springs State Park:** The largest freshwater springs in the US
- **Fort Peck Reservoir:** Famous for remote angling experiences
- **Upper Missouri River Breaks National Monument:** Offering scenic historic trails and unique geological formations
- **Charles M. Russell National Wildlife Refuge:** Locally known as the CMR, is an area of abundant wildlife enhanced by expos of the famous artist's representations

Visitors can follow in the footsteps of Lewis and Clark's historical path at the Fort Union Trading Post National Historic Site. Their path crossed several points along the river, the most iconic one being the Five Falls area, a six-mile amalgamation of five separate prominent falls.

Dude Ranches

Looking for alternative accommodation like a real cowboy? A great option for families and outdoor enthusiasts in Montana is Dude Ranch accommodation.

What Is a Dude Ranch?

This is closest to living like a cowboy! With a variety of ranches: Bespoke to family to rugged and rustic cowboy experiences, the focus remains on being outdoors. Many are similar to yesteryear, but some have a few 21st-century comforts. Some ranches date back to the 1880s, so a plethora of options await your specific needs.

What Does It Offer?

Dude Ranches offer tranquility and unspoiled wilderness. Many are combined with adventures such as scenic guided horseback excursions into rugged areas. Traversing the Old West plains like the cowboys used to do, exquisite fly-fishing experiences on the pristine water streams, or an authentic ranch experience such as cattle herding with overnight camping, rodeo rides, archery, roping, wagon rides, ax throwing, and cooking by campfires—all offer unique getaways.

Many are close to Montana's national parks and luxurious recreational amenities; some include glamping, white water rafting, gourmet cuisine and catering, spa and wellness centers, movie theaters, and bowling or golf courses. Kids activities include workshops, horseback riding, hiking, and even marshmallow roasting specialties. Many cater for romantic getaways with smaller guest numbers and intimately cozy settings in nature, others offer gravel-road remote locations deep in forested mountain areas.

Most are still working ranches to offer a hands-on experience to tourists, but they are mostly known for their warmth and welcoming community experience offering Western hospitality. Some ranches offer winter recreational experiences such as snow-shoeing, sleigh rides, or ski activities. Prices vary between $250 to $2,000 per person per night.

Agritourism

Agriculture is a big part of Montana's lifestyle, making it the perfect environment for an intersection with its other popular economic resource, tourism. Agritourism is the place where agriculture and tourism meet—where farms open their doors to the public and invite connection. With such accommodation, tourists can experience the rural lifestyle, enjoy fresh seasonal products from the farm, and enjoy unique encounters with the countryside at reasonable rates.

Agritourism furthermore offers good family options where all members can relax and enjoy the community spirit. Many include visits to farmers' markets, farm and agricultural tours, and meeting local winemakers or visiting breweries. Taking part in farming activities and educational tours or exploring organic farming and permaculture farming educate and guide the public about sustainable farming practices and informative agricultural production.

Underground Tunnels

The era of prohibition left a legacy of saloon moments in Montana. These underground tunnels housed many speakeasies in various towns during the prohibition. Evidence of these can be found in Havre, and according to records, almost 100 bars operated in the town of Butte. Billings was famous for its bootlegging rumors during the prohibition age. But just as quickly and dramatically as the law changed, the underground town of bars collapsed, and today, these sites can be seen in their state of abandonment, with coats and all still untouched.

Underground tunnels housed restaurants, speakeasies, opium rooms, bordellos, barber shops, dentists, pharmacies, and even a jail. Their sinister reputation remained and now these narrow tunnels—on average 6 ft high and 3 to 4 ft wide —provide interesting stories to soothe secret-hungry visitors. Some remind me of a sordid past, but the history is actually quite fascinating. Butte's underground houses a brothel museum originating from 1890. The brothel operated for nearly 100 years making it America's longest-running brothel.

Havre, in particular, sheltered many Chinese immigrants in the tunnels as they escaped from racist attacks. The underground city became infamous for its sinister and illicit activities. When fires ravaged the town in the early 1900s, many legitimate businesses joined these groups underground to continue their services. Its rough history remained for many years and Havre became known for being the "sum total of all that is vicious and depraved parading openly without restraint" (Wick, 2023a, para 12). In the 1930s, Havre tried to clean up its name and the tunnels fell out of use. The underground tunnels operate daily tours, showcasing historic and mind-boggling scenes

Historic Sites

Montana's Wild West buildings and historic sites ignite memories of yesteryear. The old Wild West and Native American Reserves offer countless displays and regalia at its historic sites and ghost town remains. One of these historic sites is a two-story outhouse building in Nevada City. A visit to this site reminds you to appreciate modern conveniences while savoring the atmosphere of bygone days.

Numerous battles occurred between the United States and Native Indian nations from 1865 onward—mostly Sioux wars and Nez Perce wars. The Great Sioux Wars are considered to be the biggest Indian conflict in America's history, marked by the victorious outcome of the Northern Cheyenne and Lakota warriors over Lt. Colonel George Custer and his men. These sites all hold a sacred element commemorating all the lives lost on the great plains. Other tribal clashes were more tragic and less favorable. Also, these are commemorated on the plains of Montana.

Battlefields and Monuments

Montana remains dedicated to preserving this unique historical significance through its monuments and many battlefields. Noteworthy battlefield sites include the following:

- **Little Bighorn Battlefield National Monument:**
  The famous scenic and sacred site of the 1876 battle between the U.S. 7th Cavalry (led by Custer) and the Sioux and Lakota tribes, led by Chief Sitting Bull. A few hundred American soldiers had to face thousands of Indian warriors defending their way of life and territory.
- **Bear Paw Battlefield:** The site where the Nez Perce Indian tribe surrendered in 1877, about 16 miles from Chinook.
- **Big Hole National Battlefield:** Ten miles south of Wisdom, where a memorial stands in honor of the Nez Perce who died after they were unexpectedly attacked by the U.S. military and removed to a reservation.
- **Wolf Mountain Battlefield:** Commemorating the turning point in the great Sioux wars. The arrival of

Crazy Horse at the southern flank of the Wolf Mountains led to the conclusion of the war. The Native American people were removed from the plains and couldn't roam freely again. After this, European Americans were able to settle in frontier countries, and commercial developments began.

- **Rosebud Battlefield State Park in southeast Montana:** This area comprises a 3,052-acre national park and includes the Crow Indian reservation. Heritage restrictions are maintained in the park.

- **Chief Two Moons Monument:** This was built in 1936 in honor of the Native American chief who fought in the Battle of the Little Bighorn.

- **Fort Benton:** A national historic landmark where most of the fur trading took place. It was established in 1864 as the main artery of Missouri navigation and opened up trading routes to the northwestern regions and Canada. It's also known as the birthplace of Montana.

- **Pompeys Pillar National Monument:** The spectacular sandstone rockface has significant historic drawings and inscriptions, including evidence of the Lewis and Clark expedition.

- **Citadel Rock:** This intrusive fine-grained igneous rock (shonkinite) from the late Cretaceous period in northern Montana, is accessible by boat only close to the Hole-in-the-Wall boat camp. These rocks are more resistant to weathering and thus form prominent landscape protrusions turning them into a spectacular scenic point.

Old Forts

The forts in Montana serve as reminders of early colonizer presence in Native American land. They bear memories of the Indigenous relations and activities that changed the course of history. Numerous forts were erected to manage the Native American movement and confine the tribes to reservations while "protecting" local settlers. These forts were also relay trading stations for the fur trade and other goods. Some famous Montana forts are Fort Keogh, Fort Missoula Historic District, Fort Harrison Veteran Hospital Historic District, and Fort Assiniboine Historic District. Fort Assiniboine—close to Havre—had more than 100 buildings. It was also in charge of Canadian border patrols and managing bootleggers and gunrunners.

Ghost Towns

Tourists can experience the Wild West come alive again by visiting Montana's long list of deserted ghost towns. These ghost towns are places where supported economic activity failed and led to desertion, offering a virtual stepping back into the era of vigilantes, saloons, and gold diggers. They are filled with endless mystery!

The most famous ghost town is at Bannack State Park where the first gold discovery was made in 1862. The area became Montana's first territorial capital as the gold rush set off commercial development. Now, the National Historic Landmark of Bannack's deserted streets are well preserved: over 50 log and frame structured buildings line the main street amidst outstretched prairie landscapes. A plethora of tours and activities are conducted here. The campground includes a tipi rental, and in winter, ice skating options lure family fun.

The historical ghost town treasure of Virginia City offers activities such as panning for gold, blacksmith demonstrations, stagecoach rides, train rides, ghost tours, and old-school theatrical plays for visitors in a beautifully preserved setting. The town is a state historic site, with a small friendly community close by in Alder Gulch. It was founded in 1863 with the feverish gold rush and its history paints a story of unrestrained outlaw activity, robberies and murders, executions (including the local sheriff at the time), brothels, gambling parlors, saloons, dance halls, and everything opposed to civilized concepts of societal lawfulness (such as schools, churches, and justice). A political struggle with adjacent towns, before it eventually became an obscure shadow of its former glory in the 1940s, built up over the years as World War II led to its fatal end. Now it has become a major tourism destination after careful preservation of its authenticity. A stable, small community provides ample engaging activities for inquisitive visitors.

Other Montana ghost towns are Aldridge, Diamond City, Marysville, Junction City, Rancher, and Coloma, with a very mysterious history. At Coloma, records went missing and gold ore was removed from the mines. The locals refuse to give information about the folklore, leading to much speculation. Rimini is an open-air ghost town close to Helena with a small local community. The ghost town of Granite was the richest silver mine on Earth during its heyday—now it's completely deserted. Karst's Camp was originally a Dude Ranch (1901) and operated for 50 years before its collapse, and Alder Gulch was the site of the largest placer gold strike in history—producing $10,000,000 during its first production year. This led to the birth of close by Virginia City and Nevada City. The story is told that while its discoverer and his companions were hiding from the Crow in 1863, they accidentally discovered the gold in a gulch.

Museums

A long list of museums laces the unique history of Montana and its numerous art galleries and studios, which include Native American art. Many museums are located at famous local mansions, such as The Moss Mansion Historic House Museum, which showcases architectural excellence and amenities ahead of its time.

Montana also has an unusual number of paleontological museums showcasing many artifacts found within the state. Some (like Makoshika State Park, Blaine County Museum, Fort Peck Field Station and its Interpretive Center, and the Beaverhead County Museum) have a variety of yesteryear items, ranging from fossils to automotive memorabilia and railway pocket watch exhibits.

You can literally follow the dinosaur trail and view authentic collections discovered in Montana. Many museums have dinosaur and early rancher and settler day exhibits, and, of course, cowboys and Indians exhibits. Whatever the thought of Montana brings to mind will probably be museum-cased somewhere in the state and all preserve the natural, cultural, and historical heritage of the state. Some popular museums are the following:

- **Museum of the Rockies, Bozeman:** Houses the world's largest collection of dinosaur fossils as well as a typical Montana late 1800s homestead.
- **World Museum of Mining, Butte:** Recreation of an oil mining town including an underground mine tour.
- **C. M. Russell Museum, Great Falls:** The famous Montana artist's work depicting Montana cowboy culture is displayed here.
- **Museum of the Yellowstone:** Includes a guided tour of the Union Pacific Railroad's history and other transportation narratives from the area.
- **American Computer and Robotics Museum:** Takes you back in time to the Stone Age with evolutionary information technology that started with stone tablets and continues with artificial intelligence exhibits and the space race.

Pioneer Towns

Pioneer towns offer the ultimate Wild West experiences! Some of these are Lewistown with its Old West architecture, Virginia City, Nevada City, Augusta, and Stevensville. Other notable towns are

- **Fort Benton:** Often called the birthplace of Montana, is one of the oldest towns.

- **Hamilton:** Well preserved and famous for having the iconic frontierswoman and sharpshooter Calamity Jane as a resident. The town was built by the railroad industry, lumber, and agricultural settlers.
- **Scobey:** Used to be a hangout for outlaws in the early 1800s. It also has a rich fur trading and Native American history. In 1901, settlers occupied the area and built many places for commercial use. Today, you can view the Daniels County Museum and Pioneer Town just outside Scobey. This is a town that restored its "turn of the century" former glory homes and businesses beautifully. You can view many antiques, cars, tractors, and machinery that add to the old-school charm of the town. It is also known for its "Dirty Shame Show" (a reminder of the pioneer days), held annually at the end of June.

Historic Theaters

Fort Peck Theatre was built in 1934 as a temporary amenity structure for about 50,000 workers of the Fort Peck dam project in the area, to serve mainly as a movie theater. It stopped operating as a movie house in 1968 and reopened in 1970 for live shows. The pseudo-Swiss-chalet style architecture, with its open-truss wood interior and hand-crafted light fixtures, survived and is now used as a permanent community theater with a 1,209-seat auditorium capacity. The intimate atmosphere serves the local community, keeping the arts alive by being supported by the locals through volunteer work and donations, scholarships for undergraduate performing arts students, and hosting various summer camps. Its "family theater" atmosphere provides a vital community element and offers cozy, relaxed, and intimate shows often performed by locals.

Washoe Theater, Anaconda, is one of the last Art Deco-style theaters. It was built in 1931 and officially opened after the Great Depression and has been operative for 85 years. It's still going strong, offering affordable tickets and showing the latest movies. The theater offers excellent acoustics with its original high-fidelity audio system design, and the main charm remains the venue: a 1,000-seat old-school historic auditorium with the screen flanked by vintage silk curtains, ceiling murals, and chandeliers gracing the venue. It has a distinctly Western feel with all the copper fittings, silver, and gold leaf finishes and is ranked fifth by the Smithsonian Institute for architectural significance.

Rialto Bozeman Theater is another vintage theater with an intimate atmosphere. It used to be a peanut stand in the early 1900s and was modified into a movie theater in 1924. Since then, the venue has been transformed to host concerts and offers a backdrop for creativity and authentic expression. It showcases less mainstream but more independent performances. The building incorporates a cozy theater space, bar with dining facilities, and private events venue: The Black Box Theater, The Light Box, and The Burn Box Bar—a cultural inspirational hub. Other historic theater sites include the Yucca Theater in Hysham, the Wilma Theatre in Missoula, the Opera House in Kalispell, and the Orpheum Theater in Conrad.

Art in Montana

Excellent ranges of artwork that present local scenery with an emphasis on the American Western lifestyle and local wildlife thrive in Montana. Its rich history of artists from various cultural backgrounds merges tradition and contemporary art, offering a plethora of art and galleries to choose from.

- **Blackfoot Pathways Sculpture in the Wild, Lincoln:** Offers a unique experience in the forested areas where sculptures are created from nature.
- **The Montana Museum of Art and Culture, Missoula:** This space "expresses the spirit of the American West and its relationship to the world" (Montana Office of Tourism, n.d., para 8). It hosts the state's largest publicly owned collection of art, offering a diverse and comprehensive collection of nearly 12,000 objects. The permanent collection includes famous artists such as Andy Warhol, Picasso, Salvador Dalì, and Donatello, to name a few, and will be exhibited until Fall 2025.
- **Three Chiefs Cultural Center Collection (formerly The People's Center), St. Ignatius:** Located in the Flathead Indian Reservation, a most noteworthy exhibit was painstakingly restored after a fire damaged almost 70% of its collection. This collection includes traditional local objects from the Kootenai, Salish, and Pend d'Oreille Native American cultures. The center honors their rich cultural heritage and way of life.

Charles M Russell

Missouri-born artist Charlie Russell (1864–1926) was also known as the cowboy artist. He produced almost 4,000 artworks of the American West, local landscapes, cowboys, and Native American tribes around the turn of the last century—mostly in oil, water painting, drawings, and sculptures of various mediums. His work also comprised major historical events in the American West.

Russell's work is well-known for its Native American perspective showing his knowledge of undercurrent issues of society at the time. His *Lewis and Clark Meeting Indians at Ross' Hole* (1912) is displayed in the House chambers of the Montana Capitol, Helena. His painting *Piegans* (1918) reached a record price of $5.6 million in 2005.

Famous for his storytelling and advocacy for a reservation for the Chippewa tribe, he was also an author and inducted into the Hall of Great Westerners (National Cowboy and Western Heritage Museum). The house where he lived for most of his life with his wife and marketing director, Nancy, has been turned into an exquisite art gallery and is worth a visit.

RAILWAY TRAVEL

Montana's history is closely intertwined with railroads. It is even said that Montana wouldn't be as populated as it is today if railroads were not established. During its rich mining and gold rush history, railway travel was the primary means of transportation—not only for people but also for products and materials. Railway travel ignited Montana's economy.

Today, railway travel remains mostly a scenic tourism feature. Three active passenger lines today are the Alder Gulch Short Line (between Virginia City and Nevada City), the Charlie Russell Chew Choo Dinner train (in central Montana), and the Empire Builder (connecting Seattle and Chicago while passing through Glacier Park).

According to Montana's official website, Big Sky country should not be forgotten as an outback area in the US. Instead, Montana residents pride themselves on their welcoming character (2012, para 14):

While some national observers consider Montana a part of America's "cultural outback," many Montanans pride themselves on their strong spirit of community, their close contact with the environment, and their fundamental "sense of place."

Let's find out why and tackle this vast landscape in four presentable sections: the northwest, northeast and central, southwest, and southeast.

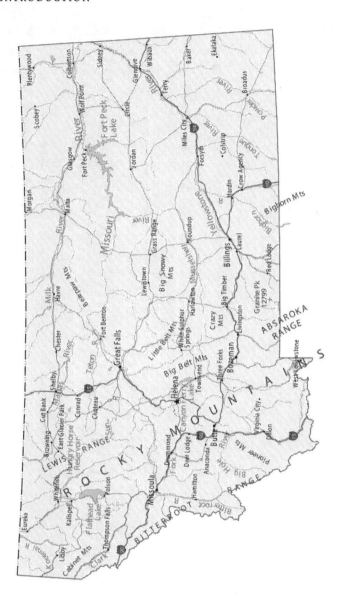

https://gisgeography.com/montana-map/

PART I
NORTHWEST MONTANA—
LAND OF MOUNTAINS AND
LAKES

OVERVIEW

> I'm in love with Montana. For other states I have admiration, respect, recognition, even some affection. But with Montana it is love. And it's difficult to analyze love when you're in it.
>
> — JOHN STEINBECK

The fact that around 70% of Montana's "streamflow originates from melting snow" (Editorial Staff, 2019, para 23), explains everything about its climate and natural landscape. Northwest Montana is glacier country and includes four national forests (Flathead, Kootenai, Lolo, and Bitterroot), three major lakes (Flathead, Swan, and Seeley), and the Glacier National Park as its prime point of interest.

The area is famous for its abundant opportunities for water and winter sports activities, including whitewater rafting, winter ice fishing, summer trout fishing, boating, snowmobiling, and cross-country snow-skiing. Whitefish (in the

Flathead Valley) was named by National Geographic as one of the world's top 25 ski towns. There are two ski resorts near Flathead Lake, while Seeley Lake is less crowded for the more introverted traveler. The area has a very low population density so chances are that you won't feel over-crowded.

The Rocky Mountains flank the area on the eastern and western sides, embracing an area filled with freshwater lakes, crystal-clear rivers, sublime forests, ancient glaciers, and prairie hills. The shielding mountains also make the winters in this area milder. Spring is a bit unpredictable with rain— although the earth comes alive under wildflower-filled meadows—but fall and summer have long days with consistently pleasant weather for traveling. Fall presents a different color palette not to be missed.

Apart from the spectacular natural vista and majestic blue skies, the area doesn't only please the nature enthusiast, but cultural and historical explorations will entice family travelers as well. Day trips, private tours, and workshops provide a multitude of social activities.

PLACES TO VISIT

Northwest Montana is a vast mountainous and forest area on the western side of the continental divide. Historical Bitterroot Valley is one of the major north-to-south valleys of Northwestern Montana. The so-called "Glacier Country" also includes two of the most popular travel destinations of the Pacific Northwest, namely Flathead Lake and Glacier National Park.

Bitterroot Valley

The 84-mile north-flowing Bitterroot River is a dominant natural feature connecting most cities and towns along the way. The main road to travel is US 93. Bitterroot National Forest embraces the valley along the surrounding two mountain ranges (Sapphire range—east, and Bitterroot range—west). The area gets its name from the hardy state flower—the pink rosette-shaped bitterroot, blooming in spring. The largest city, cultural hub, and county seat here is Hamilton with 4,000 inhabitants. Around this area you can also feast your eyes on Marcus Daly's magnificent villa built during the mining boom of the late 1800s—lavishly decorated by the Irish immigrant. The home is impressively surrounded by 46 acres of rolling grounds, ideal for a lazy picnic.

Kootenai, Nez Perce, and Salish Native tribes traveled or inhabited the area for many years. Nez Perce used the Bitterroot area as a major route during the Nez Perce War of 1877. It was also the route chosen by the Lewis and Clark expedition (1805–1806) with many historical sites of American exploration history to be found here among the towns founded by early settlers.

The Bitterroot forest, west of the valley, covers an area of 1.6 million acres and forms part of the northern Rocky Mountains. The mountain range displays spectacular heavily glaciated rugged peaks with elevation ranges between 3,200 and 10,150 feet. The forest is managed with sound principles of biological diversity: Landscape management supports healthy and diverse ecosystems, which in turn support the value systems of local inhabitants. Recreational, wildlife management, cultural resources, fishing, timber, and mineral management, as well as sustainable water provisions, are enforced. The vegetative forest management yields sustainable forest products and trout fishing is managed with fishing regulations. More than 1,600 miles of trails provide ample recreational opportunities, and the valley offers an extensive array of accommodations and recreational activities that will satisfy any need.

Flathead Valley

The Flathead Valley is the western gateway to Glacier National Park, with recreational treasures supporting "human delight in play and creativity" (Go Northwest, n.d.-a, para 1). The grand, pristine lake is nestled within the mountain ranges, offering surprisingly mild temperatures for this area. It is the largest freshwater lake in the West, embraced by the Flathead National Forest and Flathead Indian Reservation.

When you travel the country byways, you may be surprised to find champagne grapes and cherry trees. Don't be misguided by the placid lake; the adjacent rivers provide ample river kayaking rapids (in cold water!). You'll also discover the National Bison Range and Jewel Basin Hiking area here.

Apart from its abundant sports and recreational opportunities, the area provides a bustling creative and cultural component with its thriving art communities, especially in Kalispell and Bigfork. Tourism is a main source of income in the area so be prepared to share space during the busy seasonal months.

Glacier Country

Glacier National Park shares a border with Lakes National Park in Alberta, Canada. The area is cooperatively managed by the two countries in honor of the fact that fauna and flora share no boundaries. This UNESCO World Heritage Site (1995) was also designated as the world's first International Peace Park in 1932. Apart from its heritage and noteworthy names, it remains a "stunningly beautiful ice-carved terrain of serrated ridges, jutting peaks, dramatic hanging valleys, 50 glaciers, more than 200 lakes, waterfalls and thick forests covering some 1.2 million acres" (Go Northwest, n.d.-a, para 1).

In spring, the wildflowers display a colorful palette, wildlife roams the ridges in search of salt licks; and plenty of deer, elk, moose, mountain goats, bighorn sheep, as well as wolves and bears are easily spotted. There are three visitor centers with ranger-guided activities from June to September. Seven hundred miles of trails (including extended treks and day hikes) offer ample opportunities for serious hikers or families who simply want to spend time in nature.

Going-To-The-Sun Road

This spectacular road in the park climbs a daunting 3,000 feet to offer incredible vistas of the Continental Divide. It's a 52-mile trek along a narrow road, offering its spectacular views only during the warmer summer months: It remains mostly closed because of heavy snowfalls from November to May. There is a shuttle service available for the fainthearted and because the narrow road doesn't allow for oversized vehicles.

Seeley Lake

Glacially formed Seeley-Swan Valley (southeast of the park) is covered in snow for almost half of the year. This park is popular for fishing: in summer, trout fishing, and in winter, ice-fishing. It's a less-crowded area with few modern amenities as an alternative to the more touristy areas but with Missoula conveniently close by. You'll probably meet more deer than people!

St. Ignatius Mission

The Mission's historical roots go back to the 1830s, and it presents some of the most exquisite church murals in Montana. An unusual feature can be found in the adjacent log cabin, where nuns' headstones are worked into the walls and floor.

Garden of One Thousand Buddhas

The Tibetan Buddhist site, the Garden of One Thousand Buddhas is situated in the scenic Jocko Valley, just outside of Arlee. The white Buddha statues diverge in the shape of wheel spokes from the Prajnaparamita hub creating a scene of utmost serenity.

HOW TO REACH NORTHWEST MONTANA

Public transportation options are available in Montana despite its remote destination. Some scheduled bus services and limited shuttle services operate between the parks and tourist sites. However, car travel is definitely recommended. I would advise familiarizing yourself with the local transportation alternatives before your journey to help you find the most cost-effective option. Also, consider fueling options, as many remote areas do not provide this facility.

- **Fly:** Glacier Country is mainly serviced by airports at Missoula, Kalispell, and Glacier Park.
- **Country:** The prominent highways are I 90 (east and west) and US 93 (north and south). (US 93 can become clogged over weekends.) There are rental car services, private tour buses, charter companies, and an airport shuttle express. Familiarize yourself with the local road status information sites: Although most roads are maintained well and safe for traveling, it should be noted that, weather permitting, many roads can be shut down rapidly and remain closed for extended periods of the year. Secondary roads can be closed for long periods and some remote gravel roads are mostly impassable for at least six months of the year. The Going-To-The-Sun road crosses Glacier Park with scenic panoramas from west to east and is certainly one road not to be missed.
- **Rail:** The picturesque and scenic Empire Builder line (Chicago–Seattle, a 46-hour stretch of rail travel) is certainly the best option to take and view Glacier Park through the window of a train as the trip is managed in such a way that you travel this area during daytime. You can book a short trip on this line from East Glacier to Whitefish and I would certainly recommend that during the freezing months for some breathtaking views while staying

comfortably warm inside a train. Enjoy all the stops
for some brisk cultural or sports activities en route.

Always have emergency equipment handy, take plenty of
water, and prepare for drastic climate changes when driving.
Also, bear in mind when creating your itinerary that road
travel may include long stretches of driving due to the vastness of the area. In some cases, it may be more cost-effective
to fly in and spend less time on the road between sites.

WILDLIFE

As part of the Crown of the Continent Ecosystem, this area
represents one of the most intact ecosystems and expansive
landscapes in the world. You'll find a rich diversity of
wildlife. This part of Montana is home to about 19 large and
100 small mammal species. Gray wolves contribute
immensely to the health of the ecosystem, hearing an elk
bugle, and watching the bison roaming are by far the most
exquisite experiences one could have. The surefooted and
nimble mountain goats against the steep cliffs provide a
spectacular acrobatic display.

Northwest Montana is a birder's paradise with more than
200 bird species to find, including the yellow-breasted
western meadowlark (the official state bird of Montana) and
the rare, endangered whooping crane. The majestic brown
and white bald eagle can easily be spotted around waterways
where this endangered species feeds on fish. With a wingspan of up to 8 feet, they are the second largest American
birds of prey species.

You may even encounter mountain lions, coyotes, and lynx here. Of course, Montana is well-known for its fish varieties, especially trout: bull trout (a threatened species, catch-and-release principles apply), lake trout, brook trout, rainbow trout, cutthroat trout, and other species such as bass, pike, and whitefish can be found in the many streams and lakes.

When visiting Montana, keep in mind that all wild animals should be treated as such: Never feed them, be mindful of storage and disposal of your food items, maintain safe distances, and respect their territory and space. Be aware that deer can pass the roads while traveling, so remain cautious. Even if bears look very docile and cuddly, you need to stay at least 330 feet away from them, never approach them, simply back away slowly, and leave. It's advisable to avoid hiking at "bear active times" during dawn, dusk, and night and be prepared with bear spray for protection. Avoid wearing perfume and scented cream and stay on the trails. Stay at least 164 feet away from other wildlife: Remember that they can be potentially dangerous even when appearing harmless. Hike in groups and make noise to warn off any surprise attacks. Montana encourages "Leave No Trace" principles to mountain the pristine wildlife environment with respect to the animals.

CLIMATE

Temperatures vary according to topography, altitude, and geography. The weather can change rapidly without warning —prepare for this! A warm, sunny day can turn into a snowy experience at the snap of your fingers in springtime. Be mindful of hypothermia and lightning strikes. The magnificent scenery makes up for the irregular weather patterns: The mountains have to be approached with the necessary respect. Packing layered clothing is advised. Always pack rain gear, water-resistant footwear, hats, sunscreen, umbrellas, and additional warm layers of clothing. In winter, double up on moisture-wicking layered clothing like wool socks, snow pants, heavy jackets, winter boots, gloves, hats, and foot/ hand warmers.

The lowest temperatures during winter average around zero degrees, and peak temperatures in summer average around 85 degrees Fahrenheit, with generally warm sunny days and cool nights. The temperatures in Glacier Park are quite different from the rest of the area and you may encounter more wind in the eastern section of the park. The western areas of Montana also have higher rainfall and heavier snowfall (more than 300 inches).

Winter provides a paradise of frozen lakes and snowy playfields for ski enthusiasts. Summer generally calls for mountain hiking, biking, and water sports activities. This season remains the most popular visiting time as the days are longer (between 14 and 16 hours of daylight) and skies are clear. Early summer may have more rain, wildfires, and thunderstorms.

HIKING AND CAMPING

Montana has 54 state parks and more than a thousand camping and RV park sites, including dispersed and free camping in some wilderness areas. Some Montana campsites offer alternative accommodations such as cabins, yurt glamping (made from a wood lattice frame and insulated canvas walls), hike-in and bike-in sites, and authentic tipi stays (e.g., at Bank and Lewis and Clark Caverns) for the more adventurous camper.

The northwestern side of the state is an international camper attraction with forests, lakes, and scenic viewpoints of the mountainous terrain. Options of first-come, first-serve camping, hiking-and-biking campsites, or reservation camping exist. Due to its popularity, booking for the sites only opens six months in advance and then fills up within the blink of an eye. Many campsites in Glacier National Park require downloading and making bookings through the *Recreation.gov* app or website. The website *Hipcamp.com* offers a wide variety of camping options.

Strict rules apply at all camping sites: For bears, food must be stored in correctly sealed and solid containers at higher levels where they cannot reach it. Awareness of wild animals requires strict supervision of children and pets. And making fires and cutting firewood are strictly regulated to prevent runaway wildfires. Fires are prohibited in designated areas in Glacier Park. A few campsites in the northwest are the following:

- **Apgar Camping Ground:** One of the 13 campgrounds in Glacier National Park that is probably the most popular and famous. Its proximity to Apgar village on the western side of the park (with many camping shops and essentials) and the Going-to-the-Sun Road adds additional convenience to the beauty of the landscape. A tourist center, ranger station, kayak rentals, and guided horseback rides offer loads of recreational activities. Although this campsite is one of the larger sites in the park (94 campsites), it's still advisable to book your spot early.

- **Flathead Lake State Park:** Provides several camping site opportunities around the 150-mile shoreline of the biggest freshwater lake in the States. The Big Arm camping site on the western side offers the largest and most popular camping site facilities. I can also recommend the Wayfarers and Finley Point campsites.

- **Kintla Lake Campground:** In the northwest part of Glacier Park, it offers a more remote experience for solitary wanderers as the "most distant front country and vehicle camping area in Glacier National Park," according to Will Beck (2021a, para 37), who researched some of the best campsites in Montana. Running water is available between June and September. It's a paradise for canoeists and kayakers and also for trout angler enthusiasts.

- **Bad Medicine Campground:** In the Kootenai forest is a site calling for all tree-hugging enthusiasts. It's a small intimate place with wooded campsites catering to small RV's and tents. You'll find some ancient red cedars (some more than 100 years old) and family-friendly nature trails in the forest. It's also a popular recreational water activity base.

When hiking and camping in northwest Montana, be mindful and prepared for altitude sickness (leave time to adjust to the new altitudes before taking part in sports activities), giardia (drinking water from streams is not recommended as they may contain giardia parasites), dehydration, hypothermia (prevent this by dressing warmly in noncotton clothing), frostbite, and sunburn. You may not find mobile connection in all the areas so be prepared for this and make your reservations ahead of time. Always have your rule of ten essentials ready for bracing the outdoors!

Hiking

One of the most magnificent hiking options here calls for dedicated long-distance trekking enthusiasts: a 3,100 mile U.S. National Scenic Trail (the Continental Divide Trail) runs between Canada and Mexico, traversing five U.S. states along the Rockies, including Montana. Apart from this, a plethora of shorter hiking trails crisscross northwestern Montana, enough to cater to every individual need. Hiking trails of various lengths, elevation gain, and levels of difficulty are mostly in the park and around the Going-to-the-Sun road. More remote hiking sites are available further away from this road, all of them offer breathtaking views and more solitude. Although hiking in the area can be strenuous and challenging with elevated mountain hikes—mostly requiring a certain level of fitness—there are also hikes for families, day hikes, and shorter overnight hikes.

Meander through forests and along alpine ridges and landscapes, wildflower vistas, glistening with glacier lakes, clear waterfalls, and icy rivers. Enjoy ample opportunities to spot wildlife (marmots, bears, moose, mountain goats) along the walks. (For this reason, Glacier Park is referred to as the

"Crown of the Continent" as glacial valleys and breathtaking mountain peaks all inspire jaw-dropping vistas of grandeur.)

Weather dictates the best hiking season in a short period from July to mid-September, offering consistently sunny weather and only occasional rain storms in late afternoon. Shoulder season hikes during May or October require ample preparation for colder wet weather and limited campsite availability. These times may be a more inviting option for hikers who prefer less crowded conditions. (Hikers should always have bear spray and be on the lookout for wild animals. Leave no trace principles apply, and permits are often required.)

Now that we have you set up for your northwest Montana expectations, we'll first go to Glacier National Park.

GLACIER NATIONAL PARK - MAJESTIC PEAKS AND PRISTINE LAKES

66 Montana: where the elevation is usually a bigger number than the town's population.

— UNKNOWN

Known as the crown of the continent and as the first international peace park, the US and Canada present a monument for world peace through their combined efforts to maintain the park beyond man-made borders. Glacier National Park was also given Biosphere status by the United Nations in 1976. Not only does the park's status but more so its mesmerizing beauty, capture the world.

GLORIOUS PEAKS AND GLACIERS

The park was established in May 1910. Glacier National Park is one of the world's most unique glacier parks, with a sprawling one million acres of the national park set in majestic mountainous landscapes. Its "Crown of the Continent" ecosystem is part of the vast protected land of the area. On the Canadian side, visitors can use the opportunity to explore that side of the park as well via Waterton Lakes National Park, which connects with Glacier National Park from Waterton-Glacier International Peace Park.

ITINERARY LOGISTICS

It's essential to familiarize yourself with the park's restrictions and updates before you travel. Notable alerts, basic information, camping information, road user details, vehicle reservations, road status, recommended accommodations, accessibility for special needs, park entry fees, traveling with pets, eco-friendly camping info, and safety updates can be found on the park's website and these are regularly updated to make the journey for the traveler as smooth as possible. Seasonal changes regulate the park's road use and restrictions apply. The park offers a text message application assisting with immediate updates. Here is the link to the useful website: https://www.nps.gov/glac/planyourvisit/conditions.htm

The site not only provides basic info regarding seasonal closures and exceptions but also provides updates on special events, visitor center details, and operating hours, as well as weather and safety conditions. You may furthermore find hiking status updates, advice on things to do, and useful info about booking a bus, boat, raft, horseback riding, guided hiking tours, ranger-led programs, fishing, skiing, guided tours, or shuttle services, as well as tips to deal with crowds. Yes, this is real: flexibility, planning ahead, and patience will take you a long way. If you prefer a more peaceful journey, consider going in off-peak seasons or visiting adjacent areas. Other tips to consider before embarking on a journey to the park are the following:

- There are no gas stations in the park.
- For park safety, follow guidelines and carry bear spray.
- Always hike in groups and stay on designated trails.
- Be aware of rapidly changing weather conditions: Be mindful of extreme weather and hypothermia as the waters remain cold even during summer months.
- Avoid slippery rocks and wear the correct clothing when out hiking.
- Be aware of snow and ice-related accidents.

- Avoid getting wet.
- Be mindful of avalanches.
- Always have water and warm clothing at hand.

Considering the busy status of the park, especially during peak season, it's important to plan and book according to your specific needs. Consider options between lodge or wilderness camping accommodation, and gourmet dining or snacking on the go. Familiarize yourself with "Leave No Trace" principles! It is not only about not leaving your trash, it also includes things that shouldn't be done when *engaging* in the wild. Here are some logistical and helpful facts for planning your itinerary:

- The highest point in the park is Mt. Cleveland at 10,466 feet.
- Logan Pass is located at an altitude of 6,646 feet and accessible by vehicle offering postcard-pretty vistas to view.
- Siyeh Pass Trail is the highest maintained trail in the park at 8,100 feet.
- The tremendous range of topography includes forests, alpine meadows, majestic peaks, and ancient glacial valleys. The three major mountain ranges are the Lewis Range, Clark Range, and the Livingston Range.
- A variety of reasonable entry permit passes (e.g., standard, annual, or America the Beautiful) can be purchased online or on site.

When to Visit

The most popular time to visit is from June to early September, even though the park is open all year. During this peak summer season, the weather is most favorable for traveling and the famous Going-to-the-Sun road is fully accessible. It's not advisable to visit during Spring as this is the wet season, restricting most activities and limiting exploring the landscape.

Getting There

Glacier Park International Airport (FCA) near Kalispell is the closest major airport: it's 30 miles away from the western entrance and 12 miles from Whitefish. Ten airlines offer flights to the park from where visitors can arrange alternative transportation, a shuttle service, or rent a car. All these are available at Kalispell and Whitefish. Cross-country road trips connect to the park via US 2 (the main east-to-west route in northern Montana) and US 89. Amtrak's historic train stops all year at West Glacier and seasonally at East Glacier, linking tourists with shuttle access to the park.

Accommodation

A wide variety of accommodation options include campgrounds, lodges, and cabins. It's advisable to make reservations well in advance, especially during the peak visiting season. Apgar Village Lodge and Cabins at Lake McDonald, Glacier Park Lodge (original Great Northern Railway hotel), and the charming West Glacier Cabins all provide comfort, scenery, and facilities at reasonable prices. Alternatively, West Glacier RV Park welcomes your pets and provides all the facilities you may need.

PARK HIGHLIGHTS

The park boasts 350 national historic landmarks and the Going-to-the-Sun road has been granted National Historic Civil Engineering Landmarks status, which is granted to projects or structures that exceed excellence! Other high-lights include a rich fossil history of some of the best preserved Proterozoic sedimentary rocks in the world, with some of the world's most fruitful sources for records of early life. Sedimentary rocks of similar age located in other regions have been greatly altered by mountain building and other metamorphic changes. (Wikipedia Contributors, 2019a, para 24)

It is believed that some of the earliest metazoan (animal) life on Earth is found here. Threatened animal species have been dealt with and reintroduced successfully. Most importantly, wolf tribes were reintroduced to support the natural ecosystem and brought major corrections to a struggling ecosystem prior to their return. The rich formation history continues: mountains were carved by glaciers from the last ice age, leaving its heritage for all to see. Sadly, global warming poses a serious risk to glacier retreat and the possible disappearance of the remaining glaciers within the first half of this century. The effect of this on the delicate ecosystem and microclimate of the park is still being studied.

Going-To-The-Sun Road

The iconic Going-to-the-Sun (GTTS) road spans 50 miles of the park and offers breathtaking views of glaciers, cascading waterfalls, and spectacular alpine peaks. This engineering marvel can be daunting in places, so a shuttle service is available for the fainthearted since most of the westbound drive is only separated by an eighteen-inch stone wall next to a high cliff face. Portions of the road are open all year round (mostly on the western side).

Still, some sections of the higher elevations are not always accessible and they close during the severe winter months, so check the conditions before embarking on your journey. The higher elevated areas of the road have a short visiting period without snow between mid-July and the end of September. During peak season, day trippers will need a vehicle reservation to enter this road at the western gate. The road traverses the park from west to east and you won't need to obtain permits if entering from Two Medicine or the eastern side (the other roads requiring vehicle permits are at North Fork and Many Glacier). Remember to make these reservations well in advance as they are limited and you cannot purchase them at the entrance. Vehicle regulations also exist due to its narrow and winding nature and its rocky overhangs.

The entire length of this iconic road takes about two hours of a jaw-dropping experience even though it includes traffic jams and many other vehicles alongside yours. The highest point is at Logan Pass with an elevation of 6,646 feet on top of the continental divide, offering sweeping vistas and wildlife spotting—provided that you find a parking spot!

Hiking

Glacier's wilderness comes in two flavors—east and west roughly split along the Continental Divide. Each trail on a respective side offers a similar "feel." West side trails start at around 3,200 feet in elevation, are more heavily forested, and offer the greatest solitude. East of the divide, trails start at around 5,000 feet and the terrain is more sparsely vegetated, creating more open vistas and attracting more crowds.

National Park Service (2024) eloquently draws the imaginary line between the east and west of Glacier Park. It's a hiker's paradise with over 700 miles of trails to explore. Some are handicapped-friendly offering wheelchair access to the beautiful vistas. Many trails have boardwalks that protect the flora. The park offers glacial lakes to alpine hikes, and the trails provide options for a relaxing one-day trip and also more extended options for the seasoned hiker, keeping every visitor happy with the ability to explore this stunning area on foot close to nature. Many Glacier is a hiker's favorite and includes the Grinnell Glacier and Iceberg Lake hikes. Other day hikes are available in the Two Medicine area, which doesn't attract as many visitors as the GTTS road area—thus creating an off-the-beaten-track feeling.

Hiking in the park requires thorough preparation and obtaining permits from the National Park Service. They have useful videos on their site providing ample information about hiking in tune with nature and important resource protection and information before you set off into the wilderness. Remember that you are miles from civilization but also miles away from help if needed: Mobile coverage may be limited or nonexistent, so download (or screenshot) trails beforehand. Always consider drastic weather changes, rain, snow, hypothermia, frostbite, avalanche danger, and wildlife threats. In early summer, the lower-elevation trails should be snow-free, and the higher-elevation trails only become snow-free by late July.

Store your food away from wildlife when setting up camp, purify water, and be informed (and respect) the power of nature. Follow the park's trail status support page to be informed of the latest conditions and updates, but also refer to weather sites for the latest updates. My best advice is to be prepared for emergency closures and hazardous conditions that may affect your itinerary, be aware of your personal backpacking skill level and assess your group's levels accordingly, check your gear according to park sites' advice, and be prepared for emergencies. Always avoid unnecessary risks and practice good judgment by hiking in groups. Don't split up! Minimize human impact by leaving no trace. Never make contact with wildlife and use extreme caution. Here are some of the most popular hiking trails:

- **Highline Trail:** An extremely popular and breathtaking point-to-point moderate hike (11.6 miles) along the Continental Divide. Mostly a downhill walk on paths that cling to the cliffs above the Going-to-the-Sun road. It offers stunning vistas and wildlife sightings. It's not for the fainthearted and hikers with a fear of heights!
- **Grinnell Glacier Trail:** A panoramic trek of mountain peaks, wildlife spotting, and aquamarine lakes en route to a stunning glacier. It's a strenuous hike of 10.6 miles and 1,600 feet elevation gain. (The hike can be reduced by about 3 miles when taking a boat across Swiftcurrent and Josephine lakes.)

- **Avalanche Lake Trail:** A moderate 4.5-mile forest hike leading to a picturesque mountain lake. It starts off at the Trail of the Cedars and continues along Avalanche Creek to the top of the lake area.
- **Hidden Lake Trail:** Alpine scenery trail accessible from Logan Pass with mountain goats and wildflowers. It's an easy to moderate hike of 2.8 miles with 460 feet elevation gain and remains one of the most popular hikes.
- **Iceberg Lake Trail:** A scenic but strenuous trek of 9.6 miles and 1,200 feet elevation gain to an exquisite glacial lake with stunning views of towering peaks, the Ptarmigan tunnel, and falls.
- **Siyeh Pass Trail:** A challenging hike with panoramic glacier views, rugged landscapes, and waterfalls.
- **Cracker Lake Trail:** A strenuous trek for 12.6 miles with 1,400 feet elevation gain but offering the reward of a brilliantly colored aquamarine lake of the Many Glacier area. Not to be missed if you are hiking fit.
- **Swiftcurrent Pass Trail:** Offers diverse hiking trail terrain between lakes, valleys, and towering peaks.
- **Ptarmigan Tunnel Trail:** A unique trail that takes you through a tunnel carved into the mountainside with access to stunning alpine vistas. This hike is a good option for hikers who prefer to avoid the crowds even though it is a strenuous walk (10.6 miles and 2,300 feet elevation). It's getting rave reviews from other hikers.
- **Trail of the Cedars:** A short one-mile boardwalk loop trail for easy hiking under cedar trees without

much elevation to the stunning Avalanche Gorge. There are sections of gravel on the trail.

- **Glacier Viewpoint Trail:** A short trail near Two Medicine with stunning views of the surrounding mountain range. Glacier offers a shuttle service, hiking equipment rentals, and guided hiking. It's not advised to hike alone.

Scenic Viewpoints

Scenic points can be found on most roads but here are some favorites:

- **Going-to-the-Sun road** offers several designated scenic pullouts on the road with breathtaking views of valleys, glaciers, and waterfalls. Not to be missed!
- **Logan Pass,** along the GTTS road, has sweeping views of mountains, meadows, and wildlife.
- **Many Glacier** offers picturesque scenery of towering peaks reflecting in pristine lakes.
- **Lake McDonald,** the largest lake in the park, is surrounded by mountain forests and offers stunning sunsets. The historic 1914 Lake McDonald Lodge on the edge of the lake offers exquisite accommodation and recreational activities such as horse riding and boating tours.
- **Two Medicine** offers tranquil and stunning views of mountains, lakes, and the iconic Two Medicine Lake.
- **Grinnell Glacier** overlook has a panoramic view of the glacier and the turquoise-colored glacial lake.

- **Hidden Lake** overlook, along the Hidden Lake trail, pours sweeping views of surrounding alpine landscapes.
- **Many Glacier Valley** (you can either drive or hike through this scenic valley) boasts jaw-dropping mountain vistas and cascading waterfalls.

Viewpoints offer abundant wildlife scenery, including grizzly bears, black bears, mountain goats, bighorn sheep, moose, and elk. Always respect wildlife's space and observe it from a safe distance.

Tours and Programs

Various tours for visitors can be arranged and they meet every individual need. There are boat tours from one of the scenic lakes (Lake McDonald or St. Mary Lake) with its unique perspective of surrounding glaciers and mountains. Tourists will also find boating or kayaking options, fishing tours, rafting trips, and other water activities that provide ample recreational moments on the lakes.

Red Bus Tours provide the classic historic way to explore park highlights and scenery. The vintage buses have knowledgeable guides that allow you to sit back and relax while taking in the incredible vistas. These 1930 tour buses have been beautifully restored and are considered to be the oldest touring bus fleet in the world! Some tours last up to 9.5 hours and bookings have to be made well in advance.

Park shuttles are also available. Free shuttle services are available during peak season along the Going-to-the-Sun road, offering a good alternative to stressful driving and parking limitations in this area, which is the most crowded in the park.

Abundant ranger-led programs and special events happen in peak seasons: These programs and guided hikes provide interesting information about the park's natural and cultural history, geology, and wildlife providing valuable insights to enhance your travel experience. Various centers assist tourists, such as the Apgar Visitor Center and Logan Pass Visitor Center. Here, you can gather useful information and park updates about trail conditions and wildlife sightings and view exhibits.

The park offers an array of photographic opportunities with endless options for capturing stunning photographs, especially sunrise and sunset moments. Always practice Leave No Trace principles to preserve this pristine environment: pack and remove your trash, respect wildlife and vegetation, leave the park as you found it, and don't take away what belongs to nature. Stay on established trails and camp in designated locations, and avoid going off-trail, as this will widen the trail unnecessarily and damage the delicate flora. "It's a way of thinking, an attitude, and an ethic, that helps us reduce our impact on the places we love" (Glacier National Park, n.d.-b, para 1). A few travel tips to ease your visit are as follows:

- Take binoculars for wildlife viewing.
- Areas further away from parking and crowded spots have more abundant wildlife viewing.
- Have bear spray even if you venture a small distance from a parked vehicle.

- Bears, moose, mountain goats, and bighorn sheep are more commonly viewed in the park's mountainous terrain, while herds of other wildlife are mostly spotted in Montana's plains.
- Arrive early as the park gets crowded during peak seasons.
- Be mindful of traveling distances by car after flying: To experience the vast areas, you need ample time on the roads before you reach your destination.

From glorious glacial valleys and lakes, winding roads, and sunset views, let's leave the mountains and inviting peaks and find some adventure at Flathead Lake.

FLATHEAD LAKE - RECREATIONAL PARADISE

" My favorite state has not yet been invented. It will be called Montana, and it will be perfect.

— ABRAHAM LINCOLN

Flathead Lake is the largest natural freshwater lake west of the Mississippi River. It's, furthermore, the largest natural body of freshwater in the western US, and in addition to this, one of the cleanest lakes in the world. It is one of the more than 3,000 reservoirs and lakes that you'll find in Montana: well worth a visit!

LAKE DELIGHTS

The lake is an offspring of a massive glacial dammed lake, Lake Missoula, from the earlier glacial period around 15,000 years ago. In 1930, the Kerr Dam project at the Polson entry point artificially raised the lake level. Today, it generates hydroelectricity, which is owned and operated by the Confederated Salish and Kootenai tribes.

The natural lake along the Flathead River in the Flathead National Forest forms the southern tip of the Rocky Mountain trench, which extends all the way north into Canada. It's located in the picturesque Flathead Valley with Kalispell and Polson as the main gateway cities. The lake's breath-taking beauty is surrounded by the majestic peaks of the Mission Mountains (east) and Salish Mountains (west). The expansive blue waters provide a stunning backdrop for adventurous water activities and outdoor recreation. The southern area falls in the tribal boundaries of the Confeder-ated Salish and Kootenai tribes' Flathead Reservation section. Tribal permits are required for recreational activi-ties here.

It's 30 miles long, 15 miles wide, and an average of 160 to 220 feet deep (with a maximum depth of 370 feet), covering over 200 square miles of water and 185 miles of irregularly shaped shoreline. Flathead Lake is thus deeper than the average depths of the Persian Gulf. A dozen small islands cover an additional five and a half square miles of which Wild Horse Island is the biggest (2,164 acres). Another 64-acre smaller island, Melita, is close to the western shore, with a high point of 80 feet above water level.

ITINERARY LOGISTICS

The lake is open all year with a plethora of recreational activities during every season, catering to every need. Tribal recreational permits and fishing licenses are required in some instances. A multitude of camping facilities covering a wide range of needs are available. Flathead State Park offers campgrounds, picnic areas, and hiking trails. Wayfarers, Big Arm, and Finley Point State Parks are especially popular destinations for relaxation and outdoor recreation. The varied distribution of park units along the lakeshore and some more inland areas–each providing a unique feel–offer views of the lake, the valleys, and surrounding mountains.

Getting There

Located in scenic northwest Montana, seven miles south of Kalispell and 30 miles southwest of Glacier National Park, the lake is flanked along its curving shoreline by two scenic highways, US 93 and MT 35.

Accommodation

The primary populated areas are Kalispell, Bigfork, and Polson, which have many accommodation facilities and a wide range of amenities, such as groceries, supplies, information, recreational opportunities, and cultural engagement.

Resorts and Accommodations

The lake's extensive shorelines have ample hiking, picnicking, and camping sites adjacent to the water. Some of the most popular sites to visit are Finley Point, Big Arm, Wayfarers, West Shore, Wild Horse Island, and Yellow Bay. Most accommodations are found in Kalispell, Somers, Polson, Bigfork, and other adjacent towns. A range of bed and breakfasts, Airbnb, bungalows, cabins, budget hotels, motels, and glamping or camping facilities with RV hook-ups offer accommodation options close to the lake.

A vast range of alternative accommodations (like Flathead Forest Cabin rentals) can be found online—satisfying every individual need. Budget and family friendly options provide family packages, camping and jeep rental packages, alpine packages, or ranch vacation packages. Others give exquisite mountain or lake views. Visitors have the option to find accommodation on the shorelines, or others a short walking distance or driving distance from the lake. Some unusual sites are:

- **Flathead Lake Resort (in Bigfork):** For a 1950s-style accommodation experience with cabins, rooms, or cottages. The resort also has unique glamping facilities in beautifully restored retro and airstream campers. It's been operating since 1957, offering an experience of yesteryear fitted with the comforts of today. Their campers all tell their own unique story. They transport you back to slow living times! Alternatively, you can book their "intentionally designed" accommodation if full living quarters or rooms are required. These offer eco-conscious amenities but are fitted with modern-day equipment to make your stay luxurious yet still unique. Their units are dog-friendly and guests have access to their private community beach, which is a mere two-minute walk away from Flathead Lake. Water rentals (kayaks, paddle boards, or canoes) can be arranged.
- **Glacier International Lodge:** For a more luxurious stay, this renowned lodge in Whitefish offers authentic Western comfort. It's a short drive from the International Airport and has easy access to Glacier Park, Whitefish Mountain Ski Resort, and Flathead Lake.

LAKE HIGHLIGHTS

The best time to visit the lake area is in the fall and early summer. Bear in mind that although the lake offers ample space for its visitors' water-based recreational activities, this is also the busiest time of the year.

Recreational Activities

Motorized and nonmotorized water activities are both allowed on the lake. The lake's pristine waters lure a variety of water activities: sailing, waterskiing, power boating, fishing, swimming, kayaking, paddleboarding, and much more. Rent a boat to explore secluded beaches and bays while fishing enthusiasts cast a line for a trophy whitefish or trout. Adventure seekers can arrange kayaking tours, opt for private water sports, or paddleboard, jet ski, ski boat, and personal watercraft rentals. Guided fishing tours and ice fishing in winter attract many visitors.

The lake's crystal clear water is cold and crisp with pebbly bottoms. Water temperature in summer is around 55 to 65 degrees Fahrenheit, so bring a wetsuit if you intend to swim, tube, or ski. The sheer size of the lake comes as a surprise and offers opportunities for incredible water, landscape, sunset, and sunrise photography. Whitewater rafting, tranquil and scenic boat floating, or a pontoon boat tour to Wild Horse Island and some of the other islands (approximately a four-hour trip) can be arranged. Viewing the scenic wonders of the painted rock petroglyphs (only viewable by boat) is another bucket list activity.

In summer, many roadside stands offer fresh produce for sale, such as locally grown cherries, plums, apples, and a variety of other fruits. These make ideal supplies for a leisurely picnic alongside the lake's water in the milder climate. During summer, the lake is also an angler's paradise (salmon, pike, or bass, among other species), even though this requires boating out to the deeper depths for success. In fall, shoreline fishing is more popular when the trout tend to move to shallower shores. Remember to apply for a tribal recreational permit if you venture to the southern section of the lake located in the Flathead Reservation area.

Winter activities include downhill skiing (with deep powder), cross-country skiing, snowshoeing, and snowmobiling. About 200 miles of trails around the lake area provide ample opportunities to enjoy the snow. Even a scenic winter drive through approximately 2,000 miles of National Forest roads will turn your winter vacation into a memorable one. Such leisurely scenic drives along the shoreline hugging Flathead Lake provide stunning vistas and photographic roadside pullout opportunities while soaking in the beauty of the lake and surrounding landscapes.

Fauna and Flora

The 2,000-acre state park of Wild Horse Island in the middle of the lake is only accessible by boat. Tours to this state park— a scenic home to wild horses, bighorn sheep, deer, and a variety of bird species can be arranged. Other wildlife viewing here include ospreys, eagles, deer, elk, and black bears. This island has been a landmark since the Salish-Kootenai used it as a sanctuary for their horses to prevent them from being stolen by other tribes. You'll find some rare and endangered plant species here and the shoreline is a favorite for hiking trails, spotting wildlife, and soaking up the majestic views from the island's vantage point. Also, swimmers and sailboat enthusiasts hug this island's shoreline on a regular basis.

Other delights include enjoying the fresh Montana air, clear blue endless skies, and breathtaking views of the vast lake. The lake is renowned for its sweet cherries from the many cherry orchards. During summer, kids will love to visit the orchards and pick their own (go before late June!) and sample delicious cherry-based products (jams, pies). A few golf courses are located near Flathead Lake with stunning views in a picturesque setting. After a day outing in nature, you can experience the burgeoning wine and craft beer of the Flathead Valley: sample local award-winning craft beers, wines, and locally produced spirits.

Cultural Recreation

For a cultural heritage experience, immerse yourself in the rich heritage of the Confederated Salish and Kootenai Tribes: learn more about their traditions, artwork, and history at the Flathead Indian Reservation (located north of I 90 between Missoula and Kalispell, at the southern section of the lake). The reservation was created through the Treaty of Hellgate (July 16, 1855) with about 110,000 inhabitants. Sixty-five percent of the Confederated Salish, Pend d'Oreille, and Kootenai tribal members live here. There are fewer than 7,000 with only about 5,000 living on the reservation. About

1.3 million acres of land are surrounded by fertile valleys and majestic mountains.

At the Three Chiefs Culture Center at St. Ignatius (formerly the People's Center), an exhibit gallery, educational programs, and a museum tell the story of these tribes as they had to adapt to a changed environment and face many challenges. The center displays cultural traditions and dispels myths and stereotypes to maintain the rich heritage of the native people from the area. There is also a quality gift shop with tribal memorabilia and occasional art classes (beading, dream catchers, cloth dolls, adornments, mini-tipis). Through promoting "pride and respect" they encourage cultural unity and create a vision for life. St. Ignatius Mission—with its distinct backdrop against the mountain ranges—was established in 1854 when the mission church was built by Native Americans under the guidance of Catholic missionaries. The building presents 58 spectacular original murals painted by Brother Joseph Carignano.

Tourists may not always be aware that they are on a tribal reservation. Lack of awareness or noticing of tribal landmarks harms society, so getting to know the local tribal communities opens up a better sense of unity between nations. Disrespecting tribal rules and nature (e.g., over-picking berries or leaving anything behind) is an absolute negative, as this damages the pristine and sacredness of their area.

Apart from tribal features, lakeside communities dot the shores of Flathead Lake with historic and cultural charm. Polson is well-known for its shops, restaurants, and Flathead

Lake Brewing Company. Bigfork has a vibrant art scene, and Lakeside has exquisite historic charm.

Many festivals and events, such as farmer's markets and concerts, are held throughout the year. Cherry festivals or art shows will enhance your visit. In July, the tribes celebrate the Arlee Pow Wow and Standing Arrow Pow Wow, cultural events that shouldn't be missed.

The National Bison Range invites a visit where 20,000 acres of natural grassland plains are inhabited by about 500 visible bison. They roam the area after being rescued from extinction and established by President Roosevelt on the range in the early 19th century. Limited hiking is allowed and the range has a scenic loop road to view the bison. The area is maintained as a diverse ecosystem of grasslands, Douglas Firs, and Ponderosa Pine forests. Other wildlife can also be spotted and the area offers a distinct birdlife habitat.

From the vast water landscape to the mountain charm of Whitefish, let's experience some small-town Montana hospitality!

WHITEFISH - A CHARMING MOUNTAIN TOWN

> The journey of a thousand miles begins with a single step.

> — LAO TZU

An interesting fact about Montana's streamflow is that about 70% originates from melting snow. A mere 2% of this does not serve agricultural irrigation: melting snow provides an important livelihood for most of the state, its inhabitants, and vegetation.

CHARMING WHITEFISH

With its moderate temperatures and clear days, Whitefish does not get as cold as the rest of Montana. This charming town isn't only a winter resort but also a pleasant summer vacation spot with plenty of recreational activities. According to Courtney Brown, a local travel expert, Whitefish will satisfy every daily need:

It's the type of town where your day can seamlessly go from hiking grassy slopes to window shopping high-end art galleries, or where the foodie in you can enjoy a fresh açaí bowl in the morning, sip on a local ginger brew in the afternoon and finish with a classic Montana bison burger at night. In almost every aspect of Whitefish, the traditional local scene is very much alive and well, just now alongside a new wave of youthful startups offering a fresh perspective— beautifully balanced yet true to its roots. (2022, para 2)

The neat and friendly little town (with only about 6,000 local inhabitants) provides a sports adventure playground of horse trail rides, hiking, biking, skiing, fly-fishing, and a champion golf course if that's your game. Water recreational activities abound on the lake (boat rentals, kayaking, jet skiing, etc.). Whitewater rafting tours can be arranged offering around 11 rapids of category two and three intensities. These trips can take up to three hours and remember that the water remains cold, despite the season! Wildlife spotting is another favorite, and the town provides cultural nurturing for the rest of us with unique shopping delights (you can even create a custom souvenir hat or buy authentic cowboy boots), historical discoveries, a train museum, and a variety of culinary experiences after some meditative mornings doing yoga or uplifting Zen practices. The town is a family-fun-adventure spot.

In summer, families can enjoy rafting, zip lining, alpine slides, a scenic gondola ride up the mountain, or horseback riding lessons. In fall, the scenery calls for magnificent photography with its golden days and snow-capped mountain peaks. The shoulder season offers warmer weather and less crowded roads. During spring, cascading waterfalls and longer days await your presence with the season's renewal.

Popular festivals and parades are the Huckleberry Days, Under the Big Sky Music Festival, Oktoberfest, and the winter carnival (this festival includes Skijoring, which is a recreational activity where horses pull skiers). A weekly farmers market, selling locally produced products and providing live music, delights all.

ITINERARY LOGISTICS

Slightly north of Kalispell, at the southern tip of Whitefish Lake, lies this popular but quiet small ski town of Whitefish. It's about 26 miles from the western side of Glacier National Park and one hour south of the Canadian border. The small, cozy alpine town has become a sought-after destination with its perfect blend of rustic wilderness and tourist sophistication, with rising property prices as an indicator of its residence value.

Getting There

Whitefish is about twenty minutes from Glacier International Airport at Kalispell where you can rent a car or drive your own into the heart of the Rocky Mountains. For an adventurous expedition to Whitefish, Amtrak offers a train journey (known as the Ski Train) on the Empire Builder to soak up a winter wonderland while you lazily travel to your final destination. This could even be a day trip as the train leaves early and returns before sunset to get you back to work.

While you are there, renting a bike and enjoying the area with two wheels brings you closer to nature. Most hotels are within walking distance of the station, and the S.N.O.W. shuttle also operates from downtown Whitefish and renders a free service from Whitefish to the mountain activities.

Accommodation

Many accommodation options exist in the quaint town and surrounding area.

- **Downtown or Lakeside rentals and cabins:** These provide slopeside lodging for skiers, retreats, hotels, luxury stays, ski cabins, mountain lodges, and studios. There are also hideaway cabins for the introverted traveler seeking privacy.
- **Whitefish Lake State Park:** This quaint camping site offers 25 spots for your tent or a small RV (maximum length of 40 feet) right on the lake waters. It gives easy access to all amenities close to Whitefish.
- **The Lodge at Whitefish Lake:** The lodge has a reputation for providing the best accommodation

facilities as a full-service resort hotel. Lodgings are inspired by the past but offer modern conveniences, as well as mountain views in the surrounding nature setting.

- **The Quarry:** A magnificently designed and decorated house for rent for larger groups (accommodates six) between downtown and the ski slopes of Whitefish Mountain Resort. Guests have access to some luxurious amenities such as a hot tub and exercise room.

- **Montana Treehouse Retreat:** This is a top attraction ten miles west of Whitefish with its unique double-decker treehouse to rest your traveler's soul.

Quaint downtown Whitefish, with its western feel, also offers The Galleries or the pet-friendly Firebrand Hotel. Both provide traditional rustic urban but luxurious lodgings that uphold Montana's heritage.

Dude Ranches

These are a bucket-list favorite in Montana. The award-winning but still affordable Bar W. Guest Ranch is five miles west of Whitefish on US 93. It offers lodge, cabin, or glamping accommodation. Its capacity of 40 guests maintains an intimate feel. The ranch is based at the foot of Spencer Mountain and is surrounded by dense pine forests.

Their amenities depend on your selected accommodation. According to Mark Barnett, they provide an action-packed stay including the following activities: "hatchet throwing, skeet shooting, archery, arrow tag, fly casting lessons, Spencer Lake activities, lawn games, Lion Mountain hiking, line dancing, bonfire night, and much more" (Barnett, 2021, para 14). Here, you can also enjoy rodeo, roping, square dancing, cattle drives, cook-outs and campfires, trail rides, and even a scenic winter sleigh ride. Besides these, your main activity will include lots of horseback riding! Dining options cater to every individual need including vegan options. There is a strong sense of community and a friendly Western feel.

Remember to check seasonal activities and whether the ranch caters to family or adult recreational activities. Make sure their activities will satisfy the needs of your fellow travelers. It's advisable to look at the weather forecast for your planned visit and align your needs with seasonal activities. If you plan water-based activities, then make sure the lakes are not frozen over!

Horseback riding is a favorite activity but some ranches do not offer riding lessons and assume certain skill levels. If you're an expert rider, you do not want to be held back by beginner rides! So, make sure the ranch matches your level. They cater mostly to outdoor activities, which means that you have to be aware of packing the right equipment. This includes layered clothing for extreme and unexpected weather changes, as well as sun protection. Most ranches provide a clothing and equipment outline to guide you.

WINTER ACTIVITIES

It is known for its "snow ghost" trees in winter (annual snowfall is around 72 inches and on Big Mountain, about 300 inches) on a vast 3,000 acres of land. The area is known for its world-class skiing in winter. It has become *the* place to be for winter skiing. An endless variety of snow activities include snowboarding, snowshoeing, ice fishing, and snowmobiling. Additional activities are a downhill slide on a thrilling sled, tube, or toboggan ride. You could even enjoy a gentle yesteryear horse-drawn sleigh ride finished off with hot chocolate. Ice climbing is a different activity that enhances spectacular views of the winter landscape. Whitefish Vertical Adventures arranges out-of-this-world experiences with a customized ice climbing tour.

The Whitefish Mountain Resort is a snow lover's paradise. Its list of activities includes skiing or snowboarding, and in summer, the resort becomes an adventurer's playground and family attraction with tubing, strider bike rides, alpine slides, and mountain biking. Its 14 lifts and ski terrain for various levels are consistently ranked at the top in national magazines (number three in the West in *Ski Magazine*) and it's maintaining its top ten position as a ski resort. Packages of night skiing elevate your skiing adventure to another level; also, learn-to-ski packages and snowboarding packages provide ample entertainment. The fluffy Rocky Mountain snow awaits you!

The scenic Whitefish Lake (within walking distance from downtown) is a spectacular seven-mile-long and two-and-a-half-mile-wide glacier lake with its deepest point at 222 feet. Families can enjoy a day of "beach" activities by the lakeside. Lifeguards are on duty, and boats, stand-up paddle boards, and kayaks can be rented.

Enjoy a fat tire bike ride in the snowy mountainside for an additional adrenalin rush. This mountain biking activity has become all the hype in the winter season so as not to lose out on valuable adventure time. It doesn't take more than merely knowing how to ride a bicycle and bikes can be rented in Whitefish. Have an artistic cultural venture to a variety of theaters or art studios, or enjoy the winter carnival. Distinctly unique shopping experiences, vibrant nightlife, or a rejuvenating spa treatment will warm your winter bones.

Hiking Trails

More than 700 miles of hiking trails in the area leave abundant options for active outdoor adventure seekers. There are short hikes or day excursions, hiking trails for kids, and Glacier Park hiking. The large network of 43 miles of Whitefish trail systems has 14 trailheads, catering to all fitness levels and offering spectacular scenery. Mountain views, forest walks, or peaceful walks along the Whitefish River are very popular with tourists. If you prefer a quieter (and budget-friendly) vacation, this is probably not your first choice, unless skiing is at the top of your activity list. Despite the popularity, the pristine wilderness of the area and its majestic scenery are well worth a visit.

- **Spencer Trail** is set on a 2,500-acre plot where families have fun cycling, hiking, and walking while enjoying nature. It's a busy trail where you won't feel isolated.
- **Woods Lake** is a family-friendly trail with three vantage points. It offers excellent bonding time while being in nature.
- **Beaver Lake Loop** (ten miles outside Whitefish) is a four-mile intermediate hike with a 500-foot elevation gain. This longer, strenuous hike surprises you with amazing views. Bike the trail to add an additional workout. (The Beaver Lake area has a

number of hiking and biking trails to explore and join with a dip in the azure-blue lake waters.)

- **Valley Overlook** is an easy three-mile walk (720 feet elevation) to a spectacular viewpoint where you can have a picnic. Dogs can join if they are on a leash.
- **Lion Mountain Loop** is a perfect one-hour walk for beginners or the elderly. It is only 350 feet in elevation and 2.5 miles long. This easy family trail provides majestic views, phenomenal mountains, and towns and pastures scenery. Dogs are allowed.

CULTURAL ACTIVITIES

If bustling restaurants and local craft breweries don't offer enough for you, Whitefish provides many cultural delights to satisfy your needs. The infrastructure of the quaint town caters exclusively to its thriving tourism industry. Discover art galleries with local art, jewelry, sculptures, and a 328-seater theater that has been hosting acclaimed shows for almost half a century. (See their schedule at The Whitefish Theater Company.)

The historic main street used to be called Stumptown. Here you'll find a creative art studio that echoes the same name where regular classes and exhibitions are held. The White-fish Depot (the historic train station gem) should not be missed. It was built in 1928 and beautifully restored in the 1990s. Treat yourself and take a journey down memory lane while you wait for your train in the adjacent train museum: it still remains one of the busiest train depots (connecting Seattle and Minneapolis).

Local Cuisine

There are some local laws to remember when visiting breweries in Montana. The state was ranked second for breweries per capita in the US in 2020, but this is limited by only offering drinking between 10 a.m. and 8 p.m. It's also unlawful to serve more than 48 ounces of beer daily, so if you intend to go on a beer-tasting excursion, I suggest trying a few different places and doing a brewery-hop-tasting journey.

There are many award-winning craft beers available at the range of craft breweries here. Craft beers and distilleries will quench your thirst after an adventurous day out in nature. You can try the Bonsai Brewing Project or Montana Tap House for some of the 58 Montana-made craft beers on tap, and visit the Spotted Bear Spirits Distillery, Glacier Distilling Company, and Whitefish Handcrafted Spirits for distillery delights. Most of the breweries and distilleries in Whitefish offer a food option as well. At the iconic five-star rated Bierstube, you can enjoy live music while sipping your drink of choice.

According to Samantha and Chris from *Boozing Abroad* (2023, para 2), the best options for beer in Whitefish are at Bonsai Brewing Project, a microbrewery, and Spotted Bear Spirits. Bonsai Brewing has won numerous accolades and specializes in IPA beers, barrel-aged brews, and sours. They offer a lovely outdoor spot, love your four-legged friends, and are popular in summer with outside seating and shady trees. The Spotted Bear also offers a good variety of craft cocktails if beer is not your preferred choice of drink—they serve a lovely limoncello! They open at 4 p.m. and serve until 8 p.m. Spotted Bear supports local produce as well.

Other options include the Blackstar BluePub and Restaurant, where you can taste beer made from local barley malt (sourced from Montana's Golden Triangle) and boast magnificent views of Big Mountain from its balconies and rooftop. It also has a magnificent food line-up and a vibey interior that reminds you of the Great Northern Railway days.

A winery called Unleashed offers lovely locally produced wines made from California-sourced grapes in a relaxed atmosphere opposite the performing arts center. The White Raven Winery uses Montana-grown grapes (grapes that are able to withstand the cold temperatures!) to produce its wines. The winery is situated about a 20-minute scenic drive outside of Whitefish, making it an exceptional day outing.

If coffee is your thing, then try Folklore Coffee or the Huckleberry White Chocolate Mocha at Montana Coffee Traders. Top it off with delicious pastries from the French-inspired Fleur Bake Shop. This popular tourist town has endless palate-pleasing opportunities. Dining options in Montana focus on locally grown and harvested vegetables and fruit, wild game (think elk and bison), some of the best beef (being a "ranching" state), and locally sourced fish dishes.

The quaint family-owned Swift Creek Café offers a hearty breakfast or lunch. Worth a special mention is the rustic Last Chair Kitchen and Bar with its wooden interior, interesting tap handles, glasses and wine bottles display. What makes this place unique is not only the ambiance but also its exquisitely diverse dining options ranging from typically local dishes, such as rib-eye steak or bison ragu, to Asian cuisine like pad Thai, all made from locally sourced ingredients. At Abruzzo Italian Kitchen you can tempt your tastebuds to authentic in-house handmade pasta, kale pesto, and wood-fired pizza. Loula's Café offers the most unforgettable pies in town with more than twenty homemade options. Montana Tap House offers tasty pizza and pub foods alongside their craft beers.

Latitude 48 Bistro, The Wich House, the eclectic Jalisco Cantina (Mexican-infused fare), and Indah Sushi (if you can't pass Asian cuisine) are some other options to taste various culinary delights artistically prepared. Tupelo Grille (also known as one of the best restaurants in Montana) delights with creative cuisine and impeccable service. Try the crawfish cakes, elk meatloaf, rack of lamb, or dried aged bison for an exceptional dining experience.

One of the most innovative eateries in Whitefish is Café Kandahar, serving since 1983. Their refined menu is small, rotates seasonally, and surprises with unique pairings, but remains perfect for a refined palate. It's also one of the most well-known places. Or hop off to Casey's Bar and Grill for an unassuming but hearty burger made from locally sourced meat.

In Whitefish, your tastebuds can experience the world, ranging from homemade pasta to designer sandwiches to comfort food to hearty meat dishes to vegetarian options to delicious crêpes and designer cocktails while you indulge in a cozy atmosphere: round it all off with some of the best coffees or save the best for breakfast. One thing is certain: you won't go hungry or thirsty here!

Local Events

In summer and fall, on the first Thursday of the month, the Whitefish community hosts an evening of art, entertainment, and refreshments. Local art galleries support the community with gallery nights. Most fine art galleries in Whitefish feature contemporary artists of the American West and elements that define the region in their art, such as Cawdrey Gallery (fine art), Dick Idol Signature Gallery, Going to the Sun Gallery, Hoffman Gallery, For Fine Art, and Sotheby's. Not to be missed is the inspirational photographic imagery at Paul Lally Fine Art Nature, where unique views of the area's wilderness and wildlife come to rest through his camera lens.

You can indulge in many workshops: glaze workshops, fused glass classes, art explorations for preschoolers, or Art with the Masters: Mondrian Magic. The Stumptown Art Studio offers a variety of creative workshops and field trips to serve the community. At Underscore Art and Jewelry, you can feast your eyes on a collection of designer fine jewelry from around the world.

Enjoy the farmers market every Tuesday evening after 5 p.m. in summer. This market is filled with local produce, food stalls, and live music. Winter carnival events in February are ski racing and snow celebration events for kids and adults. For a unique fun-filled experience, you can book a lane of ax-throwing at Hank's Hatchets. Numerous live performances, music events, and theater productions take place throughout the year in Whitefish. Remember to recreate and explore responsibly while you support locally.

If recreational adventure is not enough for you, the culinary delights and cultural events of Whitefish will satisfy you before we head off to Kalispell—the gateway to Glacier Park and Flathead Lake.

THE SPELL OF KALISPELL

> ❝ Wherever you go becomes a part of you somehow.
>
> — ANITA DESAI

The Salish meaning of the name *Kalispell* means "flat land (or prairie) above the lake" (Historic Downtown Kalispell, n.d., para 2). Kalispell is better known as a hikers' Mecca and the "soul of Montana's Flathead Valley." The city is much more than an entry stop to Glacier Park or Flathead Lake and offers delightful options for nature and cultural recreation. When we remember that "Montana has more than a 100 mountain ranges in its western half" (Editorial Staff, 2019, para 67), the valley surrounding this gateway city is a welcome breather.

KALISPELL: THE GATEWAY

From Kalispell, it is about a 50-mile drive to Glacier Park (west entrance) and north of Flathead Lake, offering a good balance of the convenience of a city with the rugged nature of outdoor recreation or cultural enjoyment. It remains one of the most popular places to visit in the US and is a very popular tourist "town" in summer. The city has seen rapid population growth over the first few years of the century. Recent property price increases indicate a growing trend. Many homeowners have second homes in what used to be a quiet and secluded corner of Montana until it was discovered.

One of the biggest attractions is the mild weather. Being on the right side of the mountains produces cooler days in summer, and Kalispell is slightly warmer than the rest of Montana in winter. The higher mountains of the continental divide influence the weather favorably. Still, there are more overcast days in shoulder seasons and winter and the weather in June tends to be a bit unpredictable.

Popular activities include rodeo, games and action in the snow, snowmobile rentals, water activities, fishing, cultural attractions, massage and wellness, history, and some culinary and brewery explorations with a wide variety of bars, pubs, and eateries. The top attractions in Kalispell include Conrad Mansion, Lone Pine State Park, Flathead Lake State Park, Wild Horse Island State Park, and Herron Park.

The best outdoor activities (much less crowded) can be found at Thompson Chain of Lakes and Jewel Basin (in the Flathead forest). Hiking here offers a myriad of trails to explore, with stunning views of the lake and the mountains, plus wildlife encounters.

ITINERARY LOGISTICS

With its short summer peak season, the June to August period is the busiest (August has the hottest daily temperatures). Shoulder seasons become a tourist sweet spot with less traffic and crowding but cooler weather. September and October delight with fall leaf foliage displays. Freezing winters provide an adventure playground: the ski season runs from November until March with Kalispell's long, snowy winters. January generally has a high snowfall (more than seven inches) and cloudy days. Kalispell's scenic winter offers frosted tree vistas and snow-capped peaks while summer delights with green and cascading water, making it a spectacular photographic vista to be captured all year.

Getting There

Kalispell can be reached by airplane at Glacier Park International Airport (FCA), about 8.5 miles from the Kalispell city center or Missoula Johnson-Bell Field. There is also the Kalispell Airport south of the central business district (CBD).

To rent a car, you'll pay around $99/day at agencies like Hertz and Budget. Car rentals at the airport are more expensive and they may be in high demand during the season so book early. US 2 (east to west) and US 93 connect you to the city.

Accommodation

There is an array of options for family stays, camping, luxurious hotels, rustic lodging, historic accommodation, or budget-friendly stays. All of these have close proximity to all amenities. Here are a few options:

- The historic Kalispell Grand Hotel in downtown Kalispell has more than 100 years of hospitality experience. They offer delicious treats and breakfasts, are pet-friendly, and are on the doorstep of the most popular historic sites of Kalispell. According to Downtown Kalispell, the hotel has a colorful history (n.d., para 8):

Rooms in the Kalispell Hotel were originally $2 per night. Nationally known Montana author Frank Bird Linderman leased and managed the hotel from 1924 to 1926 and was able to continue writing because of the profits from the sale of the hotel lease and furniture. Artist Charlie Russell was his frequent guest.

- My Place Hotel is a popular option for convenience, comfort, and value. They are pet-friendly for an additional fee and offer fitted kitchenettes in the rooms as well as all essential amenities on site.
- The Aero Inn (downtown Kalispell) is close to the airport, Glacier National Park, Blacktail ski area, Flathead Lake, and numerous wilderness areas, resorts, and golf courses. This is the best site to have if you like outdoor adventures. It's pet-friendly at an additional fee.
- Sherman Lodge is a luxurious boutique hotel. It is a good option for couples or small groups because it is close to all amenities.
- Montana Basecamp RV Park has 50 acres of a fresh approach to camping (no limitations on RV sizes) with exceptional hospitality and amenities. Offering easy access to Glacier National Park, Flathead Lake, and downtown Kalispell with magnificent mountain views, starry skies, and miles of hiking trails right at your doorstep.
- Hampton Inn is a 120-room hotel with modern accommodations. It offers connecting rooms for families, which are convenient for sightseeing tours. The inn gets good reviews, especially for cleanliness and reasonably priced rooms.
- Outside Kalispell, the Lonesome Dove Ranch is a bed and breakfast option. It offers glamping, tipi stays, or

rustic cabins in the mountains for a true Rocky Mountain holiday.

HISTORIC DOWNTOWN AND ITS PRESERVED ARCHITECTURE

Kalispell was founded as a railroad town many years ago, which shaped its development and history. Despite this, its rail glory did not last too long even though it served as a division point for the Great Northern Railway, mainly between St. Paul and Seattle. Its fascinating history includes the story of the Demersville ghost town (four miles outside of Kalispell). Many of the buildings were transported to Kalispell across the prairie on roller logs, but soon after, the railway line was relocated to Whitefish (1904), which became the new division point. This led to an exodus of rail workers to Whitefish. Despite this, the town of Kalispell remained adamant about surviving when early entrepreneurial optimism established the town as a trading and financial post of the Flathead Valley.

Kalispell was a county seat in 1893, confirming its roots through all the amenities it now has to offer: a hospital, a variety of churches, federal agencies, schools, financial institutions, hotels, an opera house, a library, and a variety of services that any worthy town should have. Despite the railway movement, the town remained adamant about prospering (it even experienced a property boom during the early 1900s), and various regional events placed it on the map, such as the opening of the Flathead Indian Reservation and the opening of a Continental Divide highway at Marias Pass

(1930). Apart from this, it also remained a thriving lumber industry city, and its fertile lands drew many farmers.

After the opening of the Glacier National Park in 1910, Kalispell thrived on the inviting description of the "Gateway to Glacier Park" and "All Roads Lead to Kalispell" for many years (Downtown Kalispell, n.d., para 6). The close-knit community was created showcasing galleries and shops to entice every spirit and welcome its tourism opportunities.

There is an interesting 20-block self-guided walking tour down the oldest section of Kalispell (down Main Street and First Avenue East) that portrays its vibrant service history and unique architecture. This walk includes Kalispell's distinctive museums. Many of these historic buildings showcase beautifully restored and picturesque architecture, like the brick buildings that now house modern businesses offering local fare and friendly services. A beautiful report of the history of the town can be found at www.downtownkalispell.com.

Museums and Cultural Attractions

Kalispell is worth a visit for its heritage of pioneer and settler museums. The area's vibrant history can be explored here.

Conrad Mansion

The mansion was built by the founder of Kalispell and Missouri River freighter, Charles Conrad. His home remains a must-visit on your itinerary. The 13,000 sq. ft. family home reflects 1895 architecture with more than 20 rooms spanning three floors. The house was built with rare luxuries for the time: indoor plumbing, electricity, and central heating, and was thus a luxurious establishment for the Conrad family of five. It has been beautifully restored with most of its original Conrad artifacts on display in the villa. Open for viewing all year and from May to October from 10 a.m. to 5 p.m., with close proximity to more than 100 restaurants, makes this a lovely day outing. The grounds are also impeccably maintained, and it feels like making a turn in history when visiting its splendor.

Hockaday Museum of Art

This historic Carnegie Library house dates back to 1903 and is on the National Register of Historic Places. The intimate museum is worth a visit for its historical and architectural value, especially the partial woodwork interior. The museum hosts exhibitions on a rotating basis and offers children's activities and educational programs all year round. Their permanent exhibitions display well-known artists in their "Crown of the Continent" Gallery: C. M. Russell, Hugh Hockaday, Ace Powell, O. C. Seltzer, Jeanne Hamilton, Gary Schultz, and more. The rotating personal exhibitions are Native American beadwork, historic travel prints and magazines, and emerging and independent artists. Most of their art reflects the local history of the area, such as a unique film about Glacier Park and Going-to-the-Sun Road and Western-themed art. Some works are for sale through the small gift shop; their mission is to preserve the community's cultural and artistic heritage as an outlet for the enhancement of local art and cultural life of the region. Opening hours are from Tuesday to Saturday between 10 a.m. and 5 p.m.

The museum showcases two sections of the Glacier National Park Mural Restoration Project, which started in 2021. The Glacier Park Lodge had commissioned murals spanning the walls above the wainscoting, these were as majestic in size as the surrounding landscape. They were painted using casein stretched on canvas (casein is a milk protein paint that dries fast and has a water-soluble basis) and although the original artist remains a mystery, the story goes that the president of the Great Northern Railway, Louis Hill, wanted to fill the lodge with eclectic art (Hockaday Museum of Art, 2019b, para 6):

The scenic panels covered hundreds of square feet and appeared in a 1939 Glacier Park Lodge inventory as '51 watercolor panels'. There is some evidence that John Fery, the most famous of the Glacier Park artists, intended to paint these panels as he had drawn up some preliminary sketches. Instead, Hill decided to hire a muralist to expedite the process.

When the lodges were remodeled in the 1950s, these murals were removed and stored privately until they found their home back to the public eye in the Hockaday Museum in 2012. Two of the four restored murals are displayed here.

Northwest Montana History Museum

A former school building of Richardsonian Romanesque design (1894) offers six permanent exhibits, and some temporary ones, mostly about the history of Flathead Valley settlements, Native American tribes, the development of Kalispell as an economic hub, local ecology, and the vanished town of Demersville. It's quaint and smallish with an unusual presence. The oldest public building in Kalispell has a gift shop and presents year-round educational and community programs and events such as book clubs and movie nights. Opening times are only during weekdays.

OUTDOOR ADVENTURES

Kalispell offers abundant outdoor recreation in the form of whitewater rafting, fishing charters, ziplining, hiking, skiing, mountain biking, horseback riding, golfing, rock climbing, air adventures, and scenic floats. Its attractive lakes and streams are popular for water activities and fly-fishing. "Kalispell is a world-renowned destination for outdoor enthusiasts, game hunters, and those in search of blue-ribbon trout fishing" (Discovering Montana, 2022a, para 3). Blacktail Mountain ski area (en route to Flathead Lake from Kalispell) is less busy than Big Mountain at Whitefish Mountain Resort—offering quieter space for intermediate skiers without all the fuss and fancy frills. It still provides world-class skiing options.

Some noteworthy biking activities include the single-track Foy's to Blacktail trails. The single-track Beardance trails offer the best views and a bit more challenging biking (it's one of the highest-ranked single-track routes). Then there is also the Rails to Trails path that weaves in old railroad paths of the Great Northern Railway. These are relatively flat, making them perfect for scenic family leisurely biking fun.

State Parks and National Forests

Some of the most popular parks to visit in Kalispell are the following:

- **Lone Pine State Park:** There are 279 acres of nature with elevation ranges between 2,959 and 3,644 feet, overlooking Flathead Lake, Jewel Basin, Big Mountain, and Glacier National Park. The Flathead Valley provides seven and a half miles of trails to snowshoe, bike, hike, or horseback ride among the vistas, wildflowers, and wildlife. The visitor's center offers educational programs, workshops, and a gift shop. The park's seasonal amenities are archery, bird watching, and a plethora of outdoor activities. It even has an action track chair providing all-terrain accessibility for physically challenged visitors. A nominal fee gets you in.
- **Woodland Water Park:** An excellent all-year-round choice for families. In winter the water freezes up for ice adventures like hockey and skating and in summer, outdoor activities, water pool and slide fun, and ample green space for picnics enhance family relaxation. It's a small park but beautifully maintained.
- **Herron Park:** Another firm favorite here for summer and winter hikes with magnificent views of the city below. The park is well-maintained and provides biking and hiking trails.

Events and Festivals

Farmers' markets with local produce, antique stores, and shops delight every taste. Most events happen during major holiday celebrations such as Easter and Christmas. Plan your itinerary around some of these options:

- **Northwest Montana Fair:** This five-day August fair is the highlight of events in Kalispell. Enjoy fair food delights, rodeos, carnival rides, farm animals, live music, concerts, and general enjoyment.
- **Brash Rodeo:** During summer, this rodeo happens every Thursday night. Try bull riding, bareback riding, steer riding, team roping, barrel racing, breakaway roping, and calf roping events the real Montana way. Rodeo is Montana culture and this event is the longest-running open rodeo in Western Montana.
- **Taste of Kalispell:** Good for live music, food, drinks, and sheer fun.
- **Picnic in the Park:** The event takes place during summer (Tuesdays and Thursdays). Bring your picnic blanket and savor local fare from street vendors while listening to live music.
- **Fourth of July Parade:** This event offers family entertainment, fireworks, food, music, and floats. It's fun all around.
- **Flathead Celtic Festival:** Because of Kalispell's Celtic heritage, the event honors its Celtic lineage with typical dance, music, food, and crafts.
- **Kalispell Christmas Parade:** Apart from delighting in general lights displays and Christmas festivities,

this time calls for comfort hot chocolate drinks and
freshly baked local culinary treats.

Additional craft breweries and outdoor events happen
frequently, so keep an eye on the Kalispell calendar.

Now that the family slowed down in Kalispell with its
sublime nature and introduction to historic sites, I want to
introduce you to the swirling landscapes of northeast
Montana. We've seen the mountains and lakes, let's take a
journey with real history!

PART II
NORTHEAST AND CENTRAL MONTANA—A JOURNEY THROUGH HISTORY

OVERVIEW

 The winter's a little bit daunting in Montana.

— PHIL JACKSON

Parts of northeast Montana fall victim to so-called "cold waves" that happen on average up to 12 times in winter. These happen mostly eastwards of Glacier Park on the other side of the Divide. Of course, they do not hold the same dangers they did years ago before modern conveniences, but they can still be disruptive as the below-zero temperatures, accompanied by strong winds and blowing snow can cause havoc and be dangerous. They can also have adverse effects: Between January 14 and 15, 1972, the temperature range in Loma (central Montana) produced a world record for the greatest change in temperature measured within 24 hours: from -54 degrees Fahrenheit to 49 degrees the next morning! That's almost a 100-degree overnight difference.

CULTURE, HISTORY, AND VAST OPEN SPACES

Less is more! Less stress, noise, and traffic mean more authentic living. Eastern Montana embraces the lifestyle that really matters: "The soft fusion of earth and sky on horizon that seems endless" (Graetz & Graetz, 2013, para 3). The vast distances between villages and towns, especially in the stretch of the east-to-west US 2 passing through one of the richest agricultural regions in the world, make Montana a must-see location. Did you know the state was ranked fourth in wheat production in the US in 1996 (Sandy, 2023, para 3)?

This area is known as the "Great Plains" for a reason. The overpowering immensity, unique landforms, geological wonders, undisturbed space, and unending skies create an impression of no confinement and offer breathing space. Here, you have room to roam as the bison do: you have room to explore, you have room to be still, and you have room to just be.

The Missouri River became the area's lifeline as it ran like a vein through the terrain. Missouri River country faced dramatic climate change many years ago: What was once a humid dinosaur playground with forested landscapes, turned into vast and semi-arid prairies as we know Montana today. Both liquid and frozen water reshaped the landscape creating various geological and majestic rock formations. The sandstone formations were weathered by the wind into shapely sculptures. Its long and cold winter nights and sunny days support this rolling prairie landscape and fascinating wildlife that roams the sea of grass.

The protected prairie ecosystem is also one of the areas with the lowest inhabited space, adding to its wildness. Scattered bison once again roam the land along with rich birdlife such as horned larks, golden eagles, and shorebirds. Stars scatter the skies with light at night. Spectacular sunrises and sunsets frame the days. Eastern Montana is a land that is truly wild and free—an area to slow down and breathe again. It's renowned for its silence. Apart from slight human intrusion with buildings and structures, the vast open spaces allow for absolute quiet, as the air is "devoid of human created sound" (Patterson & Patterson, 2016, para 16). Apart from the breeze, occasional calls of the coyote, and bird sounds—here you can enjoy nature's silence once again.

Follow explorers Lewis and Clark's footsteps when they traveled through eastern Montana on their historic expedition to the West. Before them, pioneers, fur trappers, and ranchers settled in the area. Their trail spots many stops for discovery along their Missouri River path as they ventured deeper into unknown territory in their dug-out canoes in 1804.

You'll walk in the same steps as legendary outlaws, such as Butch Cassidy and the Sundance Kid, who roamed the undeveloped areas and badlands. Back then, an outlaw trail was established—a route between Canada and Mexico for optimistic gunslingers and robbers. Cattle barons, gold seekers, vigilantes, cowboys, and horse thieves roamed the area a mere century ago while pushing the native tribes back into the shadows of the mountains. Gangs and bar brawls wrote the history within the haste of finding gold. Northeastern Montana holds a vibrant cultural and historical heritage, ready to be explored.

These so-called badlands hold incredible paleontological discoveries dating back to the wetland era of the dinosaurs. After the dramatic climate change, the river forged a new path through these geological formations, exposing world-class fossil discoveries and a wealth of dinosaur remains. At the Montana Badlands, visitors can take part in dinosaur diggings as part of the area's rich geological heritage of these former giants.

Montana makes one feel small in its expansive landscape. These plains offer a different experience: from the rugged mountains of the western side, away from the busyness of city life, to finding thinking space. "This is classic cattle and wheat country, with grass thick and green in spring, brown and dry by fall, and blanketed by snow in winter" (Frommers, n.d.-b, para 1). It's a landscape defined by the seasons. Scenic drives in this part of Montana are as endless as the starry skies at night and the rolling prairie landscapes at day.

The area provides ample recreational opportunities for the introverted who seek quiet solitude yet yearn for outdoor adventure. It's a cultural mecca and a sportsman's paradise with ice fishing, a variety of boating options, snowmobiling, relaxing in hot springs, camping, hiking, stargazing, horse-back riding, gold-panning, dinosaur and fossil hunting, wildlife watching, rodeos, train rides, scenic drives, and many more. Montana heritage discoveries, family activities, group excursions, couples adventures, and weekend getaways offer a diverse seasonal variety—ready to be explored.

PLACES TO VISIT

Some of the most breathtaking scenery can be found along the Missouri River, especially going downstream from Fort Benton. Towering sandstone cliffs and deep canyons lace the river, known as White Cliffs or also as the Missouri River Breaks. The Milk River area has a vibrant ranching and farming community around Malta to Glasgow and Fort Peck. This is the area of vast plains where Indian tribes used to roam.

You'll experience a general "small-town" feel with comforting hospitality. The sprawling prairie wilderness and semi-desert of the badlands call for amazement. Between the town of Circle and the eastern part of Fort Peck Lake (adjacent to the Dry Arm section), there is a spectacular ten-mile stretch of unique badlands and colored buttes to delight you. The area is rich with history and remarkable cultural events that can be explored in various small towns, adjacent fields, and the waterways.

Billings

Billings is actually located in central Montana, and is farther south than the rest of the locations discussed in this section, but we had to put it in somewhere. Montana's largest city, often called Montana's trailhead, offers all the amenities for local dwellers. Billings is the main city along I 90 (which runs east to west) and is a major trade, entertainment, and medical center of northeastern Montana. Its location at the foot of a wall of massive rimrocks places it on the geological map. From these sandstone cliffs, magnificent views of the valley and Rockies in the distance can be enjoyed, and they set the scene for brilliant sunset photography.

The home of a frontier family from 1903, Moss Mansion, is a popular site to visit here. Or try your hand as a real cowboy or cowgirl at horseback riding. There is also a wide variety of accommodations and culinary delights in Billings. During summer, this is the place to visit with its long sunny days and warm temperatures. The city is a popular family vacation spot with all its festivals and fairs, Ferris wheel, shopping mall, and antique shops. Entertainment parks such as a water park and MetraPark attract sports and recreational lovers. Cave State Park is a bucket list cultural visit with kids and shows Native American's primitive paintings on the sandstone walls of the cave, dating back to prehistoric times! Just outside Billings on the I 94, the remains of Clarke's carved name in the sandstone formations is visible. It's called *Pompey's Pillar National Monument*. The *Little Bighorn Battlefield National Monument* is also close to Billings.

Little Bighorn

After the U.S. Army was sent to subdue Native American tribes and prevent them from living their traditional lifestyle, the famous Battle of Bighorn took place here. On June 25 to 26, the Native Americans were victorious in their fight against oppression as the Cheyenne and Sioux tribes were led by Crazy Horse. George Custer and many of his soldiers were killed in this futile battle, and to this day, the land where it was fought remains largely untouched and respected.

Great Falls

The largest city in the mid-northern section of Montana is a cultural and commercial center for the surrounding villages.

Covering a vast region, it remains one of the best cities to buy Western attire. The famous C. M. Russell Museum is located here—a big cultural and historical attraction. His original studio, which calls for a bucket-list visit, is located close by. The Lewis and Clark National Historic Trail Interpretive Center, overlooking the majestic Missouri River, has numerous exhibits and informative displays of their expedition to the Pacific Ocean.

If outdoor recreation is your game, some of the best fly-fishing can be done just north of the city of Great Falls. Annual festivities and fairs (such as the Montana State Fair) take place here, drawing many locals and visitors alike, with live shows, carnival rides, entertainment, and exhibits. Excellent accommodations, breweries, and eateries in Great Falls add to your comfort when visiting this charming old-world and culinary elegant Montana city.

Chateau

Choteau is a sophisticated and charming rural town on US 89, northwest of Great Falls en route to the Rockies (about 26 miles away). The small village with fewer than 2,000 inhabitants, is on the popular highway that connects Yellowstone to Glacier National Park. Here, you'll spot smaller wildlife and dinosaur fossils at the Old Trail Museum and find numerous heartwarming taverns and accommodations welcoming you. For these reasons, the town is a good stopover en route to the parks.

Fort Benton

The Missouri River area at Fort Benton is worth every visit. Following the sandstone cliffs along the river in a kayak or canoe remains one of the most favored activities in the area. It has been designated as the *Upper Missouri Breaks National Monument* offering a wildness and solitude that visitors will relish long after a visit. Just the mere knowledge of following the same footsteps as Lewis and Clark makes it worthwhile to float and reflect on a boat trip down this river. The Museum of the Northern Great Plains, as well as the *Lewis and Clark Memorial* (huge bronze statue) near the Missouri banks, serve as reminders of their expedition. The historic Grand Union Hotel offers accommodation with a touch of nostalgia.

Miles City

The southern-most city in this section other than Billings, this legendary western town was founded in 1876, and traces of its ancestry go back to soldiers, ranchmen, explorers, and frontiersmen. All played a significant role in its development, leaving historical sites and brilliant untouched recreational areas as evidence. A visit to this city with a heart of gold and a small-town feel offers an abundant recreational playground away from the crowds. It's world-famous for its rodeos, bucking horse festivities, and livestock auctions.

Fort Peck

The tiny town of Fort Peck is an epicenter of recreation! This includes the haunted but historic 1930s Fort Peck Hotel. The name is derived from an old trading post established by Colonel Campbell K. Peck and Commander E. H. Durfee in 1867. At the time, the town established a monopoly of fur trade with the Sioux and Assiniboine Indian tribes. If culture is your vibe, the Historic Fort Peck Theater (originally built as a movie house in 1934) showcases performances during summer.

Close by, the Fort Peck Dam is the largest hydraulic dam in the world. Built in 1930, it generates electricity, enables irrigation, and reduces flooding in the area. It also graced the cover of the first issue to Life Magazine on November 23, 1936. Tourists can visit the powerhouse with its spinning shaft pumping water (with the help of gravity) to spin a generator that creates electricity. The Fort Peck reservoir is like a vast inland sea (nearly four miles) with long shorelines (1,600 miles) for four-seasonal recreational activities. This dam is one of the most prominent tourist attractions in northeast Montana. Fishing at Fort Peck Reservoir always delivers success. The sheer number of fish in the lake, from boat or shore, gives it the reputation of an angler's paradise.

The Fort Peck Interpretive Center and Museum (part of the Montana Dinosaur Trail) exhibits fascinating dinosaur skeletons. The enormous Tyrannosaurus Rex exhibit (nicknamed Peck's Rex) dates back 67 million years. Visitors to the area can enjoy the lure of dinosaurs on this Montana Dinosaur Trail, which is scattered with museums. These also feature two large aquariums with native and game species. Fans of the film *Jurassic Park* may recall opening scenes referencing Hell Creek, which is located in this area.

Fort Peck Indian Reservation

The second largest Indian reservation in Montana is Fort Peck Reservation along US 2, stretching more than 2 million acres on the eastern side of Fort Peck Lake and down the Missouri River. Almost 7,000 Sioux and Assiniboine reside in the reservation.

Havre

Close to the Canadian border on US 2, you'll find the quaint town of Havre, with a population just below 10,000. The area offers many water sports activities on the Fresno Reservoir, a magnificent lake in the Milk River. Here, the Bear Paw Mountains and battlefield call for a visit. At the Battlefield, southwest of Havre, Chief Joseph and his Nez Perce Indians clashed with the U.S. Cavalry in 1877. It's known as a futile battle between a small group of Indians and the Cavalry.

Glasgow

Established in the late 1800s as a railroad town, Glasgow grew considerably after 1933 when the Fort Peck dam was constructed. The Smithsonian National Museum of Natural History houses an exhibit of the massive Tyrannosaurus rex in the Hall of Fossils, which was found (nearly intact in the sedimented rocks) here in 1988. (Fun fact - my father-in-law was a guard providing security during the excavation of this fossil.) You'll find an array of noteworthy museums here at the Valley County Pioneer Museum with its Indian heritage, cultural artifacts of early settlers, early business and aviation, geological discoveries, fossils, and wildlife collections.

HOW TO REACH NORTHEASTERN MONTANA

Cape Air and private charter options provide access by airplane, and it's the quickest way to get in. Airports include

Billings-Logan International Airport, Glasgow International Airport (Glasgow, MT), and LM Clayton Airport (Wolf Point).

A scenic train ride from Seattle to Chicago via Amtrak stops at Wolf Point, Malta, and Glasgow, offering unique views of the landscape while you relax. Apart from this, the days of easy connection with the railroads between every single town have long gone. Roads replaced the railways.

Traveling by car remains the most comfortable option. Less traffic makes this a pleasant experience. I 94 (which runs west to east), US 2, and US 191 are the main connecting routes. Car rentals are available at many points for added convenience.

CLIMATE

The semi-arid sparse landscape induces diverse temperature ranges depending on altitude, topography, and geography. The higher regions may be colder because of the effect of elevation levels, ranging from 1,800 feet to 12,800 feet. The Continental Divide has a major impact on Montana's climatic diversity: The eastern sections have more severe weather features, such as winds and unexpected thunderstorms.

Although northeastern Montana has cold winters and hot dry summers, snow may fall at almost any time of the year. Hot spells that aren't usually oppressive and a generally mild climate in summer make outdoor recreation pleasurable, especially in elevated areas above 4,000 feet. Winter can be deadly cold, but warm windy winter periods do occur along the eastern side of the Divide and are called "chinook" weather. Lakes and rivers freeze during colder winter months. That being said, be prepared for any season, any time of the year, when visiting this part of Montana!

Around 17 inches of rain usually occurs during early summer. The sunny, dry, and warm season has temperatures ranging from -20 degrees Fahrenheit to the mid-80s Fahrenheit! This is also the wildfire season, causing unexpected road closures, poor visibility, and air quality often spurred on by wind gusts. More than half of the year is sunny, with up to 16 hours of daylight during peak summer.

Eastern Montana is the coldest section of the state with the heaviest snowfall (approximately 30 to 50 inches on average), occurring in winter around February and March. This season has approximately 10 hours of daylight time interspersed with blizzards and heavy snowfall that may cause closures to mountain passes and walking trails for extended periods of the year. Make sure to have moisture-wicking clothes, layers, heavy jackets, and appropriate footwear should you venture out this time of the year. Temperatures can reach -40 degrees Fahrenheit in the coldest parts of winter.

Fall has cooler and windy conditions (especially in higher elevations) while spring brings thunderstorms and chilly temperatures. Spring also produces flowing rivers and lakes filling up with the melting ice and snow causing floods. This is the most likely season for damaging hail storms. There aren't many tornadoes, but some appear in the eastern areas.

Night-time temperatures may be cold despite the season, so always be prepared! Rainfall happens closer to the mountainous areas and mostly during spring. Precipitation levels (including snowfall, hail, etc.) are lower than 90 days on average annually, and low humidity also makes the climate more pleasurable.

WILDLIFE

The prairies are known for their abundant wildlife, including a large population of animal and bird species. They're a wildlife haven for outdoor enthusiasts, photographers, and adventurers alike.

Wildlife Reserves

Some distinctive northeastern wildlife reserves to visit are the following:

- **Medicine Lake National Wildlife Refuge:** Here, you'll find high wildlife activity south of Plentywood, a 14-mile-long scenic drive route. The bodies of water in this prairie gem provide ample summer homes for about 100,000 migrating waterfowl.
- **Leo Coleman Wildlife Park:** There is a 230-acre all-weather gravel road surrounding it, with viewing turn-offs, provides wildlife sightings of 11 Bison, a red fox family, and some deer.
- **UL Bend National Wildlife Refuge:** Situated near the Missouri River breaks, between Malta and Zortman, this refuge provides big game and other

wildlife sightings. The place is isolated with rough roads that may be affected by weather conditions.

- **Bowdoin National Wildlife Refuge (around Malta):** You'll find plentiful wildlife and birdlife, with around 230 bird species and waterfowl, as well as migrating birds here. It's best known for its nesting colonies of white pelicans at the series of lakes and wetlands.

- **CM Russell National Wildlife Refuge (CMR) on Fort Peck Lake:** This is the most prominent wildlife ecological reserve in the area. A 125-mile-long reserve is filled with ravines and creeks, canyons, and table-topped uplands. The area consists of 1.1 million acres of land for wildlife, and the vast natural habitat secures a range of animals and more than 200 bird species. The refuge is the second largest in the lower 48 states. About 229 of the Missouri River Breaks are in the area; it surrounds Fort Peck Lake and includes its 1,600-mile shoreline. The area is remote and rough, with spectacular views and a multitude of access points. Among the 40 mammal species, plenty of wildlife can be found including the acrobatic bighorn sheep (with their massive, curved horns weighing up to 30 pounds), antelope, deer, and prairie dogs.

All these parks support the delicate ecosystem influenced by seasonal changes. The area is not only a refuge for wildlife but also for sparsely inhabited human life where people come to get away from the bustling city life and find peace. It shows in their friendly attitude and calm nature: small communities living in harmony with nature and wildlife, making up the backbone of the prairies with its typical rural life profile. Here, you experience a genuine welcoming and "can do" attitude, providing hope to the weary traveler.

Species

The list of wildlife species to be found here is long:

- Bison (about 800 at present) once again roam the prairies after re-establishment as a result of near-extinction.
- The rarest animal in Montana and also the most endangered mammal in the US, the black-footed ferret, which made the IUCN Red List of Threatened Species, has a mature population count here of slightly above 200. They are also known as "prairie dog hunters" or "American polecats."
- Prairie dogs provide much entertainment with their family habits on the plains.
- Gray wolves maintain the balance of the ecosystems and were re-introduced to the state in the late 20th century. They are mostly found in the northern areas.
- The bobcat is about twice the size of a domesticated cat and is often mistaken for a lynx. It's also known as a mountain cat or wildcat. It has thick fur of various shades in red, brown, yellow, and gray, and it inhabits Rocky Mountains rimrock areas as well as grasslands in eastern Montana.
- Among the abundant fish life, you will find favorites like small-mouth bass, walleye, and chinook salmon.

- Birdlife is immense here. Game birds, burrowing owls, golden eagles, meadowlarks, and the rare piping plover in the wetlands make northeastern Montana a major bird-watching destination. More than 230 of Montana's 440 species are identified here. In spring, geese arrive for nesting, and you'll also find migratory birds and waterfowl.

- Large game in the area include whitetail deer, mule deer, antelope, elk, and moose. The largest of these, the moose, weighs up to 1,300 pounds and stands 23 feet tall. The antelope, for those who are unfamiliar, is a backward-curving branched horn species found on the prairies. It's the second-fastest land mammal in the world. When they are scared, the hair on their behind rises into a fascinating white show of fluff, visible from far away.

- Dozens of reptile and amphibian species inhabit the prairies, including the famous rattlesnake and the larger but non-venomous bull snake.

- Of course, the grizzly bear is Montana's official state animal. It may look quite cuddly, but it's one of the most dangerous animals (along with the rattlesnake and black widow spider).

- The Western meadowlark is the official state bird. It's a black, white, and bright yellow bird: a subfamily of the blackbird. These birds prefer to nest in the prairies. They stand out with their rich birdsong and remain a rare sight.

- Blackspotted cutthroat trout is the official state fish that requires a quality habitat. Montana provides that.

Notable endangered species to be found here are the whooping crane (an omnivore and tall bird spotted in the wetland areas of the prairies with a wingspan up to 7.5 feet and a very distinctive whooping cry), pallid sturgeon (a large prehistoric fish found in the Missouri and Yellowstone rivers), white sturgeon (largest North American freshwater fish with a shark-like appearance, no teeth, found mainly in the northwestern Kootenai basin), the grizzly bear, and the black-footed ferret.

HIKING AND CAMPING

Think Montana, think mountain trails. Missouri River country provides open plains, vast spaces of prairies, excellent fishing sites, incredibly dark night skies with starry encounters, and idyllic scenery for outdoor living. Who wouldn't want to savor that? There is one dominant mountain range, known as the Little Rockies or, as the Indian tribes called them, "the island mountains," that can be seen from 75 miles away, with their highest point at 5,720 feet at Antoine Butte. These create the epitome of the old west as we see in the movies. A sight not to be missed! In the northeast, are the less commanding Little and Big Sheep mountains, still providing spectacular viewing.

Hiking

Eastern Montana has 665 miles of hiking trails (more than 250), varying between challenging trails and easy trekking. Trails around Capitol Rock and Ekalaka are popular gems to explore, such as the intermediate Dead Horse trail, Bell Tower Divide trail, and the easy Halbert Gulch Crossover trail. Four Dances, Lost Lake, Cap Rock trail, and Limekiln Loop are other well-known hiking trails in the area. More trails to explore are Gunners Ridge to the Hungry Joe overlook in Makoshika State Park. The Iron Spring trail is a four- to five-hour trail in Custer Gallatin National Forest.

Hikers of all levels have found paradise in northeastern Montana. Look out for rattlesnakes (walking sticks are recommended to scare them away), come prepared for various weather conditions, and prepare your gear for challenging geographical conditions.

Outdoor Stays

Stay in bed and breakfasts, rugged log cabins, comfortable motels and hotels, lodges, ranches, vacation homes, or camp under the expansive Montana skies. You will find luxurious yurt accommodations in the Prairie Reserve at Kestrel Camp. The quaint small communities offer their unique hospitality. If you prefer outdoor accommodation, there are a plethora of camping sites, mostly around the Fort Peck Dam.

- **Tent campgrounds:** You'll find the rustic Downstream Campground below Fort Peck dam on the Missouri River. It's semi-treed and neat right on the shoreline of the reservoir.
- **RV hookup parks and campgrounds:** These can be found with boondocking or full hook-ups all over northeast Montana. It's an RV's dream!
- **Free dispersed camping:** Montana's abundant lands offer plenty of free camping sites. There are no

bathroom facilities except for the bush around the corner and a lot of wilderness while you prepare your morning coffee outside your tent. Such remoteness turns any slight inconvenience into a lovely adventure. Bruegger Centennial Park in Missouri River country is walking distance to downtown Culbertson with a free camping site right in the middle of town! A good option for RVs and tent camping is also allowed.

Camping Tips

- Make reservations well in advance, especially in peak season. Sometimes, visiting in the shoulder seasons (fall and spring) offers more options.
- Be aware of winter camping requirements and come prepared.
- Understand and respect wildlife safety, including food storage and Leave No Trace principles.

I think we are ready and prepared for some northeastern exploration. First, we go to the Fort Peck Indian Reservation.

EXTREME NORTHEAST: FORT PECK INDIAN RESERVATION - OWNING HERITAGE

66 Turn me loose, set me free somewhere in the middle of Montana...

— MERLE HAGGARD, BIG CITY

The grassy plains of northern Montana have some of the most significant native grasslands in the US with many battle sites and a long history of rife.

TRIBAL TREASURES

Fort Peck is the second-largest reservation in Montana and the ninth-largest in the US. Poplar is viewed as the capital of the Reservation. With more than 11,000 enrolled tribal members registered, only about 6,800 Assiniboine and Sioux tribes live on the Fort Peck Reservation with their own constitution and governing body. The rest of the tribal members, about 4,000, are living off the reservation.

The area covers more than two million acres in the extreme northeast corner of Montana—fifty miles south of Canada and 40 miles west of North Dakota—with the Missouri River as the southern border. A variety of industries and enterprises support their economy, including farming, ranching, oil extraction, metal fabrication, and production sewing, and about 400 work in government positions.

At the Fort Peck Interpretive Center, you can learn about the history and culture of the Assiniboine and Sioux tribes. Permanent exhibits display the culture of these tribes' heritage, and they celebrate a couple of significant days throughout the year.

The years between 1850 and 1930 marked the phase of their political and tribal turmoil and restoration, while some tribes agreed and others resisted treaties and fought battles. After 1908, land reallocation took place to reinstate tribal ownership, and today, about 380,000 acres are owned by Native American tribes, and around 550,000 acres remain allotted Indian lands around Fort Peck (Fort Peck Tribes, n.d.).

Buffalo are a metaphor for the tribal heritage, and big game hunting remains limited to enrolled tribal members. The Fort Peck bison herd is carefully monitored and managed to restore what was lost after the days of bison wipe-out. Many exhibits showcase traditional arts, crafts, and artifacts of Native American tribes and in some towns, you can even enjoy traditional Native American cuisine at local restaurants.

ITINERARY LOGISTICS

The Reservation is located in the upper right corner of Montana with the Missouri River as its southern border. Fort Peck Lake is just below the Reservation.

Getting There

To reach the Reservation, follow US 2 (which runs east or west). It's reachable from Havre, Williston, or Glasgow. From Lewiston, take US 191. To reach the Fort Peck Dam, US 191 connects you, or MT 200 and 24. The dam is 18 miles southeast of Glasgow.

Accommodation

The Fort Peck Hotel offers a unique getaway from technology, with no televisions in its rooms. For a closer-to-nature experience, you can try Downstream Campground, just below the Fort Peck Dam on the Missouri River. Nearby Glasgow also offers several hotel options.

OUTDOOR ADVENTURES AND WILDLIFE

Fort Peck Dam

This major reservoir on the river was the first dam built in the upper parts of the Missouri River basin in the Fort Peck Lake area. The Fort Peck Dam is southeast of Glasgow in the eastern prairie region of northeastern Montana, 220 miles east of Great Falls, 250 miles north of Billings, and extends 134 miles into central Montana with a shoreline length of 1,520 miles. That's more shoreline than the entire state of California, by the way. Various river tributaries feed the lake, and it covers an area of 245,000 acres.

Built in the 1930s with the aim of improving navigation on the Missouri River, it's the fifth-largest artificial lake in the US. The dam also manages flood control and provides an average of 1.1 billion kilowatt hydroelectric power hours per year. That's enough to supply a small town! History was made when President Roosevelt authorized the building of the dam and people flocked to the area to find work. Numerous villages sprang up, and new businesses boomed as the "Wild West" returned with an increased population of around 40,000 enthusiastic inhabitants. Many of the buildings are registered in the National Registry of Historic Buildings providing a fascinating look into the time of the lake's development and a glimpse into the past glory of its creation. The spillway portion of the dam even graced the cover of the first Life magazine.

The district engineer at Fort Peck between 1933 and 1937, Maj. Clark C. Kittrell explained that "No engineering job of this magnitude had ever been attempted with so short a time for planning" (U.S. Army Corps of Engineers, n.d.-b, para 13). Fort Peck was the largest earthen dam in the world when it was completed in 1940 until it was surpassed by the Nurek Dam in Tajikistan (then part of the Soviet Union) which was completed in 1980. The Fort Peck Interpretive Center has many exhibits detailing the many "shanty towns" and other activity surrounding the construction of the dam, which took seven years.

There are 27 recreational sites around the lake, including the Charles M. Russell National Wildlife Refuge. A scenic overlook on MT 24 offers Lewis and Clark's journey interpretation and unforgettable views of the lake. The dam is also an angler's mecca with fishing as one of the most popular activities. Other recreational activities include camping, hiking, boating, sightseeing, hunting, watching wildlife, birdwatching, photography, and picnicking. The remoteness from the major towns and cities makes the lake a popular getaway for nature recreation, and Fort Peck Dam remains a treasure in Montana. Your adventure starts here:

- Take a scenic hike and nature walk in the Fort Peck Recreation Area.
- Rent a kayak or take a boat tour and explore the picturesque Fort Peck Lake.
- Go fishing for walleye, northern pike, or bass in the lake's abundant waters. It's a hotspot for walleye fishing and also excellent for smallmouth bass, sauger, and chinook salmon.
- Visit the Fort Peck Fish Hatchery and learn about conservation efforts in the area.
- Keep an eye out for wildlife such as eagles, deer, and a variety of bird species.
- Visit the Fort Peck Interpretive Center to see dinosaur and dam construction exhibits.

HISTORICAL SITES AND MUSEUMS

The *Upper Missouri Breaks National Monument* has an interesting biological, geological, and historical relevance. It stretches upstream from Fort Benton for almost 150 miles into the Charles M. Russell National Wildlife Refuge. Its spectacular natural beauty has remained mostly untouched since the Lewis and Clark expedition arrived there about 200 years ago. The rivers and creeks provide ample space for the abundant wildlife to roam and hide from their predators. Many heritage sites and historic landmarks are waiting here to be explored. The Fort Peck Interpretive Center is a promising site to start your journey with its variety of exhibits, programs, and presentations. There are paved trails and other recreational amenities to satisfy any traveler. Other points of interest are the following:

- Explore the historic town of Poplar, the administrative center of the reservation.
- Visit the Poplar Cultural Museum and delve into the rich local history and heritage.
- Learn about the struggles and triumphs of the Assiniboine and Sioux tribes.
- Discover the glorious significance of buffalo in the Native American culture at Oswego Buffalo Jump.
- Visit the Sacred Heart Catholic Church, A historic landmark known for its stunning architecture.

OUTDOOR RECREATION AND TRADITIONAL ACTIVITIES

Some of the recreational and cultural highlights in the area include

- Enjoy water activities like jet skiing, paddleboarding, and swimming at Fort Peck Lake.
- Explore the Missouri River.
- Attend a powwow or cultural gathering to witness traditional dances, songs, and regalia. Fort Peck's annual celebrations include the Red Bottom and Badlands celebrations in June, the Fort Kipp celebration in July, the Wadopana celebration in August, and Poplar Indian Days in September.
- Participate in hands-on workshops or demonstrations to learn traditional crafts and beadwork.
- Attend a performance at the historic Fort Peck Theatre, which operates during the summer months.
- Attend a rodeo. One of the most popular and longest running in the area in the Wild Horse Stampede, held in Wolf Point each year in the second week of July. This rodeo usually features some of the countries top bucking horse stock.
- Visit the Phillips County Museum and the Great Plains Dinosaur Museum in Malta, and explore the nearby Bowdoin National Wildlife Refuge for more wildlife viewing.

Nearby Attractions Day Trips

Some of the most interesting site visits for short day journeys are the following:

- Fort Union Trading Post National Historic Site where you can venture into North Dakota and learn more about the tribal fur trade, join festivities and art festivals, visit the bookstore, and learn more about Native American ways at the trading post. Engage in traditional programs and educational activities as you learn more about the history of this trading spot.

- Fort Union Trading Post in North Dakota is a national historic site near the Yellowstone and Missouri Rivers junction. It is a reconstructed fur trading post that you can visit and learn about its importance in the region's history.
- Lewis and Clark Interpretive Center in nearby Williston, North Dakota where you can learn about the expedition through the area.
- Enjoy a picnic lunch along the Missouri River or a scenic spot nearby.

Return to the reservation, relax in the sunset, and reflect on the day's new experiences. Fort Peck is a good starting point for historical reflection before we go to the Little Bighorn Battlefield National Monument, the defining catalyst for victory in Native American history.

THE NOT-SO-LITTLE BIGHORN

> There are not enough Indians in the world to defeat the Seventh Cavalry.

— GEORG ARMSTRONG CUSTER

Did you know that this battle symbolized the clash of two opposing cultures: the industrialized Europeans and the horse and buffalo culture of the native tribes? The historical turning point in the history of the US, where the Native American tribes successfully defeated the American army, is famously known as Custer's Last Stand and it was one of the tribal nations' final stands against the U.S. Army to prevent forced reservation after many years of tension.

A LESSON IN HISTORY

With the discovery of gold in this part of Montana, the westward expansion of the early American settlers (who were actually there illegally) flourished. Everyone wanted their piece of the fortune. As a result, the military came in, and instead of forcibly removing the Native Americans, they protected the illegal settlers, which led to numerous peace negotiations between the US and the Native tribes. A final offer to purchase the Black Hills in South Dakota was rejected by the Lakota and Cheyenne. We all know at least part of the history of the continuous bloody conflict between Native American tribes and the westward expansion into their territory.

The Native American victory of the defiant Lakota, Cheyenne, and Arapaho tribes at the Battle of Little Bighorn against Lt. Col. George Armstrong Custer and his regiments happened on June 25 and 26, 1876. The native people were led by Chief Sitting Bull, Crazy Horse, and other brave warrior chiefs. About 7,000 tribal people were encamped there of which about 2,000 were warriors. The battle was, in fact, a successful attempt by Native American people to defend themselves against the invasion when Custer was trapped. Some tribes didn't accept the U.S. subsidies and forced relocation. Their aim was to preserve their way of life and reject the U.S. government's attempts to force them onto reservations.

This may be one of the most controversial places in the US (despite the side you may take), and the actual heritage site calls for a pause. The gold and Black Hills were sacred for the Sioux, and at this bend in the river, their war changed history. Sadly, the westward expansion was a period in history that was often misrepresented in textbooks, in stark contradiction to Native American history.

For many years, the battlefield remained a misrepresented memorial heritage site for the U.S. soldiers who lost their lives there. Only later was there a greater understanding of the true history of the site, including the Native American people who defended their rights and sacrificed their way of life at this memorable battlefield, earning its rightful place in 1991 when the site honored both the U.S. cavalry and the Native American warriors.

This is one of the last battles that the Native tribes won as they defended their nomadic way of life in a fast-changing world, hence the hallowed ground and a spiritual place for many people. The area is a very different version from the glamorized Hollywood or adapted textbook versions, leaving people emotional when they are at the site. The visitor center, with its orientational film, talks, and interpretive tours, offers a more truthful version of what took place. It remains a somber opportunity for peace and reconciliation between different cultures, here where the biggest clash caused so many sacrifices in the efforts of Western expansion.

The Battle of Little Bighorn represents the end of the Native Americans' attempts to maintain their way of life. They were all eventually forced into reservation lifestyles by an increasingly aggressive U.S. Army at the time. The area calls for a moment of somber respect in the vast prairie landscape of remembrance. To Western historians, it's remembered as the Battle of Little Bighorn; to the Native tribes, it's the Battle of the Greasy Grass—a battle that cost many lives on both sides of the fighting. It was a clash of cultures that deserves an honorable day visit.

Little Bighorn Battlefield National Monument

The park area comprises 765 acres and the battlefield 11,000 acres. Some highlights at the park not to be missed are

- The visitor center (which is the best place to start your visit) is where you will find a highly informative museum indicating the history of the conflicts and the course of the battle. It includes an orientation video showing the lasting effects of this battle. There is also a bookstore.

- Guided tours are led by park rangers to give a deeper understanding of the battle and events that took place. A 4.5-mile self-guided tour road (drive or walk) of the entire site begins at the visitor center and traverses along the east side of the river filled with interesting bits of history and memorable names of important people. The Crow Tribe offers a one-hour guided bus tour on a reservation basis (Apsaalooke Tour Company). Since the Crow was part of the historic battlefield, they offer a unique perspective, sharing viewpoints of how the Native American tribes (in particular the Crow peoples) experienced the battle.

- A self-guided driving tour along the park's roadways is marked with interpretive signs to explore key locations and viewpoints. At the Last Stand Hill, you can visit the site where the final stand occurred and pay respects to those who lost their lives in the battle.

- The most well-known section of the monument, where Custer and his men made a "last stand" against the tribes, is dotted with white headstones and one black stone (for Custer) to mark the field where the men were laid to rest. At the top of this hill, a large granite monolith, built in 1881, marks the list of names of the approximately 210 deceased, and it's dedicated to the Army's 7th Cavalry. Below this, the Indian memorial was constructed in the 1990s to commemorate the Native American men who died on the battlefield. The somber "Peace Through Unity" Indian memorial features metal castings of spirit warriors who fought as well as the women involved in the battle. The memorial was unveiled in 2003 after years of struggle to find recognition in the events.

- The Reno-Benteen Memorial is a 4.5-mile interpretive tour road with information and a trail to commemorate the other soldiers who assisted Custer's men (who attempted to defend them against the Lakota's attack). The spot marks the space where these majors tried to save their regiments. The soldiers used their horses as shields against the onslaught of the Indian tribes by shooting them when escape became impossible. Even the horses who died in the battle found an honorary stone on site to commemorate their part.
- In the Custer National Cemetery, the soldiers from various conflicts, including this battle, are buried.

On I 90 Frontage Road, in the Crow Agency, you can relive America's coming of age as you walk through the cemetery of veterans: Women, children, Indian scouts, and soldiers are all remembered with Medals of Honor.

The Civil War changed the way that soldiers who passed during battle were honored. Before this, the families were in charge of where their loved ones were buried (whether the bodies were found or not), after the Civil War and with the vast numbers of deceased soldiers from various wars, an alternative had to be found. An increasingly agonizing demand from the families to determine whether and where their loved ones died during battle and where they were supposed to be laid to rest, became a governmental responsibility.

So, in 1861, the Quartermaster General became in charge of the burial and registry of war casualties: In these national cemeteries, all were buried as equals, giving honor to every individual human being who passed in war, despite rigid military credentials and thus conferring equal honor in death regardless of military rank. Custer National Cemetery is such a site. It was created after those who died there were already buried there. By 1881, a memorial in honor of these soldiers of the 7th U.S. cavalry was erected at the site and approximately 5,000 people are interred here.

Reenactment Events

Annual reenactments provide a historical portrayal of the battle and take place between June 24 and 26 as a joint effort between the local residents and the Crow tribe. These events showcase the battles. There is also a Park Junior Ranger program for the young ones. You can experience history with demonstrations showcasing the life and culture of both Native Americans and soldiers during the time of these battles.

 Reenactments of the battle on site (off East Frontage Road) as the Crow Real Bird Family tells of the clash that happened at the Medicine Tail Coulee once they crossed the Little Bighorn River, have been presented annually since 1990. During these presentations from mid-to-late June, with associated activities, local events, and inspiring history lessons, you can learn more about the battle. The script for these reenactments was written in 1965 by Joe Medicine Crow, recounting significant events leading up to the battle.

Many people are confused about the historical truth of what happened on that day. Reenactments help to share the reality of what truly happened. Jim Real Bird orchestrates such an enactment with about 150 participants, focusing on the downplayed victory in order to "heal people." His group shifts the focus away from one "victor" to a mutual lesson in healing and moving forward.

Explore Native American Culture

A 20-minute ranger talk at the visitor center provides ample information about the Plains' Indian tribes, the weapons used during the battle, the history, and Custer's life. Visitors can take part in cultural events and activities organized by the Native American tribes in the area, which provide insights into their traditions, art, and music. When you arrive, you can visit the nearby Apsáalooke (Crow) Nation and learn about their rich heritage through museums, cultural centers, and powwows.

Getting There

Bighorn is situated in the Crow Indian Reserve in the south-eastern part of Montana. On I 90, you can take Exit 510 and follow signs to the park entrance on the Battlefield Tour Road 756. The battlefield is located near the junction of I 90 and US 212, just before you reach the Crow Agency on I 90.

Billings-Logan International Airport and Sheridan County Airport are both within 60 to 75 miles away from the battlefield if you intend to arrive by plane.

Make sure to stock up on snacks before you arrive or have a proper meal beforehand, since there are no eateries on-site.

Accommodation

The closest town is Billings, around 65 miles away. The site is closer to Hardin (around 12 miles away). If you want to stay in a smaller town, away from Billings, I'd recommend Hardin. It has a variety of hotel options at reasonable rates.

OUTDOOR ACTIVITIES

It's open all year round but windy and ice-cold conditions with snow on these prairie hills can make a visit challenging in winter. The best time to visit is during May up until early October when the sun makes walking around enjoyable. When the trails are covered with snow, walking is nearly impossible. Storms can develop rapidly with changing weather conditions and temperatures may drop below freezing. For this reason, the park has set its winter opening hours from the first of October to the end of March, and trails close at 4 p.m. while summer operating hours are from 8 a.m. to 8 p.m. daily. (Remember sun protection as the trials have no shade and summer can be hot!)

Enjoy hiking and nature walks along the park's designated trails while you immerse yourself in the breathtaking landscape and wide open spaces, taking in scenic vistas. Pack sturdy boots for walking, sunscreen, hats, and comfortable hiking clothes, and layer them. Always have a jacket, plenty of water, and snacks for energy.

The monument trails are on gravel or paved paths and driveways in the flat prairie and slight hills. Remember that there is usually limited shade, and be wary of rattlesnakes. You need a minimum of two hours to see the site and more to take in all the history and understand the full effect of what happened on that day. Making it a day outing is much better to explore all the sites in the area. Most of the trails in the area surround the Last Stand Hill section.

The Deep Ravine Trail is a hiking trail originally established by the U.S. Army to bury the dead and assess the casualties of the two-day battle. The trail starts from the ridge above the river to the adjacent ravine below where the last shots of the battle were fired. Markers (white marble for the U.S. Army and red granite for Native Americans) can be found alongside the trail, indicating where the warriors and the cavalrymen were buried. The trail ends with informative and interpretive signs.

While you take in all the splendor here, visitors can also enjoy birdwatching (look out for various bird species that inhabit the park, including eagles and hawks), or photography to capture the dramatic landscape and historical landmarks of Little Bighorn and preserve memories. Alternatively enjoy a relaxing picnic at a designated area within the park surrounded by the serene beauty of the landscape.

NEARBY ATTRACTIONS

The most notable attractions in the area include the Medicine Tail Coulee, which played a significant role in the battle and offers stunning views of the surrounding area. The other option is the Bighorn Canyon National Recreation Area. Here, you can take a short drive to the scenic area, known for its breathtaking canyons, boating opportunities, and diverse wildlife. About 58 miles west of the monument, the 120,000 acres Bighorn Canyon National Recreation Area cover a vast area of wetlands, prairies, mountains, hiking trails, valleys, and a lake but mostly gapes at dramatic twisting canyon walls alongside the Bighorn River: A sight not to be missed!

The Crow Indian Reservation annually hosts a Powwow and Parade Celebration, including traditional highlights such as dancing and singing, Indian rodeo, horse racing, and parades. The Chief Plenty Coups State Park has tribal artifacts and historical exhibits on display as well. Other nearby attractions worth a day trip outing when you are in the area are the following:

- Rosebud Battlefield
- Pompey's Pillar
- Chief Plenty Coups State Park
- Pictograph Caves State Park
- Bighorn National Forest Medicine Wheel (Wyoming)

EDUCATIONAL PROGRAMS AND EVENTS

Many programs and events enrich the area's history and culture with information. Attend presentations and talks by historians and experts to gain deeper insights into the battle's history and significance. In addition, visitors can participate in educational programs offered by the park, such as ranger-led walks, discussions, and workshops.

AFTERTHOUGHT

Opposing perspectives of this battle state that Custer was the martyr (or glorified soldier) against the threat of "innocent settlers" and a westward push against "threatening tribes." Another perspective indicates that mere owners of the land were defending their right to live freely.

Regardless of your viewpoint, the site creates a somber pause and reflection on what drives mankind. The peaceful echoing of the hills out there is a testament to the bravery and sacrifices of all who fought on that day. It is said that the Indian tribes made a pact of silence after the battle—to seal the tragedy of loss.

Even though many books were written about this day and many stories told, the site remains shrouded in mystery and the real truth of what happened on that fatal day beckons investigation. Regardless of what we know today and where we choose to lay our beliefs, many lives were lost, and tragedy still rings in the whisper of the wind on these plains. If only you visit for this moment in time, to hear the whispers of the wind on the plains, I urge you to go.

From a place of sacred reverence to Miles City—Montana's plains are as vast as her history.

TRAVELING TO MILES CITY

> Spending that many hours in the saddle gave a
> man plenty of time to think. That's why so many
> cowboys fancied themselves Philosophers.

— CHARLES MARION RUSSELL

Interestingly, almost half of Montana's inhabitants live in rural areas.

EXPLORING THE COWBOY CAPITAL

Miles City was an important cattle town in the 1800s. It used to be the livestock and horse trading center of the country and retains this heritage today. There are still weekly livestock auctions and the town celebrates everything about horse country annually! Rodeo is a way of life here—it's nothing extraordinary. As are cowboy boots instead of sandals. Don't expect a cosmopolitan atmosphere when visiting Miles City; here you'll find good ol' Western vibes.

Recreation happens in the middle of nowhere and on the outskirts of the small town in its huge rural area. It offers endless miles and solitude for breathing space and relaxation. Bighorn National Forest is a short three-hour drive away (in Montana language, that means close by!)

The small city has around 8,500 residents and does not provide a club scene or hectic daytime activities. However, you will find some real essential and purposeful amenities (including a bar dating back to the 1800s—still serving brews —and an art museum.) The general feel is one of stepping back in time at a leisurely pace.

Main Street and Historic Downtown

Stroll along the historic downtown and admire its preserved architecture. A first stop could be at the 1800s-themed historic Montana Bar offering classic brews. This bar has traditional architecture and features, making your tasting experience much more interesting. Vintage & Rustics is another option offering a mall, antique shop, and flea market combined in one. Here, you can find retro items, trinkets,

Montana-made items, upcycled items, custom-made items, western clothing, unique souvenirs, handmade Native American jewelry, and, of course, your handmade cowboy hat. Exploring the local shops, boutiques, and art galleries among the old-west architecture buildings calls for a pleasant stroll about town. Some places house typical Wild West artifacts, and you may even find some dinosaur fossil displays.

Cultural pleasures include a visit to the Range Riders Museum, a typical "old West" museum with real cowboy and pioneer lore in a 13-building complex filled with Western artifacts, that shares the stories about Miles City's history and cowboy culture. This should be on your bucket list. The Waterworks Art Museum showcases classic art detailing the town's evolution and surrounding landscapes. Both museums provide interesting snippets of yesteryear and are a welcome visit on rainy days. Alternatively, experience western-themed events and festivals held downtown.

ITINERARY LOGISTICS

The Miles City Chamber of Commerce is a tourist site where you can find all the info you need or download a travel guide to the area from their website to help you plan your itinerary.

Getting There

Miles City is situated where the Yellowstone and Tongue Rivers meet and can be reached from the I 94, MT 59, or US 12. It's the transition point between the badlands and the western mountain ranges. The two main roads in town are

Main and Haynes Streets and the city's historic part can be reached via Main Street. I would suggest renting your own car and keeping it during your visit since there aren't many public transport or taxi services available. Public transportation depends on making a booking on an on-demand one-day-in-advance reservation with Custer County Transit.

The Miles City airport does not provide commercial services —only charter air services. Billings-Logan International Airport is about 140 miles west, and from here, you can travel via car on scenic roads. Jefferson Bus lines operate to Miles City. Bear in mind that in the remote part of Montana, emergency services are sparse. You probably want to take additional supplies of any regular medication if you intend to stay for long.

Accommodation

Recommended lodging includes a reasonable range of hotels, motels, bed and breakfast options, guesthouses, vacation rentals (VRBO), camping, RV parks, ranches, and wine farm accommodations. These all provide a sense of tranquility and a small-town atmosphere. Consider staying at a guest ranch for an authentic Western experience. Many accommodations offer small-town hospitality with a Western feel. I would make use of the ambiance of the area's historic buildings, which are mostly within walking distance of the amenities. Park the car, slow down, and enjoy some slow living for a while!

ANNUAL EVENTS AND FESTIVALS

Miles City mostly attracts hunters and anglers for recreational activities. The rest of the family can enjoy its family-friendly festivals. Main events happen around bucking horse sales and activities in spring. Check the town's calendar for major events such as the Eastern Montana Fair and PRCA Rodeo. Or attend the Mile City Bluegrass Festival for live music and performances. During the third weekend of September, Bluegrass artists from across the country arrive to join in the fun.

For a winter wonderland, the family can take part in the local Christmas stroll while enjoying the holiday lights and festive activities. Just pack warmly! Other events include several outdoor events, nonstop cultural events, fairs, a barbeque cook-off, music festivals, theater, brew festivals, and general small-town hospitality. There are too many to mention, so stay informed via the town's website. People out here enjoy the company of others: true old-school human connection.

Annual Bucking Horse Sale and Rodeo

Every third full weekend in May, the annual world-famous horse sale takes place. This major event features bucking broncos, wild cow riding, and horse races. The best part is that many celebrities attend the auctions, so you may just bump into your idol. Enjoy thrilling rodeo events in this rodeo capital of the world with its bull riding, barrel racing, parades, live entertainment, concerts, and street dances during celebrations. It can be cold this time of year in Miles City, so plan accordingly. Also, book accommodations early if you plan to attend this event as rooms tend to book up as much as a year in advance. Many people stay in RVs for this event as well.

DINING AND LOCAL CUISINE

Although some fine dining options are available, you will mostly find comfort food and informal eateries. Indulge in hearty Western cuisine at local steakhouses and barbecue restaurants, where you can sample popular regional specialties such as bison burgers and Montana beef. In Miles City, you can experience farm-to-table dining with locally sourced ingredients.

Pubs and bars offer Western-style grub, while tap rooms, craft distilleries, wineries, cideries, and breweries delight with their locally produced products blended with the area's glacial water. Alternatively, enjoy strolling through some farmers' markets and sourcing locally produced products.

Tongue River Winery and Brewery

The Tongue River Winery prides itself on using only local grapes for their fermentation. Take a tour of the winery and learn about the winemaking process, or sample a variety of locally produced wines and craft beers while you enjoy scenic views from the winery's tasting room and outdoor patio.

RECREATIONAL ACTIVITIES

As with most of Montana, be prepared for severe weather conditions. If you don't like severe winter conditions, you probably won't like Miles City. Be aware that such conditions may lead to road closures and unexpected weather warnings, so don't get caught in the rain! Stormy weather may include occasional tornadoes, flash floods, and extreme temperatures all year round. The winter here can be brutal. Blizzards reduce visibility, making driving conditions very dangerous. Be informed about wildfires, wildlife, and wilderness safety. Water temperatures may drop suddenly or be deceiving. Average temperatures range between 30 and 90 degrees Fahrenheit, but maximums can easily top 100 degrees in the summer and well below zero in the winter. The average rainfall is low at around two inches annually.

The area offers abundant outdoor activities, such as bird watching, rock collecting, golf, and sightseeing scenic vistas. Explore the nearby Yellowstone River for fishing and water sports: kayaking and floating are popular, but bear in mind that some parts of the river may not be safe for swimming. Avoid flowing water, as currents can be deceivingly strong.

Go hiking, camping, or wildlife watching in nearby state parks and recreation areas. The Yellowstone River offers a river walk along the northeastern side of the city. The Yellowstone Jewel trail offers magnificent vistas of Custer's camping site (1876) and the valley below. Alternatively, take a scenic drive through the rolling plains of eastern Montana and feast your eyes (and soul) on the vast spaces.

The Spotted Eagle recreational area offers beautiful picnic sites, horseshoe pits and grills, walking trails, nonmotorized boating, fishing, or scenic drives for a tranquil day outing. Twelve Mile Dam attracts teenagers for water activities (tubing, canoeing, etc.), and there are many recreational parks in the city. (Wibaux Park, Hillemann Park, and Bender Park all offer something special.)

You can go primitive camping at Strawberry Hill (on Baker Road). This 4,200-acre recreation area is a place to slow down and enjoy nature. It also offers climbing and hiking. Watch out for ticks and snakes.

You will need licenses and documents for fishing and hunting, and different rules apply in the Native American Reservation areas. To avoid disappointment, stay informed via local websites and check state parks' access information online before heading out.

Pirogue Island State Park and Nature Walks

A visit to Pirogue Island State Park, a tranquil retreat along the Yellowstone River, bears excellent wildlife spotting without the risk of meeting a bear or angry moose along the way. The Spotted Eagle Recreation site is popular for swimming, picnicking, birdwatching, and fishing opportunities. Explore nature trails in a vast 123-acre area and admire the scenic beauty of the river and surrounding landscape. The Holy Rosary Story Walk is popular for kids. Matthews Wildlife Habitat Management Area offers paved paths for ease of access to physically impaired persons or the elderly.

Miles City Saddlery and Western Shops

The Miles City Saddlery is a historic saddlery and western supply store where you can purchase authentic cowboy gear, including hats, boots, and saddles. They've been in the saddlery business here for more than a hundred years, and the business has been passed down from generation to generation! This is where you can get your cowboy gear before you leave Montana, just as many famous people have done here.

You might as well explore some of the other western shops here before having a relaxing sundowner with your new booted heels up on the table.

Miles City was featured on a list of the most boring places to visit! But if you have the correct intention, visit at the best time that suits your bucket list, or merely pass through, it remains worth a visit as one of the most favorable places for outdoor recreation in solitude and experiencing cowboy culture: a quiet respite away from the crowds before we arrive in Billings.

SPOTTING BEAUTY AT BILLINGS

> I travel not to go anywhere, but to go. I travel
> for travel's sake. The great affair is to move.

— ROBERT LOUIS STEVENSON

Billings is the only city in Montana with more than 100,000 residents, making up about ten percent of the state's population. If you are flying into Montana, it is likely that you will fly into Billings. It's a central location in the middle of the prairies, yet not too far away from the mountains. The Absaroka Beartooth mountains are a mere 60 miles away where you can take in some beauty. Billings is the largest city in Montana, and its metropolitan population is around 130,000. Billings also has the most prominent hospital coverage within a more than 500-mile radius, which makes up much of the economic activity. The city is the main entrance to the Yellowstone National Park (via scenic Beartooth Highway). It has been nicknamed the "Magic City" from its railroad booming days in the 1800s. Sadly, today, there are no more rail services here. The vibrant culture of this crossroads city is by far the best attraction.

ITINERARY LOGISTICS

Don't be put off by the industrial side of Billings as you come from the interstate; once you get into town, it can be quite refreshing. According to the Billings Chamber of Commerce, "Billings is your trailhead to Little Bighorn Battlefield, Pompey's Pillar National Monument, the Dinosaur Trail, Yellowstone National Park, and so much more" (n.d.-a, para 1). You will even find the only skyscraper in Montana right here: a high-rise office building soaring 20 stories into the sky. Well, remind yourself that you're in the prairies, not New York!

How to Get There

By plane, the city can be reached via Billings International Airport, which is also the busiest airport in the Montana.

Bus services here are serviced by Jefferson Bus Lines. When you arrive by car, you can take the I 90, US 310, I 94, and US

87. In the city, shuttle services, cab services, transit (MET), and Uber and Lyft ride-sharing services help conveniently. There are also bike trails in the city for leisurely cycling and sightseeing.

Accommodation

Billings is generally affordable. You will find a variety of hotels, motels, inns, lodges, bed and breakfast options, and budget-friendly options. Nearby guest ranch accommodation for some unique experiences should not be missed. The affordable Dude Rancher Lodge, dating back to 1949, is a historic hotel in downtown Billings. If you prefer something more luxurious, the Northern Hotel was built in 1940 and recently renovated offering a touch of something different. The DoubleTree by Hilton Hotel Billings is the tallest free-standing brick structure in the world. Imagine! In this prairie landscape of space.

CULTURAL ENRICHMENT

There is a thriving art and cultural scene. Billings has many museums to visit, such as the Museum of Women's History, Western Heritage Center, and the famous Yellowstone Art Museum. After a museum visit, you can spend some money in the Rimrock Mall for shopping delights or watching a movie. If modern amenities do not fit your taste, take a stroll downtown and explore the historic downtown area and its preserved architecture. And then there are always some culinary delights to enjoy.

Downtown Billings

Visit the Western Heritage Center to learn about the region's history and culture, or shop at local boutiques, art galleries, and specialty stores. Sample local cuisine at diverse restaurants and cafés, where industrial chic, Eastern food, comfort food, American fare, and bar food delight every taste. The Burger Dive has won national awards for its burgers—definitely worth a stop.

Local Montana-crafted beers, craft breweries, cideries, and microbreweries call for a leisurely stroll and savoring. Afterward, attend live performances at the Alberta Bair Theater or Babcock Theater and enjoy Billings' active nightlife. All in all, Billings offers a wonderful blend of activities to keep the whole family happily occupied.

Yellowstone Art Museum

Discover the art scene of downtown Billings, showcasing and promoting contemporary and historic art of the area. The gallery has diverse collections with works by prominent artists, including contemporary and Western art. A stunning outdoor sculpture garden, with its combination of art and nature, provides a serene space for true reflection. Art exhibitions include painting, sculpture, and mixed media. The museum also hosts workshops.

Moss Mansion Historic House Museum

Tour the beautifully preserved historic red-stone mansion on the National Register of Historic Places. The Moss mansion is the beautifully preserved Preston Boyd Moss family homestead dating back to 1903. The mansion is a testament to the family's influence and prosperity in the area.

Learn about the wealthy family who once resided there, its original furnishings and artifacts show their lifestyle as part of the elite. Guided tours provide interesting insight into the family's interests and the architectural features. Explore elegant architecture and period furnishings, or simply step back in bygone days.

POMPEYS PILLAR NATIONAL MONUMENT

A short drive (25 miles east on I 94) to *Pompeys Pillar National Monument* is a sure bucket list event. This 120-foot sandstone formation has become a landmark in Montana. Visitors flock to the site and the views of the river valley from here are quite spectacular. Its main attraction has become the signature of Captain William Clark (of the Lewis and Clark expedition) carved into the sandstone pillar. It remains the only physical evidence of their expedition.

Learn about the expedition's journey and history at the visitor center. The 200-step, well-maintained boardwalk (about 1,000 feet long), with its interpretive displays along the way, is a wonderfully informative lesson in history and takes about two hours. Pets (leashed) are allowed, and picnic areas invite leisurely recreation. Even if history is not your main interest, the sheer miracle of nature's rock formations here will call for a jaw-dropping experience.

OUTDOOR RECREATION

The beauty of Billings does not stop at cultural experiences. Explore nearby hiking and biking trails of the famous Rimrocks. These huge sandstone cliffs, rising up vertically at the escarpment by about 500 feet, can be reached by a road connecting at Billings' west end. At the top of the rims, magnificent views and impressive vistas inspire calm after a test for your driving skills. The road up there is not for the fainthearted! Be mindful of rock slides at the rims. There are also opportunities for horse rides on the rimrocks.

Alternative outdoor recreation includes fishing, boating, and water sports at nearby rivers and lakes. Hunting closer to the forested areas is also popular. Abundant hiking and skiing opportunities exist with a wide scope for various kinds of camping.

A bucket list drive along the scenic 68-mile drive of the Beartooth Highway is worth every second. The Bear tooth Mountains have the highest peaks in Montana. From here, you can explore nearby dense forests and glacial lakes and enjoy alpine views via the winding road. The road is the gateway to the northern entrance of Yellowstone National Park.

Always check the weather and road conditions before venturing out, especially after winter snowstorms in Billings. (Look out for the locally named "slick streets" warning.) Summers are short and you may have constant winds due to the flatlands. The only trees are around the water and mountainous areas. However, the winds are not as strong as in other parts of the prairies. Temperature ranges are a different story, ranging from an average of 37 degrees Fahrenheit to 79.

Summer and late spring, around July and August, are the best tourist seasons, especially for outdoor activities.

ZooMontana

A visit to ZooMontana, the 70-acre wildlife park in Billings, is a fun family outing. The area includes a botanical garden, more than 80 indoor and outdoor species, including some rare species like the Siberian Tiger, a sensory garden, and a farm area where visitors can feed goats.

Discover a variety of animal species, like wolves, bears, and birds of prey. The beauty of this zoo is that all the animals are conditioned to the local climate and have lots of roaming space. It's a good recreational option for a day out with kids as the zoo offers many play parks, walking trails, picnic areas, and educational programs.

Pictograph Cave State Park

This park is known for its ancient rock paintings dating back 2,000 years and excavated in 1937. The prehistoric archaeological cave paintings can be viewed in the three main caves alongside interpretive displays from the loop walk to the site.

There is also a guided tour to learn about Native American History and culture. The area invites leisure with easy hikes and picnics amidst scenic natural surroundings.

SAVOR LOCAL JOYS

Sample locally brewed craft beers at Montana Brewing Company. Enjoying your craft beer is like a local culture. I suggest a walking beer tour to take in the true culture of Billings. Explore this vibrant craft beer scene in Billings with visits to other breweries and taprooms.

Attending the Montana Fair is a popular, lively annual event featuring concerts, a rodeo, and carnival rides. The fair takes place in August and features amusement rides, commercial and agricultural expos, local talent competitions, music shows, a rodeo, and fun all around. Stock shows and live-stock events draw visitors from afar. The Magic City Blues Festival, showcasing local and national musicians, happens annually in August. The festival hosts talented musicians for an outdoor weekend of entertainment.

Sourcing local products and fresh products at the Yellow-stone Valley Farmers Market makes you forget you are in a city. It evokes a feeling of yesteryear and slow living where quality and community are all that matter.

The greatest attraction of this area remains the vast open spaces and the enjoyment of solitude as you travel around. Fresh air and relaxed laid-back vibes make you feel whole again—giving you time and space to breathe. The north-western vistas team up with the echoes of history to render an unforgettable introduction to the ecological wonders, trails of heritage, mining mysteries, and forested ski slopes of southwest Montana.

PART III
SOUTHWEST MONTANA—A
TAPESTRY OF HERITAGE

OVERVIEW

 It is not the mountain that we conquer but ourselves.

— EDMUCH HILLARY

In the 1880s, 30% of U.S. copper was supplied from Butte. Copper King William Clark, from Butte, was the richest person on Earth at the time. His copper riches delivered 15% of the global market. He earned $17 million every month, while his hardworking miners earned only $3.50 for a day's labor—they only got a small raise 40 years later.

Nevertheless, southwest Montana is an explorer's paradise with a touch of history, culture, nature, and adventure all in one breathtaking package. It's not surprising that this part of Montana is one of the favorite areas attracting tourists. Let's have a look at what you can expect to see when traveling to the south.

- **Helena area:** The gold rush spurred its rich history and left a legacy of charming communities with quaint historical villages filled with museums and pretty main street architecture to explore. Apart from its cultural appeal, there are many lakes and numerous trail systems for hiking and biking.
- **Deer Lodge area:** This is a typical rancher area. Back in the day, the valleys were prime cattle breeding grounds to supply the surrounding mining towns and have now become an outdoor paradise to enjoy.
- **Anaconda and Philipsburg area:** Known as the gem mining area (Anaconda was founded by another copper king—Marcus Daly—and Philipsburg was a trading town). It's a wonderful recreation area all year round, with skiing in the Discovery Ski area and Georgetown Lake area for water-based activities.
- **Butte area:** This is often called "the richest hill on Earth" as immigrants flocked to the mining town of Butte from all over and created its vibrant culture. Its location right in the middle of magical landscapes calls for outdoor recreation galore.
- **Dillon and Beaverhead County area:** Heritage, heritage, heritage! The area was the main point of the first major gold rush and includes a section of the Continental Divide hiking trail. Also, the Centennial Valley, Pioneer Scenic Byway, and Red Rock Lakes National Wildlife Refuge delight with their magnificent landscapes. Not to mention the trails of Lewis and Clark that can be explored here.
- **Virginia City and Ennis area:** History and blue ribbon fishing are calling all visitors here. Apart from

the Madison area, the Ruby Valley combines the joining of three major rivers (Big Hole, Beaverhead, and Ruby) into the Jefferson River, which is a famous fly fishing destination. Ghost towns, dating back to the 1800s, return fond memories of yesteryear—and a couple of spooks!

When visiting this part of Montana, make sure to leave enough time for off-the-beaten-track discoveries and surprises that divert from your itinerary.

A RICH HISTORY

The historic Victorian mansions, rich with the mining boom industry's fascinating heritage, left elegant ghost towns and interesting museums to explore. They are all entwined within the richly diverse landscape of mountains, waterways, and grasslands—making this part of Montana a discovery of landscapes and heritage in one.

Southwest Montana hosts 3.2 million acres of forests, snow-capped mountains, spirited rivers, national parks with abundant and diverse wildlife, and vast spaces of untouched grasslands. The southwestern section epitomizes the picture that comes to mind when the name Montana is mentioned: endless skies, wildlife grazing in rolling grasslands, a cowboy greeting you, and a pace that slows you down to bare essentials. Sweeping spaces between the northern Glacier Park with its snow-capped peaks and southern Yellowstone Park with its geological wonders offer you Big Sky Country at its best with friendly locals to welcome you.

The cultural significance is shown in its rich history of cultural events and festivities. You will satisfy your senses with history, art, culinary delights, ghost towns, as well as natural vistas that go beyond your expectations. This part of Montana's diverse outdoor recreational opportunities enthralls with many of the best outdoor recreations in Montana: outdoor adventure remains its main attraction. The pristine landscapes, mesmerizing views, and unique natural wonders such as hot springs and lakes call for bountiful enjoyment. Some favorite recreational activities here include fishing and angling in Montana's meandering creeks.

The area's historic landmarks are plentiful. Helena is not only the capital of the state but it was also the major stopover for the Lewis and Clark expedition, making it a worthy historical visit in the northern corner of the area. You can take in history while you follow their footsteps in the stunning landscape. Eclectic communities, friendly locals, and historic towns with beautifully restored gold camps, national monuments, museums, art galleries, heritage, and architecture all call for sightseeing. Tours can be arranged for these.

PLACES TO VISIT

Since mining was a big part of the state's history, the legacy remains and can be seen in southwest Montana's range of museums: Exploration Works (Helena) for science-based exhibits and activities, the World Museum of Mining (Butte), Beaverhead County Museum (Dillon), Madison Valley History Museum (Ennis), and Montana Historical Society

Museum (Helena). Butte was famous for its copper mines (also silver, zinc, and lead) and the museum showcases many insightful exhibits, a memorial wall, an underground tour, an informative trolley tour, and a vast collection of minerals. For a more intimate experience, consider a sapphire sifting at Philipsburg. (Montana is known for her many sapphires.)

Apart from these, art galleries and museums like the Holter Museum of Art (Helena), and the Ohrmann Museum and Gallery (Drummond) will delight all art lovers. For an architectural display, Helena's turn-of-the-century cathedral is worth a visit. Helena, alongside Butte, are two places that form the cornerstone of Montana's rich legacy.

Other architectural visits entice visitors at the Copper King Mansion and Clark Chateau in Butte, as well as the Old Montana Prison (Deer Lodge). This quasi-medieval prison was constructed by convicts in the 19th century (1871) and is said to be haunted. The site now houses a formation of five museums (guided tours or self-guided tours are available). One of the museums here houses more than 165 vintage cars (the Montana Auto Museum) and was listed as one of the country's top 10 car museums. Part of the Nevada City museum exhibits automated music machines, the largest in the country, and also the world's biggest music organ—most still working! This is a wonderful visit with the kids.

Some of the best preserved and famous ghost towns can be seen in Nevada City and Virginia City. At Virginia City's theater, you can sit back and relax while being entertained by Vaudeville shows or 1800s melodramas. Virginia City has been the backdrop for many movies. Here you can also enjoy the famous Bale of Hay Saloon while you feast your taste-buds and immerse in history. The bar is the oldest running bar since Virginia City's gold mining boom days. Others include Alder, Marysville, Philipsburg, Boulder, Drummond, Bannack, Nevada City, and Garnet. The dusty streets of Bannack ring of the Wild West. This is where the first notable gold discovery in Montana was made in 1862. The nearby Vigilante Campground offers camping accommodation as well as tipi stays. If you want to feel like a real cowboy on a night out, go and feast your eyes on the way it was done a couple of centuries ago.

Alternatively, you can immerse yourself in the Native American traditions of a powwow's captivating dancing, music, and regalia or visit the Grant-Kohrs Ranch for an eye-opening visit to a former cattle empire (10 million acres big). This ranch is now a national historic site (Deer Lodge) with a blacksmith shop and anything "horsey" to fancy your cowboy sentiment.

Many breweries and distilleries include tasting tours and opportunities for culinary visits. The Headframe Spirits boutique distillery and tasting room in Butte is a must-visit for something different based on its rich heritage. Every spirit is named after a mine from the area, a testament to Butte's rich mining heritage. Lots of artifacts are displayed in the bar. Here they host bottling party options, sell bottles, and also house a bar dating back to 1920. Also, old-school saloons, upmarket restaurants and grills with quality products, homely bars, friendly diners, and casinos keep the nightlife alive in this part of the state. There are plenty of bistros, bakeries, and coffee shops famous for their local hospitality. And of course, with all the homegrown produce, there are farmers' markets aplenty; the most popular one is the Boulder County Farmers Market, which has been in operation since 1987.

Craig

At the Missouri River Ranch in Craig, a fly fishing lodge, you will find diverse outdoor activities including hunting opportunities, canoeing, snowshoeing, boating, and much more. But Craig is most famous for its trout fishing on the Missouri River, a premier trout stream. Here, you'll find everything related to fishing: fishing lodges, fishing shops, and fishing access sites for ease of access and relaxation. I suggest finding a log cabin or ranch, staying close to the river, and slowing down again!

Accommodation in southwest Montana will suit any budget. The area has been a welcoming host to tourists and visitors for many years due to its plethora of attractions. You'll find a wide range of accommodations catering from family-friendly, pet-friendly, and budget-friendly to all-inclusive resort stays, upmarket and luxurious hotels, mountain chalets, winter lodges, ranch stays, and camping sites. For something more extraordinary, indulge in hot springs resort stays. (These can be found in Boulder, Anaconda, Jackson, and Polaris.) Popular ranch stays include the Blacktail Ranch (Wolf Creek) and Iron Wheel Guest Ranch (Whitehall).

HOW TO REACH SOUTHWESTERN MONTANA

Helena Regional and Missoula International Airports are the main entry points. You can also enter at Bert Mooney Airport.

When driving, be aware of the long distances between remote places, watch out for wildlife on the roads, fill up regularly, and be prepared for breakdowns and intermittent mobile reception. Take your old-school map with you! Always verify updated weather conditions and road closures and travel with emergency supplies.

CLIMATE

Southwestern Montana is perfect for winter getaways. Apart from being renowned for its miraculous winter beauty, the landscape creates an outdoor recreational paradise for cross-country skiing, fly fishing, ice fishing at Georgetown Lake, ice skating, or visiting one of the various hot springs—with options at Helena, Anaconda, Butte, or Boulder. Norris Hot Springs' other name is aptly "Water of the Gods" offering a muscle-relaxing mineral soak in its comfortable average 110 degrees Fahrenheit water: a welcome release from the city-life rush!

You will find unpretentious ski areas (Maverick Mountain, Great Divide, and Discovery Basin) and fewer crowds around here. For some unique adventures you can try ice boating at Windswept Canyon Ferry Reservoir or snowk-iting at Philipsburg. Winter activities abound.

In summer, mostly hiking, camping, water recreational activities, long forest walks, and simply enjoying the fresh air and open spaces lure visitors to this area. The average high in summer is around 83 degrees Fahrenheit, and in winter, around 35 degrees, with about nine inches of snowfall in January. The short summer weather is dry, warm, and with clear skies but winters are cold, freezing, and generally partly cloudy. Winters can last up to six months.

WILDLIFE

The area is rich with wildlife that can be easily spotted. Moody moose, playful deer with their white spots, stern-faced pronghorn, and elk bugling away all call for a visit. There are many wildlife refuges and state parks that offer not only spectacular vistas and landscapes but also lots of wildlife spotting. At Ennis, Helena, and Anaconda, you'll find loads to see. Also, golden eagles, black bears, and gray wolves abound. The area has bobcats, bighorn sheep, and bison. If you are very patient with good eyes, you may spot a lonesome and shy mountain lion, something that will make a bucket-list entry!

Birdwatch at Red Rock Lakes National Refuge: The site combines a diverse landscape of wetlands, steppe, sagebrush, grassland, and forest. This is the last known breeding spot for trumpeter swans and the refuge offers many bird species as well as a variety of wildlife. Bald eagles are easily spotted around the lakes and mountains, as well as peregrine falcons and the golden eagle. The area is a birders' paradise and also a photographer's mecca. Besides this, southwest Montana is renowned for its trout rivers (Upper Missouri, Big Hole, Madison, Gallatin, Jefferson, Beaverhead, and Upper Yellowstone). The section south of Butte and Helena is famously known as the Trout Triangle and is a sought-after area for fly fishing.

HIKING AND CAMPING

Recreational activities include zip-lining, cross-country skiing, biking, snowmobiling, horseback riding, golf, bird-watching, and a multitude of watersports. For an adrenaline rush, mountain bike the single-track Mt. Helena Ridge with its beautiful vistas. A few popular hiking trails in the area are Agnes Lake Trail (Dillon), Bar Gulch Trail (Townsend), Arrastra Creek Trail (Lincoln), Bear Creek Trail (Ovando), Bear Gulch Trail #108 (Butte), and Anderson Mountain Road Ski Trail (Wisdom).

Campgrounds vary according to individual needs. Some provide many facilities while others are wild and remote. The popular campsites often have more facilities and should be prebooked, but the less touristy sites may come with a more isolated ambiance—getting away from the city, right? Planning a bit and making sure you get what you want, makes the difference between an enjoyable camping experience or an absolute disaster. Some favorite camping spots are the following:

- **Swan Creek Campground at Gallatin Canyon,** 31 miles from Bozeman, is a quaint campground in a dense fir and spruce tree forest away from the traffic noise. You get privacy at your single-family resting spots and lots of wildlife. The Gallatin River flows through the campsite. It is also the perfect location en route to Yellowstone between Big Sky and Bozeman. There are vault toilets and drinking water available.

- **Bear Creek Campground** signifies roughing it! Situated in the west Absaroka Mountains, the campsite offers lots of space and privacy on a first-come first-serve basis. Vehicles longer than 21 feet are not able to access the road.

- **Branham Lakes Campground** in the Tobacco Root Mountains offers two mountain lakes 13 miles up Mill Creek Road for lots of relaxation. At the top of the hill, you'll find only six sites and some picnic areas. This is wild camping with plenty of water recreation activities.

- **Cliff and Wade Lakes** are a two-hour drive from Bozeman outside Yellowstone National Park. The clear, blue-green lakes and pristine countryside attract tourists. There are 27 campsites offered on a first-come, first-served basis.

- **Woodbine Campground,** along the Stillwater River, offers wild camping with 44 sites and lots of privacy in the forested area. Toilets are on site, and firewood is available. It's a quiet campground with plenty of space between campers, but the site can be prone to getting cut off during flood seasons. Water and general facilities are available, and the trailhead to Woodbine Falls starts here.

- **Pine Creek Campground** in Paradise Valley, south of Livingstone and close to Yellowstone, is a family-friendly camping site. There are many local trails including a horseback ride trail. The adjacent streams and the Chico Hot Springs are the main attractions in the area.

- **Chisholm Campground** on Hyalite Reservoir is 20 miles from Bozeman. Here, you will find only ten high-demand campsites, which should be reserved beforehand. The area includes many biking and hiking trails, and water recreational activities, including fishing, are available.

- **Langohr Springs Campground** is in Gallatin County, 11 miles south of Bozeman, and situated on open meadows next to Hyalite Creek (6,200 feet elevation). Nineteen sites are scattered around fir trees, and restrooms are available. It offers close proximity to hiking trails and fishing, but you do need to reserve your spot at $20 per night.

- **Ruby Valley Campground and RV Park** is a more commercial site close to the ghost towns (Virginia City and Nevada City). It's popular and offers lots of recreational activities. Besides the adjacent mountain ranges for hikes, there is a pond on-site, and it's pet-friendly with lots of touristy things to do in the area —but you are literally on the road to the next town.

- **Fairy Lake Campground** in the Bridger Mountains (26 miles north of Bozeman) is a great place to stay if you feel like roughing it. Nine campsites are available on a no-reservation basis and there are no fees. However, the road to the site can be treacherous and not suitable for RV or trailer vehicles; it requires high-clearance vehicles.

Many tours operate in the area (for hunting trips, horseback riding tours, and hiking). At Ennis you can take a horseback riding day tour through the rolling hills of the lush Madison Valley, operated from the guest ranches.

At Lewis and Clark Caverns State Park, you can enjoy cycling, hiking, and camping. A relaxing weekend hike on the Belt Mountain Divide trail offers stunning views on the moderate 6.7-mile trek.

A popular activity is fly fishing where the Big Hole River (a famous spot close to Twin Bridges) converges with the Beaverhead River. Here, 160 miles of free-flowing tannin-colored waters home to more than 3,000 trout per mile: any fly fisher's dream! Enthusiasts will find brown and rainbow trout as well as graylings.

Does rafting or boat tours sound interesting? At the Gates of the Mountains Canyon, north of Helena, with its rugged limestone cliffs, you can enjoy a leisurely canoe or kayak trip through majestic 1,200-foot cliff faces on both sides of the Missouri River. Look out for bighorn sheep on these cliffs while you appreciate their splendor.

Stand-up paddleboard or windsurf on the 3,700-acre Georgetown Lake (Anaconda) at 6,000 feet elevation while taking in the surrounding mountain views and wildlife. And most incredible of all, with its limited light pollution, stargazing is a wonderful experience under these perfect big skies!

Southwest Montana is an outdoor lovers paradise. Boasting many of the Big Sky Country's best outdoor activities, the southwestern corner of the state is home to a collection of eclectic towns brimming with personality, mountains just begging to be explored, and wild-running, iconic rivers ready to be fished and floated. Let's find our way in!

THE BUTTERFLY OF BUTTE

> The real voyage of discovery consists not in seeking new landscapes, but in having new eyes.

— MARCEL PROUST

The streets of Butte cover 250 miles, but the tunnels beneath the Butte streets cover more than 2,500 miles! I don't know about you, but I prefer the streets—where I feel less confined. Montana is probably the best place to live if you suffer from claustrophobia because no matter which way you turn, endless space and big skies abound.

Every Montana county has its own appeal but Butte's charm is quite unique. It's known as the state's "richest hill on Earth," and, therefore, Butte has an undeniably eerie charm laced with its rich mining history. Labor is written on this hill and that's exactly Butte's mining appeal. It's America's acropolis—the copper served wars, assisted with electricity, and powered the world, leaving a visible footprint that is frightfully beautiful. What used to be Montana's largest city maintained its enduring characteristics of a town that never died. It was founded by the resilience of immigrants from all over the world–mostly Irish.

When approaching from the northern section on I 15, the following words appear as you near the town: "The 'greatest mining camp on earth' built on 'the richest hill in the world.'" According to *Wikivoyage*, these descriptive lines summarize Butte's heritage well (Wikivoyage, n.d.-b, para 3):

That hill, which has produced over two billion dollars worth of gold, silver, copper and zinc is literally honeycombed with drifts, winzes and stopes that extend beneath the city. There are over 3,000 miles of workings and shafts [that] reach a depth of 4,000 feet. This immediate country was opened as a placer district in 1864. Later Butte became a quartz mining camp and successively opened silver, copper and zinc deposits. Butte has a most cosmopolitan population derived from the four corners of the world. She was a bold, unashamed, rootin', tootin' hell-roarin' camp in days gone by and still drinks her liquor straight.

If you ever visit Butte on St. Patrick's Day, you'll whole-heartedly agree.

HISTORY

Around the early 19th century, this town was one of the most notorious boomtowns in history. The copper and mining industry lured the development of many saloons and even a red-light district. The town survived its wild history and, during the copper boom, became one of the richest mining towns in America's West. The landmark town developed quickly and stayed, leaving its industrial relics, historic structures, diverse cultures, and fascinating architectural heritage. Modern-day Butte has a small population of about 35,000 inhabitants, making the town still a pleasant friendly place to visit.

Historic Mining District—Butte Underground

The focus of your visit is notably the historic mining district. Here, you can visit the World Museum of Mining to learn about the city's mining history. It comprises an actual mine yard landmark spread over 22 acres of land filled with history. At the original mine yard, you can experience what it was like to work in the mines and make some interesting discoveries. Explore mining artifacts and exhibits at the museum. There are interesting outdoor and indoor displays and exhibitions, such as a stunning reproduction of an old mining town, and plenty of original mining equipment. The museum offers underground mine tours as well. The shafts are eerily beautiful at dusk and dawn, so I recommend you take a half day for this on your itinerary: To take in this huge marvel, you need time.

Take a sobering guided tour of the 1,700-foot-deep Berkeley Pit, a massive open-pit mine that, in its heyday, turned into a toxic lake after work was halted. This frightening Butte feature is perhaps its most interesting site to visit. The old copper mine is now filled with toxic runoff after it filled up with water and is listed as a governmental program to clean off toxic waste. Regardless, visiting the site's informative historic operation allows for interesting debates despite its "horrifying" description.

Historic Architecture

Stroll through the uptown historic district and admire the architecture and mining head frames, all part of the urban spread. Visit the Copper King's 34-room mansion that belonged to W. A. Clark, one of the world's richest men and one of the three famous Copper Kings of the area. This is a beautifully preserved historic home and a novel experience to visit. The ornate mansion returns nostalgia and makes you feel like you are on the set of a movie. It now offers lush bed and breakfast facilities with luxurious mahogany sleigh beds, definitely a bucket list visit! Further your historic journey by exploring the Butte-Silver Bow Courthouse—an architectural gem.

ITINERARY LOGISTICS

Butte is on an incline in the Rocky Mountain range, part of the Continental Divide.

How to Get There

Butte's nearest airport, Bert Mooney Airport (BTM), is a few miles away from the CBD. Other airports in the area are Bozeman Gallatin Field, Missoula Johnson-Bell Field, and Helena. Most international airlines serve Butte.

Car rentals can be arranged in Bozeman (75 miles from Butte). Butte's bus station is near the city center with the Jefferson line and the Salt Lake Express line operating in the area.

There is a developed biking trail system. Walking is possible but the town is large and spread out, so it's more convenient to drive with a car, a taxi, or the local bus lines servicing the town's main streets.

Accommodation

There are a range of hotels, motels, and bed and breakfast options in Butte. Some are historic and others a bit spartan—but affordable. The Toad Hall Bed and Breakfast hails its name from the English classic *The Wind in the Willows,* and it offers an elegant, relaxing hideaway as well as a charming romantic element.

Resort cabins and RV parking are available. But for a typical Big Sky Country vacation, consider staying at a historic hotel or guest ranch for a unique experience.

Day Trips From Butte

I would recommend day trips from Butte to the following places:

- Explore the historic Anaconda Smelter Stack with its interesting legacy.
- Experience life on a cattle ranch the way the cowboys used to do at Grant-Kohrs Ranch, a National Historic site.
- Find natural beauty at Big Hole Valley or Beaverhead-Deerlodge National Forest.

CULTURAL AND CULINARY DISCOVERIES

Take a walking tour of the city's uptown business district to discover hidden gems and historic landmarks. You'll find well-preserved Victorian architecture with stately mansions and vintage signage.

Cultural Attractions

At the Mai Wah Museum, you can learn about Butte's Chinese heritage. The museum is one of the only original buildings of Butte's former Chinatown, which was once the largest one between Seattle and Minneapolis.

The notorious Venus Alley is the home of the Dumas Victorian Brothel Museum, one of the last Victorian architectural style houses of ill repute that still exists in the US. This was the longest-operating brothel in the US (1890–1982)! Although the remaining items, after a few burglaries, may not be authentic and original, they still represent an eye-opening display of the red light district's operations. Reservations have to be prebooked, and I would strongly recommend taking a tour with a guide who will fill you in on the history. At face value, it looks like an old haunted and forgotten house, but that is exactly where the fascination lies. Don't go with expectations and be quietly surprised. It looks as if everything was just left as is. The museum calls to memory the vices of yesteryear's mining world and how the predominantly male population was entertained.

At the Mineral Museum, you can feast your eyes on precious crystals. Their exhibit includes about 1,300 specimens from around the world. The museum conducts tours, lectures, and workshops about the mining industry as well as the seismographic industry. The Montana Bureau of Mines and Geology Earthquake Studies office shares the site with the museum and you can have a look at active seismographs as recorded in real time from Montana's seismic history.

For a cultural experience, Arts Chateau features local artworks and exhibits. Alternatively, attend a performance at the Mother Lode Theatre, a historic venue for live shows. Uptown Butte has a vibrant art scene and many galleries to enjoy. The Butte Trolley tours visit historic sites and explain the memories of Butte's mining days (it's a two-hour tour).

Festivals and Events

Attend the Montana Folk Festival, a three-day celebration of music, arts, and culture in mid-July. Experience the Evel Knievel Days, a festival honoring the famous daredevil and featuring motorcycle events and stunts. It's held annually every fourth weekend in July. Enjoy the An Ri Ra Irish Festival, celebrating Irish music, dance, and heritage. It takes place annually in August.

Dining and Local Cuisine

An interesting story is that the miners used to heat their food underground with their mining helmet candles. These were mostly closed self-contained meals that we know today as pasties (a meat, potato, and onion mix enclosed in a semi-circle of pastry dough). The dough had a crimped edge for a reason: it used to be discarded after the miners heated the pastry with their dirty hands. Nowadays, you can taste these same pasties at many of the Butte eateries called Joe's Pasties–and you are welcome to eat the crimped edge! Butte pasties and Butte pork chops are local favorites. Meat is definitely a must-have on your culinary visit to Butte. Sample the local flavors and cuisine at Butte's diverse restaurants and cafes. You'll find coffee at many places with light lunches and on-the-go meals. I suggest trying traditional Montana dishes, such as bison burgers and huckleberry treats.

Enjoy craft beers at local breweries and pubs, which offer a variety of exotic beers, classic indulgence, slow pub crawling, and tasting rooms. Headframe Spirits, a mining-inspired tasting room rich with Butte history, offers endless tasting opportunities in a friendly environment.

OUTDOOR RECREATION

Apart from its range of arts and crafts, cultural, and historical recreational activities, the surrounding area calls for outdoor pleasure with a variety of adventures. The surrounding landscape is vast and inviting. Make sure you are prepared for the Montana climate. In summer around July, the average temperature is around 60 degrees Fahrenheit with highs of 80 degrees, making it sheer fun to spend outside. The coldest month is December when temperatures average around a cold 17 degrees, but be warned: it can fall to 5 degrees Fahrenheit! Most rain falls in June while February is the driest month.

The landscape offers magnificent wilderness reserves and panoramic views. Maney Lake, Elkhorn State Park, Sheepshead Recreation Area, the Anaconda-Pintler Wilderness, and Beaverhead-Deerlodge National Forest are all worth a visit. Explore nearby trails and hiking opportunities that are extensively developed. Alternatively, go fishing, floating, boating, or swimming in nearby reservoirs and rivers. Play a round of golf at the beautiful Highland View Golf Course or Eagles Nest golf course.

For a more cultural outdoor trip, take in some panoramic views of Butte from Big Butte Open Space or the Granite Mountain Memorial Overlook where you can honor the miners who were killed in the 1917 mining disaster: a poignantly somber visit with spectacular views of the Butte valley.

Another option is to visit the 88-foot-high statue over-looking Butte called *Our Lady of the Rockies* on the Continental Divide. This is the second tallest statue in the US and is dedicated to the Blessed Virgin Mary. This magnificent statue was built (from donated material) by volunteers to honor women, especially mothers. It gets lit up at night and is a beautiful sight both from below and at her feet. If you only visit her for the views, it's worth it. You have to make a booking because the trip to this landmark is on private land. Be mindful that everything is managed by volunteers, it's not a commercial tourist site. And then you have recreational activities like natural hot springs, horseback rides, hunting, and in winter—cross-country and downhill skiing, ice-skating, and snowmobiling. Outdoor recreation does not stop in this valley!

Let's move from copper to gold, and find the glamor of Helena.

THE GRANDEUR OF HELENA

> Of all the memorable views, the best have been
> framed by Montana windows.

— WILLIAM HJORTSBERG

Bannack was the first territorial capital of Montana, but today, it is a mere ghost town. History had other plans for the state and the story involved gold. The new capital city, Helena, has a history tracing back to a significant gold discovery at Last Chance Gulch (1864). The Gold Days legacy is still evident in the copper-covered dome of the State Capitol building and the name of the main street—Last Chance Gulch. Helena was the wealthiest city in the world at some point, and its inhabitants flaunted their investments in establishments and private or public enjoyment. These riches can be seen today in their well-preserved Victorian buildings. Helena used to be called the "Queen City of the Rockies" during its mining boom and former gold camp days and has many sites on the National Register of Historic Places as a testament to her mining glory days.

Yet, the city maintains a relaxed and laid-back atmosphere with hardly any traffic issues as most locals walk to work. Despite being quite big, the underrated gem offers a small-town feeling. Many attractions and major events lure visitors to the city, including the Great Northern Carousel, the historic Governor's Mansion, and the city's impressive cathedral. It is strewn with heritage architecture like the historic Reeder's Alley of the charming village originally built for miners with fire safety in mind, hence the brick complex. Lewis Reeder started using stone for his buildings and the red brick homes became iconic. This complex still has most of the original historic buildings intact from the late 19th century. Among the old historic buildings, you will find top-notch eateries with local culinary delights. Another popular visitor site is the Treasure State area. During winter, this is the best for a delightful play of festive lights and historic architecture.

There are many highly-rated museums here, such as the Holter Museum of Art, Exploration Works, and the Montana Historical Society. For outdoor activities—all year long—most people venture out east to the Canyon Ferry Reservoir. The city rests at the foot of Mount Helena, and Mount Helena City Park provides a plethora of outdoor activities: world-class skiing, horseback riding, forests, trails, view-points for camping and exploring, and exquisite waterways for water-based recreation. This one-mile-high mountain offers panoramic views of the prairies, craggy limestone cliffs, woodlands, and pine forests, with the city at its base.

ITINERARY LOGISTICS

Helena is situated halfway between the Glacier and Yellowstone parks, offering all-season comfortable weather that supports many outdoor activities. In winter though, the mountain trails can be challenging. The best weather is in May, June, and September with maximum temperatures in the low 65 degrees Fahrenheit. January has below-freezing temperatures. Depending on the time of your visit, prepare correctly: hydration and sun protection in warmer seasons and warm layered clothing for winter. Bear in mind that there may be more rain in summer.

How to Get There

Helena can be reached from I 15 and US-12. Coming by car or renting a car is the most efficient means of transport here as the city's grid street system makes navigation easy.

The town has its own regional airport, Helena Regional Airport, a mere three miles from town. Missoula International Airport is a two-hour drive away. There are no airport shuttles, but most hotels provide transport. Taxi services from the airport are available.

A Greyhound bus station and two bus lines service the area (Capital Transit System).

Accommodation

There are many accommodation options varying in price and facilities. Choose from a wide variety of hotels, motels, and bed and breakfast options in Helena. A range of self-catering *VRBO* and *Airbnb* rentals exist here as well as a range of camping and RV sites. Helena is a popular tourist city catering for ample accommodations. Off-season prices are more affordable, but even though June to August is the most expensive, accommodation rates are still reasonable.

DOWNTOWN HELENA

Have a leisurely stroll along the downtown pedestrian mall of Last Chance Gulch, the main street, and enjoy diverse shopping and dining. Explore this historic downtown area of Helena and its well-preserved architecture within its thriving culture. You'll find old buildings and vintage stores laced between modern eateries and shops: jewelry stores, lovely eateries, fascinating shops, antiques, and much more. It's indeed a downtown area that will satisfy everyone. This historic area is also a favorite place to stay. The popular Highlander Bar and Grill is a favorite among locals and for your sweet tooth, try the Dirty Dozen Donuts. There are numerous taprooms and microbreweries here. The Blackfoot River Brewing company has a wide range of beers and tours of the brewery and beer making. In this area, you'll find anything from fine dining to relaxed pubs and grill eateries. This iconic street has entertained people since 1864 and still does with its wide variety of merchants, visual stimuli, sculptures of Helena's history, entertainment venues, cultural events, and breweries.

For a cultural experience, visit art galleries and attend exhibits showcasing local and regional artwork. Visit the Montana Historical Society Museum to learn about the state's history. This is one of the most popular museums in town, and it houses a superb collection of C. M. Russell's art (the largest in the world). The museum also has a beautiful display of Native American arts and exhibits. It presents a meaningful Montana travel experience with around 50,000 artifacts and ethnographic objects, native American exhibits, and several workshops.

A variety of festivals and events take place throughout the year to entertain outdoor-, history-, and culture enthusiasts. Experience the annual lively atmosphere during the Alive at Five music concerts, hosted at various spots between June and August.

Helena Walking Tour

If you do not want to take the self-guided walking tour of historic Helena, try the historic trolley tour or one of the many sightseeing history tours in the city. Feast your eyes on the colonial revival mansions in the Mansion District, including the famous Governor's Mansion, which was home to the state governor for half a century since 1848. The riches and wealth are harmoniously flaunted in graceful Queen Anne-style architecture and abundant antiques, fireplaces, and lavishly decorated rooms.

For family entertainment and adventure, have fun at the Northern Carousel for kids. It offers 37 hand-carved animals to ride, providing much joy! Ghost towns a short distance away are incredible sites of frozen time as they were left a few centuries ago, fun for young and old! The city has informative plaques and markers to teach about its vibrant gold rush history, which can be turned into a historic family treasure hunt.

HELENA'S PRIDE

The historic mansion district was once the home of mining millionaires and the birthplace of the legendary actor Gary Cooper in 1901. Now, the city has become Helena's pride and joy.

. . .

Montana State Capitol

Learn about Montana's government at the Montana State Capitol. The building has been a beacon of freedom since its beginning in 1896. The neoclassical design's most notable feature is the massive rotunda surrounded by four circular paintings depicting archetypes of Montana history (a cowboy, Native American, explorer and fur trapper, and a gold miner). The building is filled with memorabilia and an impressive art piece by C. M. Russell of the explorers, Lewis and Clark. The exterior is dominated by its magnificent copper dome topped with the Lady Liberty statue. Guided tours to explore the historic architecture and legislative chambers are available from Monday to Saturday. Enhance your experience by enjoying the beautiful capitol grounds and the Montana Veterans Memorial.

Cathedral of Saint Helena

Many visitors call this their highlight. The Cathedral of Saint Helena is a stunning architectural masterpiece with its iconic red twin-spired skyline towering high above the city and looking as if it has been placed there directly from Europe. The building is awe-inspiring. Crafted at the turn of the century, in 1908, the Neo-Gothic structure has 59 intricate Bavarian stained glass windows, a grand interior, and a magnificent pipe organ. The exterior is topped with gold leaf crosses and limestone sculptures.

For an unusual experience, you can attend a special event or religious service at the Cathedral. Guided tours are available and special services are held. Special masses happen during the week, and the church is always open to people of all faiths.

Holter Museum of Art

This fascinating museum exhibits a contemporary art scene featuring local, regional, and national artists. They pride themselves on excellence and innovative exhibitions and inspire creativity with educational programs, art workshops, and classes offered by the museum and community participants. They aim to build meaningful connections and showcase established and emerging artists.

Annual Events and Festivals

A plethora of events take place in Helena so keep an eye on the local calendar. Some to look out for are the Last Chance Stampede & Fair, rodeo events, and the carnival. The Alive at Five concert series showcases live music performances. For outdoor enthusiasts, hiking, biking races, and trail runs happen often and there is the famous Helena Ice Fishing Derby during winter months.

OUTDOOR RECREATION

Outdoor enthusiasts have an endless canvas to explore. Find some solitude in silence and fly fishing with no humans in sight in the Blue Ribbon trout areas, mountain bike endless trails of Silver Level Riding in the mountainous terrain, go horseback riding, float on water, kayak and boat, find some rock-climbing on craggy cliffs, have a family picnic, or simply take in the endless vistas and photographic scenery.

Helena National Forest and Outdoor Recreation

The natural beauty of the Helena National Forest provides loads of opportunities for hiking, biking, or horseback riding on numerous trails. Go fishing, boating, floating, or swimming in nearby lakes and rivers. Simply enjoy the panoramic views from Mount Helena Park and the 1,300-foot mountain. Pack a picnic lunch and enjoy a relaxing day in nature. For an alternative historical visit in nature, venture out to the Lewis and Clark Cavern State Park with its limestone caverns, trails, and resounding caves and rock formations in gorgeous nature.

Gates of the Mountains

The top outdoor visitor attraction of Helena is the Gates of the Mountains Wilderness area. This magnificent recreational area is filled with wildlife viewings, water activities, and breathtaking views. The Gates of the Mountains is Montana's smallest wilderness area, an hour and a half drive away from Helena. It was named after the epic limestone cliffs lining the river on both sides. These were first spotted by Lewis and Clark, and they called them the most remarkable cliffs they had seen and named them the "Gates of the Rocky Mountains."

Presently, a rich trail system abounds in narrow gorges and streams with lots of wildlife. This gateway to the wilderness is best viewed from the water, so I suggest hopping on any kind of boat and taking a slow journey through these cliffs alongside the Missouri River. For a two-hour river cruise with guided narration to discover all about the area's history, the expedition, and the legendary places these men discovered, make a booking on one of the several daily boat tours in summer. There is no better way to experience the magical scenery! Spot wildlife and enjoy some peaceful surroundings.

Helena provides a mix of opposites: past and present, wilderness and hometown comfort, solitary isolation in nature and the company of engaging venues for recreation. From here, I'll take you on a journey to the past: the ghost towns of Virginia and Nevada City.

THE TWIN PLEASURE OF TOURING VIRGINIA AND NEVADA CITY

> Wyoming is good, but Montana is like heaven on earth.

— HENRY WINKLER

There are many reports of haunted places in Montana. One of the most popular is the ghost of a woman walking down the stairs at the Demas Hotel in Butte. Some have spotted some eerie events in the ghost towns of Montana. It seems like there remains a lingering presence of the past. A visit to Virginia City and Nevada City in Montana may just clarify this for you!

The glorious days of a saddler and a barber shop are written on the landscape around these twin towns. Connected to the rough and tumble old west, here you  can step back in time, to the time of frontier settlement 150 years ago in 1859. When small gold deposits were discovered, many immigrants from other countries arrived to find their fortune. Hotels and businesses sprang up instantly to create a vibrant hub for daily life. Today, the towns resemble the wave of prosperity that made them alive in the 19th century. Some of these buildings date back to the early 1800s. Unique places lace the heritage of that life in these ghost towns, such as the last four-story wooden school in the US. The many churches are a testament to the cultural diversity of the miners. Their opulence and sizes reflect the wealth of the city. One example is the rare gothic-style wood construction of the St. Paul The Prospector Episcopal Church (1861), which is a national historic landmark.

With only a one-mile distance between the two towns, both of them make magnificent backdrops for photos. These towns attempt to keep history alive and fresh in the minds of visitors today. The surrounding landscape provides vistas and wildlife to enjoy. It is one of the last remaining symbols of the Wild West: wild horses roam the area and there are approximately 2,000 protected wild horses here (including mustangs).

By 1896, Nevada Mining generated more than half of the precious metals in the US, and at The Way It Was Museum, you can view the exhibits of the miners' lives and the tools they used. There is even a canary memorial to illustrate the miners' habit of taking caged canaries with them to warn them of imminent danger, making you aware of the dangers of their work. They left a legacy well presented through historical markers and a memorial to the miners. The Ponderosa mine has been reinforced and is open to the public. According to Knapp, once gold was found in the area, Virginia City instantly became a boomtown filled with fortune seekers (2017, para 3):

On May 26, 1863 Bill Fairweather and Henry Edgar discovered gold near Alder Creek, so named because the banks were lined with Alder trees. They discovered the largest surface field of gold in Alder Gulch. No matter how hard they tried to keep their discovery a secret, the word got out and within three weeks the town of Virginia City was thriving. Some built log cabins, some of which stand to this day. Others built makeshift brush shelters while others pitched their tents. By the Fall of 1863 between 7,000 and 10,000 souls called this place their home.

Needless to say, such discoveries prompted vices and crime, and together, with a lack of a legal system, all flourished. Vigilantes, gunfighters, houses of ill repute, and many saloons thrived as the money went around. But when the gold ran out, it all changed drastically. Everybody left except for a few hardy residents who could keep their businesses occupied. By the 1950s, Virginia City was frozen in time and was restored to its heyday glory as a tourist attraction and open-air museum. Nevada City suffered a similar fate and was destroyed by dredging in the early 1900s.

ITINERARY LOGISTICS

The ghost towns are located in the famous Alder Gulch area between the Custer Gallatin National Forest and Beaverhead-Deerlodge National Forest, where Interstates 15 and 90 converge.

How to Get There

These ghost towns are highlights of a magnificent small-town route between Bozeman and Butte on MT 287. Virginia City and Nevada City are southeast of Butte, close to Yellowstone National Park, which is only a 90-mile drive away. Ennis and Sheridan are close towns.

Accommodation

Consider staying in a historic hotel, bed and breakfast, or guesthouse in Virginia City or nearby Ennis. Enjoy the unique charm and hospitality of the region's accommodations. In these two quaint ghost towns, I would recommend a log cabin or a home with a charming Victorian interior. Other options include vacation rentals, inns, camping, and RV sites.

- Rambling Moose Campground is a well-maintained camping area with level gravel sites for no-nonsense RV parking.
- In Nevada City, at Nevada City Hotel you can find

cabins with magnificent mountain views. They are close to amenities but still in nature.

- In Victoria City, try Elling House Inn, which is a historic Gothic revival stone house (1876) with a lush garden and stunning Victorian furniture including quilt-covered beds. The Inn is an easy walking distance to all amenities and famous attractions.
- Fairweather Inn in Virginia City has a homely Victorian interior and relaxing atmosphere. There is a grand old terrace on the street where you can have a drink, close to all amenities, museums, and eateries.
- Just an Experience Bed and Breakfast is one of the top review-rated places to stay close to these two ghost towns. It offers cabins and guest rooms with warm hospitality and a relaxing atmosphere. With its large yard, gardens, hot tub, fire pit, and plenty of games for the kids, it's the perfect place to stay for families.

VIRGINIA CITY

Explore the streets of Virginia City, a living ghost town with all the spooks, nooks, and crannies of the old Wild West. Mark Twain started his writing career in Virginia City. He got a job as a reporter at the local newspaper, changed his name, and gained a national reputation as a writer. He also wrote about the hazardous mining conditions. Today, the ghost town honors him with the Mark Twain Museum. Every single structure in this town writes heritage and history on the surrounding landscape.

Virginia City started after the discovery of gold at Alder Gulch in 1863. It remained a boom town during the post-Civil War era, but sadly, the city did not last very long, and as soon as the gold ran dry, the town's population decreased drastically. It was a dying town until Charlie and Sue Bovey saw its value as a glorious frontier town and initiated a restoration of the storefronts, boardwalks, and exhibits. Now, Virginia City is on the National Register of Historic Places. The following attractions call for a visit:

- **Boothill Cemetery:** One of Montana's most popular attractions, and the last resting place of five infamous road agents who were hanged by the Vigilantes (1864).
- **Bale Hay Saloon:** Experience the lively atmosphere of Montana's oldest operating bar and feel the blast from the past.
- **Nevada City Museum:** Learn about the era's gold rush history and relive the frontier town atmosphere while visiting this interesting museum. You can

engage with interpreters over the weekends for interesting history snippets.

- **Virginia City Opera House:** An old livery stable was remodeled into a 19th-century theater and still has a beautifully restored Cremona Player Piano which was used to accompany silent movies. The Opera House presents Vaudeville variety shows and 19th-century melodramas.
- **Virginia City Players:** Enjoy live performances (Vaudeville shows and melodrama) at one of the oldest theaters.
- **Virginia City Historic Steam Train:** Take a historic ride and enjoy scenic views of the countryside between the twin towns.
- **Virginia City Stagecoach:** Historic coaches take you up to Alder Gulch like a real vigilante with a narrated tour. Slow stagecoach journeys were a popular travel means for almost 200 years.

NEVADA CITY

This family-friendly ghost town is sheer fun. It's another Bovey couple restoration project and a living history outdoor museum featuring original log buildings and historic structures from the Gold Rush era. Here, you'll find a marvelous collection of old-time music boxes, calliopes, player pianos, and even an automatic violin player. You'll find the biggest music organ in the world in Nevada City! The Music Hall hosts live performances and entertainment events on weekends.

The town is open annually between Memorial Day and Labor Day weekends when you can take a self-guided tour and learn about the history of the town. Experience a ride on the 30-inch Nevada City Narrow Gauge Railroad. The number 8 Bovey train connects the two cities with a one-and-a-half mainline tour. Discounts apply, walk-ins are accepted, and groups have to book in advance. There is a fascinating exhibit of the 1910 Baldwin Steam Locomotive on site as well.

LIVING HISTORY EXPERIENCES

If creepy attracts your senses, ghost stories make these towns the biggest attraction. There are many supernatural accounts, and these spooked sites attract tourists. The Old Washoe Club is the epicenter of tall tales with a real-life history of several murders and suicides, missing prostitutes, and an explosion to account for the spirits. History and ghosts come alive in the collection of 150 historic buildings that recreate a past. It's a lovely experience for the whole family.

The best part of the historic visit is the blending of museums and actual shops: one may be an 1800s shop filled with memorabilia, but the next may sell homemade ice cream (like The Virginia City Creamery) as well. The Museum in Virginia City has a shop where you can buy memorabilia. Meticulously assembled exhibits allow the visitor to step back into yesteryear and experience what life was like or entice imaginative stories of the people and the children who lived here. Some even show the accumulated 150-year dust!

Enhance your visit by engaging in living history demonstrations and activities throughout both towns. Watch blacksmithing, gold panning, and other period crafts being practiced. Or interact with costumed interpreters who bring the history of the towns to life. Attend reenactments and historical events showcasing life during the Gold Rush era. Opening hours are mostly between Memorial Day and Labor Day and the towns have historic reenactments of the 1800s on weekends.

Alder Gulch Short Line Railroad

Take a ride on the Alder Gulch Short Line Railroad (about 1.5 miles) connecting Virginia City and Nevada City. The railroad activity was initiated by the Bovey couple in 1964. They created a vintage railroad to enjoy the scenery between the two villages with a 15-minute train ride. The rides run between May and September on an hourly schedule. There are no ticket reservations, tickets can be obtained on a first-come first-serve basis at the Virginia City train depot, or the Nevada City Museum. It departs across the road from the Bovey Visitor Center and the Music Hall. From here you can enjoy a scenic journey through the historic mining district and learn about the area's transportation history and railroad operations.

RECREATIONAL ACTIVITIES

Nature and history combine to provide a plethora of recreational activities around these towns. Horseback and pony rides, scenic drives, water-based activities, historic tours, and yesteryear celebrations will keep the whole family occupied.

Dining and Shopping

Dine in historic restaurants and cafes offering a taste of the past. Sample local treats like homemade fudge and ice cream. Have a local beer in the historic Bale of Hay Saloon and fill up with fuel food at the Pioneer Bar, which made the list for one of the top six best burgers in the country. Browse unique shops and boutiques for antiques, handmade crafts, old-fashioned candy stores, and souvenirs.

Annual Events and Festivals

Attend the Virginia City Grand Victorian Ball: a celebration of the Victorian era with live music and dancing. Or experience the Virginia City Players' summer theater performances. Alternatively, join in the family fun at Nevada City's Living History Days where regular reenactments and demonstrations are held. Keep your eye on the town's lively calendar for regular festivities.

Outdoor Recreation

Outdoor fun abounds here! Take advantage of the many outdoor recreational opportunities in the surrounding area. Go fishing, boating, or swimming in nearby rivers and lakes. Enjoy a picnic or take scenic drives through the mountainous landscape. The wide open spaces call for hiking, biking, and wildlife viewing in the scenic countryside.

If these twin towns didn't spook you enough, explore nearby ghost towns like Laurin, Granite, and Pony while you experience the remnants of once-booming mining towns around Alder Gulch. From here, I take you to the fascinating Lewis and Clark Caverns State Park.

THE FANCY LEWIS AND CLARK
CAVERNS STATE PARK

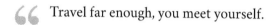

❝ Travel far enough, you meet yourself.

— DAVID MITCHELL

The notable and colorful limestone caverns in southeast Montana have fascinating dripstone formations of stalagmites, stalactites, columns, helictites, and flowstones inside. It takes around two hours to hike two miles in the caverns. The hikes are only through guided tours with knowledgeable guides. The caverns are a delicate ecology of a world without light and can now be viewed with 538 feet of underground tunnels.

ITINERARY LOGISTICS

The caverns can be found between Beaverhead-Deerlodge National Forest and Helena-Lewis and Clark National Forest, just south of Helena.

How to Get There

Lewis and Clark Caverns State Park is situated in the middle between Butte and Bozeman on MT 2E. It's 19 miles west of Three Forks and 15 miles east of Whitehall. The park is next to the Jefferson River. Bus lines service the park from both towns.

Park Guidelines and Safety

The park has an informative visitor center, picnic area, fire pits, a large campground, and an amphitheater. The water supply is limited in winter—the camp water is turned off between October and May.

Follow park regulations and guidelines to preserve the natural environment. Leave No Trace principles apply here. Be aware of potential wildlife encounters and take necessary precautions. Check the park's website or visitor's center for updates on trail conditions and closures. Come prepared with plenty of water, comfortable shoes, sunscreen, a hat, and a warm jacket.

Accommodation

Consider staying in a nearby cabin or lodge for a more comfortable overnight stay. There are many lodgings available in Whitehall and Three Forks, a short distance away from the park. The websites *Expedia.com*, *Booking.com*, *VRBO*, and *Airbnb* are useful sites to search for the type of accommodation that will suit your needs.

Camping and Overnight Stays

Well-equipped campgrounds and rental cabins service visitors all year round. They provide a peaceful atmosphere and starry nights in the remote Montana wilderness. The park has 40 campsites, some tipis, and three cabins. You could also reserve an RV camping spot from the camping options.

CAVE TOURS AND EXPLORATION

The caves were discovered by local hunters in 1892 and it became Montana's first state park. Take a guided tour of the caverns to explore its stunning limestone formations. The tours provide entertainment for the adventurer, the inquisitive, and the geologist in you where you can let your imagination run wild by observing the fascinating formations.

Guided tours are between May 1 and September 30. There are two tours available: the Classic Tour is more strenuous and longer, and the Paradise Tour is the easier one for physically challenged or elderly people. The caves have 90% humidity and a temperature of around 50 degrees Fahrenheit all year round. They are dimly lit and some passageways are narrow, so dress appropriately (have a lightweight jacket and wear comfortable shoes). The caverns may be slippery and wet.

- **Classic Tour:** For the more adventurous, this is a longer (in total, a two-mile walking tour) and more strenuous walk with 600 steep cave steps (100 ascending and 500 descending) and a three-quarter mile uphill walk to the cave entrance. It takes about 30 minutes to get to the cave and then turn, bend, duck, and bum slide through narrow cave openings once inside to see the various cave rooms. After this, you continue with a return walk outside on gravel for about half a mile back to the visitor center. It's highly rewarding for your efforts but not for visitors who are afraid of confined spaces and the dark. You need to be reasonably flexible to get through narrow openings and slide down some on your behind!
- **Paradise Tour:** This is for families and people with claustrophobia or mobility challenges. The tour takes you to the largest and most decorated area of the cave, called the Paradise Room, and one other room. It takes about an hour and a half to complete with ease.

To enter the caverns, visitors have to take safety precautions. According to the Montana State Parks website, visitors have to take precautions for a lethal threat to bat safety (n.d.-e, para 9):

Visitors will pass near a nursery colony of bats. White-nose syndrome, a fungus that affects bats but not people, has reached Montana. Bat mortalities from the disease are higher than 80%. Managers are requiring precautions from visitors to reduce additional stressors for this fragile cave resource: Visitors cannot bring or wear any item that has been to another cave or mine.

This means that you will have to disinfect eyeglasses if you wore them to another mine or cave five years prior to this visit. It's advised to wear a mask and sterilized gloves. Limited tickets are available and are made on a first-come first-serve basis. Arrive 30 minutes prior to the start. For a unique experience, a limited number of candlelight tours are available during December. The Candlelight Cave Tour tickets have to be reserved online, and it's a challenging two-mile walking tour with 600 steps and a slippery interior (similar to the Classic Tour). However, this experience enhances the unique underground environment and awe-inspiring darkness and silence.

INTERPRETIVE CENTER AND EXHIBITS

Explore the history of the park with many interpretive programs to start your cavern journey. Learn and engage about the history, geology, and formation of the caves from knowledgeable guides, interpretive and interactive displays, educational programs, and events. The park's Interpretive Center also has information about the Lewis and Clark

Expedition. Explore the exhibits showcasing the flora, fauna, and geological features of the park but also discover the fascinating historical significance of the expedition's journey through the area.

OUTDOOR RECREATION

Apart from the variety of camping opportunities, discover nearby attractions and activities like the following:

- A scenic drive along Madison River Valley with breathtaking views.
- Madison Buffalo Jump State Park provides Native American history and hunting techniques.
- Visit Three Forks, a charming town where the Missouri River begins.
- You can enjoy water recreational activities such as fishing, boating, canoeing, or floating on the Madison or Jefferson Rivers.
- Other recreation activities include hunting, biking, hiking, wildlife watching, and photography.

Hiking and Outdoor Recreation

Hike or bike the many trails near the caverns. Scenic hiking trails wind through the park's beautiful 3,000-acre landscape. Some of the ten trails have 1,600 feet elevation gain. The two main trails are strenuous, with steep elevation gain and loss, while the others are more relaxing, such as the floral Short Nature loop trail in the picnic area (a quarter-mile track). The Fishing Access Trail to the Jefferson River is a little bit more than one mile long with only a 100-foot elevation change. At the river, you can relax and swim or fish your heart out. The moderately challenging Cave Gulch Trail (a 4.7-mile loop trail) offers panoramic views of mountains and valleys. Pack a picnic and relax in designated areas within the park.

Wildlife Viewing and Nature Photography

Diverse wildlife viewing for elk, bighorn sheep, mule deer, and birdwatching for raptors and a wide variety of bird species attract many visitors. Alternatively, capture the beauty of the park's natural landscapes and unique rock formations with photography. Remember to practice responsible wildlife viewing and photography, maintaining a safe distance, and respecting the animals' habitats.

Picnic Areas and Recreational Facilities

There are designated picnic areas in the park offering recreational facilities such as park playgrounds and sports fields. Organize a family gathering or group outing amidst the scenic surroundings and smile at yourself for gliding through slithery caves on your bum.

From miraculous limestone features and cave mysteries, let's get back to some serious history at the Big Hole National battlefield, the place where the Nez Perce were forced to surrender to the onslaught of a relentless army.

HISTORIC REALM OF BIG HOLE NATIONAL BATTLEFIELD

> Inside of me there are two dogs. One is mean and evil and one is good and they fight each other all the time. When asked which one wins I answer, the one I feed the most.

— SITTING BULL

The Paleo-Indian culture established itself in Montana after the last glacial era more than 10,000 years ago. The prehistoric Native American tribes thus share a long history with the Montana landscape. But life inevitably changes.

Big Hole Battlefield imparts one of the most epic Indian war stories. The conflict took place between five bands of the Nez Perce Indians and the 7th U.S. Infantry in 1877. As with most Indian wars in the area, this one also symbolizes the differences between the two sides with their different cultural and political viewpoints, goals, social organization, and individual responsibility. In 1855, the Nez Perce reluctantly signed over 5.5 million acres of land to the U.S. government. The remaining 7.5 million acres became an Indian Reservation and the treaty prohibited Europeans on the Reservation land.

The tribe held peaceful relations with the white men at the time. They even assisted Lewis and Clark on their expedition and gave them food, shelter, horses, and guides for their expedition and nursed their weary and sick. They were thus instrumental in the exploration history, helping European explorers to navigate the rivers that they knew so well, and sharing their information with them.

About 800 Nez Perce Indians who didn't want to sign the treaties, left in June 1877 to meet up with Sitting Bull in Canada in an attempt to find safety. (Sitting Bull's tribe was relatively free in Canada at the time.) They managed to elude the U.S. forces, but by October, they surrendered because of exhaustion and starvation. By this time only about half of them were still alive. The turning point started when gold was discovered in 1860, intensifying their problems, and forcibly removing them to reservations. There were some incidents in the reservations when Europeans invaded and started squatting on their land without permission. Tensions increased in the ensuing years. The tribe was forced to relinquish more of their land until they were left with only 750,000 acres. Many Nez Perce were murdered during this time. The catalyzing incident that raised alarm in 1877 was after some enraged Nez Perce youngsters ignored the elders' advice and took revenge for the death of an earlier murder of one of their fathers. They hunted down and killed four white settlers. The army was called in and the rest is a battle history.

Much of the tension started in Idaho, and once they reached Montana, they thought their problems were over, and set up camp in the Big Hole Valley. A mere two days later, they were overcome while sleeping and that incident is what is now commemorated as the Battle of Big Hole. The Big Hole National Monument commemorates their heroic five-month flight, which covered about 1,200 miles of rough country of the High Plains and much of Yellowstone Park. Many battles took place between them and the much larger U.S. Army—one of the most devastating ones at this site. Between 60 and 90 Indians died, mostly women, elders, and children and only 12 were warriors. It was the largest battle between the U.S. military (who suffered 29 dead and had 40 soldiers wounded) and the Indians.

Various versions of the battle exist. Some say the revenge was initiated by reservation demands and agreements that left them with too little of their traditional homeland. Others share the story of the tribes' revenge on the loiters on their land. The one thing we do know is that the Nez Perce tribe's tragic long fight for freedom happened over the vast area of four states: from Wallowa Lake in Oregon to Montana. There are now 38 sites spread over these four states (Idaho, Washington, Montana, and Oregon) to lace the threads of their brave story. They certainly left a tapestry of change and a distinctive mark on the history of the frontier counties.

The area (1,000 acres) became a national monument in 1910 and a national battlefield in 1963. The site where the tribe set up their camp is considered a sacred place. The big-sky landscape of broad plains with mountains offers a scenic backdrop of austere tranquility in the area. It's hard to believe that such a bloodied battle took place on these serene plains.

VISITOR CENTER AND EXHIBITS

The journey of your discovery starts at the visitor center in Wisdom. Here, you can watch a highly informative and touching 26-minute introduction video of the incident, visit the interesting museum, and shop at the bookstore. Explore the exhibits of the Nez Perce war showcasing the events leading up to the battle and its aftermath. Gain insight into the culture and traditions of the Nez Perce people. All provide helpful information and an overview of the battle. From here, a well-laid-out self-guided tour with a one-hour walk on the paths takes you to all the points of interest.

During summer there are various interactive ranger-guided activities, including ranger programs and education programs for school groups. At the museum are exhibits of personal items and thought-provoking photographs of those affected by one of the bloodiest battles in Nez Perce history. There is no entrance fee to the park. You may have limited mobile reception in the park, pets are not allowed, no drones are allowed, and there are no gas stations. Remember to bring insect repellent for mosquitoes, wear comfortable clothing, and bring your own water and snacks. (No plastic bottled water is sold in the park, and the nearest restaurant is a 12-minute drive away, so come prepared.)

ITINERARY LOGISTICS

The historic site is located in Beaverhead County, between Chief Joseph Pass and the Continental Divide. It is open all year, although the walking trails may be closed during inclement weather in winter. The best time to visit is during the summer months, especially in July when the weather is the warmest.

How to Get There

Little Big Hole Battlefield is 76 miles west of Dillon, 106 miles south of Missoula on MT 43, and 10 miles away from the little hamlet of Wisdom, which has less than 100 inhabitants with limited services and amenities. From Butte, take I 15 SW to Divide, then MT 43 to reach the battlefield location. It's a two-hour drive through the scenic Beaverhead-Deerlodge National Forest.

You'll find bus stations at Dillon, Butte, and Missoula, and the closest airport is Bert Mooney Airport in Butte (90 miles away).

Park Guidelines and Safety

Follow park regulations and guidelines to ensure the preservation of the sacred battlefield. Stay on designated trails and respect the natural and cultural resources of the park. Always be aware of potential wildlife encounters and practice proper safety measures.

Accommodation

There are limited accommodation options close to the battlefield and no accommodation or campgrounds within the park. Nez Perce Stay and Play Cabins are about a mile away. These are very rustic cabins offering accommodation for one group, with limited and basic amenities. You have to walk a bit to your cabin from the parking area. You'll have no running water (but it does include jugged water from the local well), and there is a heated bathroom outside the cabin for a "roughing it" feel. Your pets will love it here, they are welcome! Nez Perce Motel is ten miles away in Wisdom: a basic place with only five rooms but a little gem off the beaten track. Big Hole River Park provides RV parking close by and there's a variety of camping sites and RV parking sites in the wider area—into Idaho as well.

A variety of lodgings can be found in the wider area such as the Bitterroot Valley or outside Montana (Salmon, Idaho). A two- to three-hour drive away from the battlefield will provide camping, lodges, fishing lodges, cabins, and vacation homes around Butte and Dillon. For a luxurious, all-inclusive outback adventure, try a ranch booking in the wider area. There are some amazing remote ranches a mere 25-mile drive away, offering farm hospitality and peace and quiet. For more luxurious accommodation, you'll have to drive more than 45 miles. The battlefield is remote and serene.

THE HISTORIC BATTLE

After the battle, Chief Joseph led his people toward the border of Canada and another battle ensued. After nearly a week-long siege between the U.S. Army and The Nez Perce bands at the Bear Paw Mountains, the chief surrendered and his words still echo on the fields. This battlefield is located on Road 240, south of Chinook in north-central Montana. From the Big Hole Valley, the prominent mountain ranges can be seen. According to Tillison, it was the end of an era and their time in Reservations had begun (2023, para 33):

This is the place where Chief Joseph surrendered to the U.S. Army. His famous quote at this location has echoed through the centuries: 'Hear me, my chiefs. I am tired. My heart is sick and sad. From where the sun now stands, I will fight no more forever.'

Battlefield Tour

Take the well-presented self-guided walking trails connecting the siege area, the Nez Perce camp, and the Howitzer capture site to experience its historical landscape. It's about an hour's walk, laced with flowers and the harrowing reminder of the tipi camp poles standing eerily desolate on the plains. Follow the interpretive signs and markers to key locations as you learn more about the strategies and tactics employed by the Nez Perce and U.S. Army forces. Reflect on the events that unfolded during the battle within the nostalgic landscape setting.

Nez Perce Camp and Tipi Village

The battle took place while the New Perce group was heading to Canada for safety and asylum. They were passing slowly and peacefully through the Bitterroot Valley with about 2,000 horses and their families. The group set up camp and did not think that their lives were threatened. They were unaware of the approaching army, led by Colonel John Gibbon, who attacked them at dawn on August 9th and 10th, 1877. The surprised women and children fled to safety. Their tipis were burned and it was the turning point in the Nez Perce wars. Now, the tipi poles are a silent reminder of the ravaging battle and tragedy—it's also a sacred site to the people. You can visit the reconstructed camp and tipi village, learn about the traditional ways of life and cultural practices of the Nez Perce people, and engage in educational programs and demonstrations offered at the village.

OUTDOOR RECREATION

Be aware that the park is situated at 6,300 feet elevation above sea level. This may affect your fitness levels and you may have to slow down a bit, which is not a bad thing when you visit this sacred site!

Nearby Attractions and Activities

Take scenic drives through southwest Montana's landscape and discover Wisdom with its charming western small-town atmosphere. The landscape calls for scenic photography and meditative lookout spots. There are many water-based recreational activities such as fishing and kayaking around the Big Hole River. Fishing is strictly regulated and thus maintains a high-quality fishing experience with the main species brook trout, mountain sucker, and mountain whitefish. Check out Bannack State Park, a registered historic landmark near Dillon, and Beaverhead County from here.

Hiking and Nature Walks

Engage in hiking and wildlife viewing in the surrounding area. These trails are like meditative pilgrimages, and it's encouraged to be respectful of the people who died here. Nature walk trails are closed during winter starting from the first snow falls until the snow melts. February has the highest snowfall and December is the coldest month. The road leading to the trail parking lot is also closed for vehicles during this time, but it remains open for skiing and snow-shoe activities.

The battlefield has three hiking trails: the longest, 1.6-mile Nez Perce camp trail, takes about one hour; a 1.2-mile Siege Area trail with ascending steps takes about 45 minutes; and the Howitzer trail with a steep climb takes 40 minutes. Trail guides are available, and all trails are moderately easy for families. (A one-dollar fee is charged for them, and you have to drive from the visitor center to a lower parking area for access.) The trails take you to the sacred place where the Nez Perce were sleeping before the fatal attack, and also the other significant battle sites. They all have impressive scenic vistas. There are covered picnic facilities, interpretive signs, benches, and restrooms.

A slightly longer trail, the Big Hole National Battlefield trail is a 2.9-mile trek with only about 330 feet elevation. Even this one is still moderately easy and accessible for family hikes. The trail takes about an hour and has an informative guide at the trailhead explaining the historic battle. No dogs are allowed. The trail provides some solitude and stunning prairie vistas.

One-day and multi-day hiking trails are dotted around the area at Anaconda, Bitterroot National Forest, and Beaver-head-Deerlodge National Forest. As you immerse yourself in the natural beauty of the area, enjoy scenic views of the surrounding mountains and valleys all year round. In winter, enjoy hiking, Nordic skiing, and snowshoeing on these trails.

Nature walks offer wildlife viewing (wolves, bison, black bears, mountain lions, etc.) as you learn about the fauna and flora of the region. Birdwatching is a favorite activity here with around 80 species. You'll encounter northern pygmy owls and bald eagles, and in winter, the redpoll and American tree sparrows set up nests here.

Ranger Programs and Guided Tours

Take advantage of ranger-led programs and guided tours offered by the park. You can engage in a two-mile hike with a knowledgeable guide that leaves a better understanding of the fatal event. There are also 30-minute "deck talk" tours with scenic views from the seated site for immobility-challenged visitors. In the summer, various speakers (Nez Perce tribal members and cultural experts) give talks about the event and other related subject matters at the visitor center. Participate in talks, demonstrations, and interpretive activities to deepen your understanding of the battlefield's history. Check the park's schedule for specific programs and events during your visit. The Junior Ranger program is open to all ages where you can learn about the history of the park. There are frequent ranger-led deck talks on weekends.

The annual commemoration of the battles happens at both Bear Paw Mountains (Chinook) and at Nez Perce Camp of the Big Hole National Battlefield. These provide pipe and drum ceremonies (no photos are allowed). Entry is free, and remember to bring blankets, mosquito repellents, umbrellas, lunch, and sunscreen.

Picnic Areas and Visitor Amenities

Utilize the designated picnic areas for a relaxing and pensive outdoor meal. Take advantage of the informative visitor amenities, restrooms, and bookstore at the visitor center to enhance your understanding of this tragic event. The battlefield is remote, so prepare for limited accommodation and dining options unless you drive to the bigger towns.

From serenity to luxury—let's take a trip to Big Sky, an outdoor adventurer's paradise.

THE WONDERS OF A BIG SKY

> 66 Don't let your luggage define your travels, each
> life unravels differently.

— SHANE KOYCZAN

There are 14 operational ski areas in Montana, and
14,000 acres of ski slopes and more than 500 downhill runs make Montana's mountains a winter playground for
ski enthusiasts. One of the most luxurious ski resorts is in

Big Sky. Its allure is alpine and golf resorts with many hiking trails traversing into nearby forests. The valley beneath the Lone Mountain peak demands visits from the world's best skiers. Unlike some of the other glamorous ski resorts in the world, this one offers incredible nature and vistas on top of some of the best powder for ski adventures. Big Sky covers 5,800 acres of ski paradise— the most in the US. There are more than 250 ski trails here. The world's first extreme skier, Helena, born Scot Schmidt, lives here.

Private ski clubs and members-only golf clubs lend themselves to the area's sense of exclusivity. More relaxed cross-country ski trails provide scenic ski experiences. State-of-the-art ski facilities and lifts, many chair lifts and ski runs, top-rated after-ski enjoyment, some of the best ski lounges, Michelin star dining, luxurious accommodation, and magical sunsets and sunrises for nature lovers make this a snowy paradise. Nowadays, the town comes alive beyond its ski delights making it a perfect Montana year-round attraction. In summer, all the hiking trails appear with the melting snow. Big Sky is mainly a tourist town with a small local population.

ITINERARY LOGISTICS

The town is part of the Yellowstone ecosystem (a mere hour away) with its undisturbed land teeming with wildlife. The nearby Gallatin River is famous for its high-quality fishing. Mountain Village and Meadow Village are the two main areas of Big Sky. The latter is located six miles away from the ski resort base. (Mountain Village is closer to the ski slopes.) Plan accommodation according to your needs as Meadow Village provides more nightlife while Mountain Village gives ease of access to sports activities and is quieter at night.

Be prepared for cooler weather—even in summer. (There have been snowfall reports in June!) The weather is cooler in the morning and evenings and temperatures can shift drastically so pack layered clothing and be prepared for the outdoors: "function over fashion" works best here as they say in Montana. Always have bear spray and sunscreen. Winters can be extremely cold with temperature ranges well below 30 degrees Fahrenheit.

Big Sky Town Center and Meadow Village are where you can buy provisions for your trip, find your base camp and ski rentals, rent or buy sports-related equipment, get fuel, and find the main ticket offices or a hospital. The main base is located at Mountain Village, but you will also find Madison Base, which is on the other side of the peak and less crowded.

How to Get There

Big Sky is located in southwest Montana, about 45 miles south of Bozeman Airport. It is surrounded by the stunning Gallatin National Forest and the Gallatin Canyon and is the gateway to Yellowstone National Park.

Airport shuttles, Uber (only to the town and back), and car rentals are available at the airport. Big Sky is on US 191, midway between Yellowstone's north entrance and Bozeman. In winter, the best option is to have a car (and remember snow tires). The resort offers free transportation, just book in advance, and there is also the Skyline Bus transportation service.

Accommodation

Being a popular tourist attraction for its winter activities and having a world-class ski resort since 1973, many are drawn to Lone Mountain with its iconic peak surrounded by the vast Montana wilderness. Big Sky offers some luxurious accommodations with alpine charm and modern designs. Choose from mountain homes, condominiums, wooden cabins, elaborate mountain mansions, or a small hotel selection. (Summit Hotel offers comfortable rooms at Mountain Village Center at the base of the main ski lift.) But the variety in the popular area also provides a vast mix of historic and avant-garde lodgings, such as Montage Big Sky and 320 Guest Ranch.

The area has plenty of dude ranches: Elkhorn Ranch, 320 Guest Ranch, 9 Quarter Circle, Cinnamon Ranch, and many more. Huntley Lodge and the state-of-the-art Lone Mountain Ranch provide rustic hotel facilities or guest ranch facilities in private cabins. At these two lodgings, you'll find alternative recreational activities arranged by the ranch, such as horseback riding, guided hiking, kids' activities, live music, fireplace rooms, archery, and exquisite local cuisine.

Bookings to these places can be made via *Big Sky Resort* and *Moonlight Basin.* They have a wide range of sophisticated and comfortable lodgings for short stays and longer stays. Some offer self-catering facilities or guest rooms, and others provide larger family residences. There are also backpacking and camping options at Gallatin and West Yellowstone.

OUTDOOR PARADISE

Big Sky offers a plethora of outdoor activities year-round. In summer, explore the vast network of hiking and mountain biking trails, go whitewater rafting on the Gallatin River, or fly fishing in the pristine waters. In winter, experience world-class skiing and snowboarding on the mountain slopes, known for its expansive terrain and deep powder. Or try your hand at snowmobiling for wildlife viewing in Yellowstone.

Big Sky Resort

This is one of the largest ski resorts in the United States. Winter activities include skiing, snowboarding, snowshoeing, and snowmobiling. The resort boasts a vibrant base of village shops, restaurants, and après-ski options. It's an exceptional ski resort with consistent snowfall (around 400 inches annually). The peak tourist season is over Christmas and New Year with the highest snowfalls in January. Because of its popularity, it's important to book ski lift tickets, lodging, guides, training, and rentals well in advance. The popular one-mile hike to Ouzel Falls can also be done in winter to see its beautiful waterfall of a winter cascade of ice. Sleigh ride experiences can be booked at Lone Mountain Ranch or at 320 Ranch (this ranch dates back to 1898!).

Summer activities include numerous hiking trails, some to glacial lakes and others to Lone Peak. When you stay at guest ranches, you can enjoy horseback riding and ranch experiences. Play some golf, go zip-lining, or do world-class fly-fishing here. There are more than 40 miles of mountain biking trails for various levels of cyclists. Another secret that not many visitors notice is Lake Levinsky at the base of Lone Mountain (especially in winter when it's covered in snow).

During summer, this is a perfect spot for water recreation (stand-up paddleboard, canoeing, pedal boats, etc.). The website *bigskyresort.com* provides all the necessary ski tips, preparation, and information you need to know before you arrive.

Big Sky Hiking

Some of the many hiking trails, mostly open during summer, are the following:

- **Ouzel Falls:** A 1.6-mile round trip of 45 minutes to a stunning waterfall in the Gallatin River. The trailhead is outside Meadow Village.
- **Beehive Basin:** A 7.1-mile round trip with wildflowers and alpine lakes to the base of the Spanish Peaks. The trailhead is a few miles from the resort.
- **Uplands Trail:** A 2.2-mile round trip that loops around Big Sky Town Center with great views of the landscape.
- **Cinnamon Mountain:** An 8.5-mile round trip with meadows and forests to the old fire tower on top of the mountain. There are beautiful views of Lone Mountain, Spanish Peaks, and Yellowstone National Park from here. The trail has a steep elevation gain of 2,500 feet and the trailhead starts at 230 Guest Ranch on US 191.

Two off-the-beaten-track trails a bit further away are Lava Lake and Golden Trout Lakes, both around 20 miles away from Big Sky. These are longer hikes with streams, forests, and uphill climbs.

Lone Peak

Ride the Lone Peak Tram at Big Sky Resort with a knowledgeable guide. It takes you to the summit of Lone Peak, Montana's highest scenic overlook, at an elevation of more than 11,000 feet. Enjoy stunning panoramic vistas of the surrounding mountains and the chance to dine at the renowned Everett's 8800 restaurant.

Gallatin River

This river flows through Big Sky offering an excellent variety of water activities such as fishing, whitewater rafting, and kayaking. Enjoy the scenic beauty as you cast a line or navigate thrilling rapids. In early summer, rafting is extra adventurous when the first melting snow adds to the water's rush. The Gallatin River originates in Yellowstone and flows north and is a top-rated fly-fishing river. (The Madison and Yellowstone rivers share this status.) There are many blue-ribbon trout streams here, and catch and release is encouraged to maintain their health. Gallatin Canyon is also a top-rated rafting river, besides its Blue Ribbon trout status.

Scenic Drives

Take a scenic drive along the Gallatin Canyon, a picturesque stretch of road that winds through towering mountains, following the course of the Gallatin River. Another scenic drive is the route from Big Sky to West Yellowstone, offering breathtaking views of the surrounding landscapes. There are widespread wild flowers in summer along the Gallatin river and plenty of wildlife en route. It calls for epic photography.

Golfing

Big Sky is home to several beautiful golf courses that blend seamlessly with the natural surroundings. Play a round of golf while enjoying stunning mountain views, magnificent vistas, and pristine fairways. One of the courses was designed by Arnold Palmer.

Wildlife Viewing

Keep an eye out for wildlife while exploring Big Sky. Spotting deer, elk, moose, bears, wolves, bighorn sheep, and various bird species is not uncommon in the area. Remember to maintain a safe distance and respect their natural habitat.

YELLOWSTONE NATIONAL PARK

The 2.2 million acres of Yellowstone National Park have astounding geological wonders and geothermal features, which include 500 geysers that erupt regularly. Apart from this, you'll also find many fossil forests and glacier valleys. Old Faithful erupts every two hours. According to Sara from *Travel à la Mer*, Yellowstone's geysers are a plentiful sight (2021a, para 34):

Upper Geyser Basin, home to Old Faithful, has the most geysers per square mile of anywhere in the world and [is] a popular winter destination. Plus the heated visitor center next to Old Faithful is a welcome site. Other popular thermal features in the basin are Grand Geyser, Castle Geyser, Riverside Geyser and Morning Glory Pool.

This unspoiled wilderness was the first national park in the US (since 1872), and the geological marvel is just a short drive away from Big Sky and serves as a convenient base for exploring Yellowstone National Park. (The north-eastern section of the park is in Montana.) Take a day trip to witness the park's iconic geysers, wildlife, and awe-inspiring natural wonders such as Old Faithful and the Grand Canyon of Yellowstone.

A heated snow coach or a snowmobile guided tour can be booked in winter when most of the Yellowstone roads are closed. Wildlife viewing of Yellowstone megafauna and abundant flora roam the backcountry serenity and space with a touch of wildlife danger in its ecological diversity (bison, grizzlies, and sulfuric acid geysers are stunning but can be lethal). The 1995 reintroduction of wolves has been highly supportive of Yellowstone's delicate ecosystem.

The park's high season for tourism is in summer with most visitors arriving in July and August. Overcrowding can be an issue at these times, so plan to visit in shoulder seasons, arrive early at the main attractions, or enjoy hiking off the beaten track to escape the crowds. Most of the park roads are closed during winter except for the headquarters at Mammoth Hot Springs (north entrance) and the east entrance at Cooke City. By mid-December, some areas can be accessed via snowmobiles, snow coaches, snowshoeing, or skiing. Fall is the best time to visit, providing exciting wildlife viewing and fewer tourists (and mosquitoes!) as well as cooler weather.

Park Entrances

The northern entrance of the park in Montana is located at Gardiner. This entrance (a 90-minute drive from Bozeman) provides easy access to popular attractions within the park and is open all year. The park roads are in good condition and you don't need vehicles with extra clearance or four-wheel drive cars. Stay informed about road closures and sudden changes in weather, as you may have to cover long distances and don't want to be disappointed or get caught.

Entrance fees are reasonably priced and there are options of an annual park entrance pass or a seven-day pass priced according to your means of entry. Entrance passes can be purchased online. There is limited to nonexistent mobile reception in the park.

Main Features

Yellowstone is famous for its geothermal features including the iconic Old Faithful geyser, the Grand Prismatic Spring, Mammoth Hot Springs, and the colorful geothermal pools scattered throughout the park. The park rests on a dormant volcano. Be sure to explore these unique natural wonders. Old Faithful hails its name from its regular and predictable eruptions. You can view them from the boardwalk surrounding the geyser but this path is very crowded. An alternative route is the Observation Point trail, which provides stunning elevated views of the eruptions.

The Grand Prismatic Spring is probably the most iconic and fantastic sight in the park. It's as deep as a ten-story building and the third-largest hot spring in the world. It pushes up extremely hot water that appears in all shades of the rainbow due to the bacteria inhabiting the various rings. Apart from this, petrified trees, many waterfalls, subalpine forests, grass-lands, and alpine meadows form a stunning backdrop for the 360 species of wildlife roaming here.

Wildlife Viewing

Yellowstone is home to a diverse array of wildlife. Keep an eye out for grizzly bears, black bears, mountain lions, coyotes, wolves, elk, bison, moose, and a variety of bird species. Lamar Valley and Hayden Valley are known for their excellent wildlife viewing opportunities and the Upper Loop road provides ample wildlife viewing.

Scenic Drives

Enjoy the beauty of Yellowstone by driving its scenic roads. The Grand Loop Road takes you through the park's major attractions in an infinity shape, offering breathtaking views of mountains, rivers, waterfalls, and wildlife: a photographer's dream. The Grand Loop road is divided into the Upper Loop and the Lower Loop. You can access Upper Loop Road from Gardiner and Lower Loop Road from West Yellowstone. Mammoth Hot Springs is close to the northern side and is a must-visit geothermal feature as they are different from the others. Also, make sure to visit the Albright Visitor Center here for information.

Hiking Trails

The 900 miles of hiking trails in Yellowstone offer options suitable for all skill levels. Options range from short walks to multiday backpacking adventures. Some notable trails are Uncle Tom's Trail, Mount Washburn (10,243 feet), Fairy Falls Trail, and Grand Prismatic Springs overlook trail, which is about a one-mile trailhead with a stunning view of the multi-colored hot springs.

Pathways and boardwalk loop trails around the thermal features include Porcelain Basin, Back Basin, Artists Paint Pots, the Lower Terrace Interpretive Trail (1.5-mile round trip trail in the Mammoth area), the Lone Star Geyser trail (4.8-mile trail near Old Faithful), and Mystic Falls (a 2.5-mile round trip hike), which features a dramatic waterfall and Old Faithful in the background on the horizon as it erupts.

Safety measures for your hike in Montana include bear spray, making noise, staying on designated paths, and remaining in groups. The same applies to Yellowstone, as all of it is bear territory. You can find all the information needed for outdoor recreation on the National Park Service website (nps.gov).

Fishing

Anglers can enjoy fishing in Yellowstone's rivers and lakes, but check and respect the regulations and obtain a fishing license before casting a line. The National Park Service website (nps.gov) provides all the useful information.

Camping and Lodging

The park has nine hotels. Old Faithful Inn is probably the best bet in this area and closest to Montana. It's a sight to see as the largest log structure in the world. If you prefer more nature-based accommodation, try some of the 12 Yellowstone developed campgrounds, or 300 backcountry campsites. (These have to be booked in advance starting from April 1.) Ninety campsites are available on a first-come first-serve basis but fill up fast in high season. (The sites can only be reserved up to 48 hours in advance only.) Most accommodations in Yellowstone have to be booked well in advance.

West Yellowstone (just outside the park on the Montana side) has many hotel and short-term rental accommodation options and also provides the biggest choice with dining options. It's centrally located and provides easy access to the main sites within 90 minutes. Lamar Valley is a two-and-a-half-hour drive from West Yellowstone. Consider lodgings at Kelly Inn, Explorer Cabins, or the Yellowstone Park Hotel.

Northern parts of Yellowstone are closer to Gardiner. This entrance is well located for Mammoth Hot Springs (a mere six miles away) and Old Faithful (an hour and 40 minutes away from Gardiner). At Gardiner, consider Absaroka Lodge with its magnificent views.

Ranger Programs

Attend ranger-led programs and guided hikes to learn about the park's geology, wildlife, and cultural history. These educational programs offer valuable insights and enhance your experience. You could also join a ranger program, but be aware that they vary seasonally and never happen in spring (the transition time in the park).

Picnicking

Numerous picnic areas throughout the park allow you to enjoy a meal surrounded by nature's beauty. Take advantage of these scenic spots for a relaxing break. Always practice park safety, never feed animals, don't leave food unattended, and make sure your fires are out before you leave. (Fires are only allowed in areas with fire grates.)

Photography Opportunities

Yellowstone is a photographer's paradise. Capture the park's geothermal features, wildlife, stunning landscapes, and vibrant sunrises or sunsets. Be respectful of wildlife and follow safety guidelines while photographing. This is not a place for selfies and up-close cellphone photos! Bring your camera and binoculars to view and capture wildlife without threatening them: "Zoom with your lens not your feet" (National Park Service, n.d.-d). Drones are not allowed in Yellowstone. Popular photographic sites are Old Faithful, Grand Prismatic Springs, the lower falls of the Yellowstone River, wildflowers in Spring, Lamar Valley for wildlife, winterscapes, sunrise and sunsets, and majestic night skies.

Visitor Centers

Various visitor centers in the park offer information, an array of exhibits, and updates on trail conditions and wildlife sightings. The Old Faithful Visitor Education Center and Canyon Visitor Education Center are among the most popular. Here, you can gather information, talk to a park ranger, visit the souvenir shop, attend a ranger program, or view interpretive displays.

Park Safety

Follow park regulations, stay on designated trails, and maintain safe distances from wildlife. Carry bear spray, be aware of changing weather conditions, and practice Leave No Trace principles. Don't attempt any illegal activities, such as stepping on thermal features, taking anything, not keeping safe distances from wildlife, obstructing their paths, and general common sense when intruding on wildlife territory! Familiarize yourself with the park's well-written safety regulations for its delicate ecosystem, and drive and park responsibly. Easy distances to remember for wildlife safety is keeping a minimum of two bus lengths (75 feet) away from all animals and eight bus lengths (about 300 feet) from bears and wolves. Another way to know that you are dangerously close is if your presence causes an animal to move. If an animal approaches you, back away slowly—don't run and respect their territory! They are also afraid of you and they were there first.

Nearby Attractions

Consider exploring the surrounding areas near Yellowstone National Park in Montana such as the charming town of West Yellowstone or the scenic Gallatin National Forest. This forest makes up a part of the bigger Custer Gallatin National Forest.

RECREATIONAL ACTIVITIES

Big Sky offers all-year-round fun. If you're not a keen ski enthusiast, many other activities will provide joy. The Crail Ranch Homestead Museum in Big Sky is an interesting visit for history buffs, exhibiting documents, information, photographs, and artifacts of pioneer families from the area.

Dining and Shopping

Big Sky offers a range of dining options, from casual eateries to upscale restaurants where you can savor locally sourced cuisine. Many eateries at Big Sky are between Mountain Village and Meadow Village, some along the river, others on the slopes. Shedhorn Grill (in a yurt on the mountain) caters to hungry skiers and hikers with light burgers and beers. Vista Hall in Mountain Village provides lots of scenic seating, Headwaters Grill is good for families, and Everett's 8800 is exceptional for rustic alpine dining.

A unique experience is the Montana Yurt Dinner: a candlelit cowboy dinner at a secret location in the woods, with a campfire, stargazing, and torch-lit sledding. The nighttime low-light sledding under the starry skies is incredible.

Explore local boutiques and galleries for unique Montana-made souvenirs. Shop local artisans' crafts, artwork, and gifts. All your sports adventure shopping is catered for here with leading technology outfitting and appropriate gear for the whole family at Big Sky town center.

Music and Festivals

Various festivals and events are hosted in Big Sky throughout the year, including music festivals, culinary events, and art exhibitions. Check the local calendar to see if any events coincide with your visit. Some events include art events, dance and trivia nights, wine nights, art classes, photography, and visual media exhibitions. The Lone Peak Cinema movie theater shows big-screen productions. Another performing arts center attracts a variety of local, national, and international artists. There is also a children's musical theater company called Big Sky Broadway hosting many music events. In mid-summer, have fun at the professional bull riders event called the Big Sky PBR with its farmers markets, vendors, local food, and crafts. In winter, never get bored—with ice skating and hockey events, sleigh rides, and dog sledding.

From here, I'd like to take you to Southeast Montana to follow the dinosaurs' trail.

PART IV
SOUTHEAST MONTANA—
EXPLORING THE PLAINS

OVERVIEW

> The world is a book and those who do not travel read only one page.

— ST. AUGUSTINE

The Montana Dinosaur Trail provides a range of sites where evidence of their existence can be seen. The Judith River Formation, close to Lewistown, indicates that the area was once an inland sea. Evidence of that is the 75 million-year-old dinosaur embryos that are preserved here. Now, if we go just slightly southeast, the dinosaur trail takes us to Southeast Montana—where history is made.

INTRODUCTION TO SOUTHEAST MONTANA

Less is more. Here, you can settle down and breathe again, away from the crowds. We've traveled across this vast Montana landscape of endless space and long distances, changing landscapes from mountains to plains with uninterrupted views and starry skies. This part of the journey is where you slow down, where the waters are the only thing rushing, where you find optimal space for adventurers and thinking space for free-spirited souls. Big Sky meets adventure here where you fall in love with the country chasing endless horizons. This part is where adventure meets landscape, and where history meets dinosaurs in an unforgiving climate.

It's a highly contrasting area: contrasts in cultural activities, landscape, outdoor recreation, and entertainment. Adventure here includes hunting, hiking, never-ending fishing, and horse riding in one of the few places where cowboys still ride them on the plains. Popular cultural activities include rodeo events, celebrations and festivities, concerts, ethnic attractions, horse shows, art galleries, and culinary charm.

Southeast Montana is rich in Native American tribal culture, predominantly the Northern Cheyenne and the Crow, and explorer history. On top of that, you have world class national wonders, cultural treasures, national monuments, and uniquely abundant dinosaur fossils ever present and waiting to be discovered. This area provides interesting activities for all ages and a variety of attractions to interest every kind of tourist, plus an added bonus of Western hospitality. If you like solitude and fewer crowds, this is your place. With the isolation, there are also fewer amenities but lots of discovery of fascinating culture, wide open spaces, adventure, and history far beyond what they teach you in books.

HISTORY ASSOCIATED WITH SOUTHEAST MONTANA

The bonds that connect this corner of Montana's history, culture, and the land are Lewis and Clark, railroads, ranching, rolling prairie landscapes, and dinosaurs. Museums in southeast Montana exhibit frontier, tribal, prehistoric dinosaurs, agriculture, prominent families and their lavish homesteads, state-of-the-art steam engines and cars, locomotives, railroads, pioneer life and old buildings, weaponry, art, and artifacts. The list is endless! The old west remains alive, and even the smallest county museum here in Montana has stories that still echo the big sky landscape. Small communities shared collections of stories from generation to generation. This part is made up of hardy pioneers and native tribes offering a powerful history and heritage. An active cultural calendar provides events including powwows, artisan events, fairs, native days, rodeos, and bucking horse sales.

Makoshika State Park is famous for its badlands scenery, geological stories, and prehistoric exposed dinosaur fossils and stories. The highest concentration of fossils has been found here and the Montana Dinosaur Trail connects you to Montana's 14 dinosaur museums. You can even dig up some bones while you are here. Prominent places to visit for history are the Frontier Gateway Museum, Glendive Dinosaur Museum, and The Gallery. According to Tyler & Premier Travel Media, (2022, para 1) the top sites to see here are the following:

The best places to visit in Montana for heritage, fossilized treasures and natural beauty are located in the southeast portion of the state. Discover the rich history and culture of Southeast Montana in a half dozen museums, and breathe the outdoor air along the magnificent Yellowstone River. Visit Montana's largest state park at Makoshika, with its picturesque vistas and remnants of prehistoric residents. Southeast montana (sic) has it all. From the billings brew trail and glendive history to idyllic makoshika state park and scenic yellowstone river.

PLACES TO VISIT

With fewer crowds, there's more to see! You can rockhound minerals and petrified wood from the Yellowstone River and tributaries and visit many museums: the Range Rider Museum has 13 buildings on 13 acres with exhibits dating back to the Mesozoic period, the Frontier Gateway Museum covers history from prehistoric times to modern-day with an incredible display of exhibits under one roof, and the Glendive Dinosaur and Fossil Museum hosts 24 full-sized dinos and many fossils.

The *Canyon Creek Battlefield Monument* commemorates the September 13, 1877 battle between Nez Perce and the U.S. Army, enhancing the area's tribal heritage. You'll find a unique culture of ethnic celebrations and historic reenactments. To mirror this, Western cowboy culture has many county fairs in small cow towns, like Glendive or Ekalaka, with livestock shows and rodeos. Interestingly, the town Ekalaka hails its name from Chief Sitting Bull's daughter.

Scenic drives around historical sites, battlefield tours, tribal sites, significant legends, dinosaurs, and a badlands drive where prehistoric meets the outdoors will all entice your curiosity. The Warrior Trail highway through scenic Custer National Forest and the Cheyenne Reservation toward Little Bighorn connects here. Two places provide 360-degree panoramic views: the Terry Badlands overlook and Four Dances (500 feet above Yellowstone River). The Tongue River Reservoir holds exceptional fishing spots and offers space and solitude for campers.

If your palate comes first, culinary curiosities won't disappoint you. There are many breweries and wineries, burger bars and serious steaks to be tasted here. Many special events are held throughout the year, such as Dino Shindig in July and the Crow Fair and Rodeo in August.

Custer Battlefield Museum

Custer Gallatin National Forest between Broadus and Ashland offers excellent hiking and horseback riding between the mountains and Tongue River. There are also rich archaeological and paleontological resources to be found and some history at the battlefield. The Custer Battlefield Museum in Garryowen has an acclaimed collection of the Custer Battlefield and important Indian war artifacts and manuscripts, including the only signed contract by Chief Sitting Bull, a lock of Custer's hair, battle vintage beaded clothing, Little Wolf's eagle feather war bonnet, and a range of frontier memorabilia.

Makoshika State Park and Glendive

This is where you will see jaw-dropping bones and fossils of giant dinosaurs that roamed the area millions of years ago. The Badlands scenery enhances the feeling of eerie yesteryear struggles between nature and animals larger than your house! You can view their skeletons and relish in their landscape while your hiking shoes follow in their footsteps.

Montana's unique and largest state park (11,000 acres) in Glendive has sinkholes, dinosaur fossils, and badlands to make you gasp. This is *the* place to visit for dinosaur fanatics and paleontologists. The Montana Dinosaur Trail leads you to discover fossils, visit museums and dig sites, and engage in guided excursions—like gigs and digs at Glendive and Makoshika State Park. The Makoshika Visitor Center has interpretive displays and the fossils of triceratops and tyrannosaurus rex! The park has educational and culturally enriching workshops for any age. Park facilities include fascinating exhibits, hiking, biking, camping, archery, picnic sites, outdoor amphitheater events, disc golf courses, and scenic drives.

Hiking trails take you to partially excavated sites to see dinosaur vertebrae among topography with unique and immense sandstone formations, cap rocks, fluted hillsides, and dinosaur fossils. Unique tour group journeys include cowboy cookouts, tribal reservation excursions, nature trips, and horseback rides. Wet weather asks for indoor recreation as the site's walkways get quite challenging to walk on. Operating hours are reduced in the off-season.

When the moon hides, make sure to go outside and see the starry skies for some stellar stargazing in the wide-open night skies of Montana. Because it has largely rural areas, it's farther from city lights, and due to less pollution, the clear skies present more stars, and here you can see the billions of stars that make up the Milky Way. On very cold nights the skies are even brighter. Keep your eye on the aurora borealis forecast to see the northern lights from here! And top it off with sleeping in a tipi in the park camping site to enhance tranquility.

Tongue River State Park

Ten miles north of Decker, you'll find a tranquil man-made 12-mile-long lake. This is a hidden fishing paradise and ice-fishing favorite. Tongue River Reservoir angling has produced four state records up to date. You'll have Scenic views of red-shale rock formations and juniper canyons to frame your days. The lake is popular for water sports like paddle board, canoeing, float, kayaking, or a scenic pontoon trip. There are many camping sites—some with boat ramps and a beach area. If you don't have a boat, don't stress, rent a pontoon!

HOW TO REACH SOUTHEASTERN MONTANA

The main connecting routes are I 90 and I 94. Southeast Montana borders on Wyoming and Dakota. Billings-Logan International Airport (BIL) is the primary airport. Southeast Montana is a three-hour drive from Yellowstone and six hours from Glacier.

Climate

The corner of the state has hot, dry, and short summers with clear days and cold weather the rest of the year. Winters are freezing, snowy, and partly cloudy. Peak winter has about six hours of sunlight. The average daily summer temperature is 75 degrees Fahrenheit—with hottest days around 85 degrees in July. Wintertime temperatures are around 42 degrees Fahrenheit, down to 14 degrees Fahrenheit in January. Warm weather clearly calls for water recreation to fish, boat, or float on some of the many rivers and mainly on the rare lake in the prairie landscape.

Wildlife

Wildlife in this part centers around fishing. The Yellowstone and Bighorn Rivers have plenty of lodges that provide guides and support. Ice fishing is a favorite in May and June at Tongue River Reservoir, and you can travel to a rocky stretch of the Yellowstone River at Glendive to experience angling prehistoric paddlefish (during May and June). Sustainable hunting is practiced with plenty of outfitters. Wildlife spotting here includes lots of deer and elk, pronghorn, bighorn sheep, black bears, mountain lions, and raptors as well as 400 bird species.

HIKING AND CAMPING

And then get active with hiking trails in southeast Montana! You will find beginner-friendly to challenging trekking and most without the crowds. Famous trails include the Hungry Joe trail at Makoshika State Park (4–6 mile loop) and many trails close to Yellowstone, Pompeys Pillar, and Four Dances Natural Area. There are 40 trails around Billings and almost 200 around the Custer National Forest area. Makoshika State Park offers six trails, and Red Lodge has 17 trails, ranging between one-day hikes and extended trails. With more than 30 stunning stargazing sites in the region, Southeast Montana is a stargazer's paradise (Visit Southeast Montana, n.d.-c, para 3):

Designated as an International Dark Sky Sanctuary, Medicine Rocks State Park is the darkest of the dark spots—in addition to being a really cool place during the day. Nestled along the rolling prairies of Montana's eastern edge, between Ekalaka and Baker, we promise you will fall in love with this remote, mystical place of 'big medicine.'

Rough it with camping under these outstretched big starry skies, RV in developed campgrounds with amenities and state parks, enjoy unique camping in Makoshika State Park tipis, or Bighorn Canyon National Recreation Area with boat-in-only campgrounds, or reserve Custer Gallatin National Forest and Diamond Butte Lookout fire tower for alternative unique sites. Try Medicine Rocks Campground or Campers Point Campground at Tongue River Reservoir for space and solitude beyond measure.

Let's start our journey at Custer National forest.

INSIDE THE CUSTER NATIONAL FOREST

“ Everything is so big—the sky, the mountains, the wind-swept flatlands—it sinks into you, it shapes your body and your dreams.

— CHRISTOPHER PAOLINI, ABOUT MONTANA

M aybe a surer way to determine your heart is to go to a forest. Feel the breeze whisper on the leaves and hold the forest silence in your heart for a moment. Then let the trees show you that love and peace lie within—live with your senses beside a campfire and find company in nature.

A multitude of recreational trails are in this vast area. There are 19 family hikes in Custer Gallatin National Forest and much more for the adventurous hiker. The two forests, Custer (1.2 million acres) and Gallatin (1.8 million acres) are administered jointly from Bozeman. Custer-Gallatin National Forest together has some of the most popular hiking trails in Montana. It's a gateway to Yellowstone, the Absaroka-Beartooth Wilderness, and Lee Metcalf Wilderness, some of the most ecologically diverse forests in the north of America. It's a vast terrain of uninhabited space.

Custer-Gallatin National Forest has 172 named mountains! The Custer National Forest is an alpine terrain with diverse ecosystems and rugged peaks. Parts are covered by glacial ice and the western part is dominated by trees (fir, spruce, and pine), while the eastern part boasts grasslands of the great plains. It has ten sections with elevation levels ranging between 1,000 feet and almost 13,000 feet. These sections include three further topographical sections: Beartooth Ranger section in south central Montana, Ashland Ranger east of Billings, and Sioux Ranger section on the border of the three states, and all combine to the greater Custer Gallatin National Forest.

ITINERARY LOGISTICS

A vast and ecologically diverse landscape of mountains, buttes, buffs, trees, and wide open spaces all combine here at the south-central and southeastern parts of Montana, right on the border of the northwestern parts of South Dakota and some sections leaning into Wyoming. The forest covers seven ranger districts namely Bozeman, Hebgen Lake (Yellowstone), Yellowstone (Livingston), Gardiner, Bear Tooth (Red Lodge), Ashland, and Sioux (Camp Crook, SD). It's the gateway to Yellowstone National Park, Lee Metcalf Wilderness close to Missoula, and also the Absaroka-Beartooth Wilderness near Bozeman.

How to Get There

Custer National Forest is near of Billings, between the Powder River and the Yellowstone River, alongside the Crow and Northern Cheyenne Reservations. You turn off on the 212 from US 87. It's directly south of Miles City toward the Wyoming border. The wider Custer-Gallatin National Forest can be reached from Bozeman, between Livingstone and Gardiner on US 89, which runs along the Yellowstone River toward Wyoming. In this book, I'll focus on the wider Custer Gallatin National Forest.

Accommodation

Choose from a variety of campgrounds and dispersed camping options within the forest. Or if you prefer something more solid, consider nearby lodging options in towns such as Red Lodge, Cooke City, or Livingston. However, dispersed camping remains the number one accommodation option here. This way, you get close to the real Montana: starry skies, scents of forests and wildflowers, sounds of creeks and brooks, and the wild calls of animals around you.

HISTORICAL AND CULTURAL SITES

Most of the Native American tribes lived here: the Crow, Blackfeet Nation, Nez Perce, Northern Cheyenne, Salish and Kootenai, Sioux, Mandan, Hidatsa, and Arikara nations. Their heritage leaves traces of cultural evidence along the mountains and the valleys. Medicine Wheel National Historic Landmark is an ancient Native American site where you can marvel at the stone medicine wheel.

OUTDOOR RECREATION

Outdoor recreation is the main activity here. Forests, glaciers, water streams, gushing rivers, and prairies all call for exploration.

Hiking

Explore the numerous hiking trails that wind through the forest, ranging from easy strolls to challenging treks. Because of the elevation, many peaks maintain snow cover throughout the year, leaving trekking options limited. During warmer months, these invite hiking enthusiasts from all over. Some of the popular hikes include the following:

- **Lava Lake/Cascade Creek Trail:** A popular six-mile round trip hike with a gradual elevation gain to a stunning alpine lake.

- **Storm Castle Peak:** A five-mile hike about 30 minutes from Bozeman with spectacular limestone bluffs and a five-hour hike into Custer Gallatin National Forest.
- **Sacagawea Peak:** A 4.2-mile summit and back hike offering the best views of the Tobacco Root mountains where you may spot mountain goats.
- **Baldy Mountain Summit:** An almost ten-mile day hike with steep elevation (4,000 feet climbing). This hike is not for the faint-hearted but provides spectacular views of the Gallatin Range.

For climbing enthusiasts, the most famous Granite Peak, with its three trails leading to the summit, is challenging but highly rewarding. The mountain peak calls for respect, so take caution and prepare well. In the Beartooth range, you'll find Parkside, Silver Run, and Wild Bill hikes, as well as backcountry trails for horseback riding and mountain biking. There are too many hiking trails to mention here. Even simply meandering around your campsite on the paths will bring enormous delight.

Camping

Choose from about 50 campgrounds (20 in Custer Forest) to enjoy a peaceful night under the stars. Campgrounds are usually open between May and September and there are also day-use areas all along the main and west fork of Rock Creek, east Rosebud, west Rosebud, and Upper Stillwater Valley. There are more than 50 campgrounds to choose from in the greater forest area. You can find all the information you need on the Forest Service website at www.fs.usda.gov/activity/custergallatin/recreation/camping-cabins/.

Fishing

Cast a line in the forest's lakes, rivers, and streams, known for their abundant rainbow and cutthroat trout as well as other fish species.

Wildlife Viewing

Observe wildlife such as the glorious elk, majestic bison, deer, bighorn sheep, and various bird species in their natural habitats. Take scenic drives through the forest to enjoy breathtaking vistas and panoramic views in the wilderness areas. Remember your camera! Adjacent areas to explore are the Absaroka-Beartooth Wilderness, for the rugged beauty of a pristine wilderness area offering opportunities for backpacking, wildlife viewing, and mountaineering, and the Ashland Ranger District—to explore the remote wilderness of a district known for its diverse wildlife and scenic landscapes.

Scenic Byways

Two scenic byways deliver stunning vistas. The Beartooth Highway is an iconic scenic byway known for its alpine landscapes and high mountain passes. US 212 connects Yellowstone and Red Lodge and another scenic route is the Chief Joseph Scenic Byway. Journey through scenic valleys and mountainous terrain following the route taken by Chief Joseph and the Nez Perce Tribe.

Winter Activities

Custer National Forest lures winter adventurers:

- **Snowmobiling:** Enjoy snowmobiling through the forest's winter wonderland on designated trails. At Cooke City, the average snow depth of 500 inches per year is a sledder's heaven. It's close to Yellowstone.
- **Cross-country skiing:** A long list of ski trails in Custer Gallatin Forest—varying in distance—can be found on the *AllTrails* website.
- **Snowshoeing:** Explore the forest's trails and winter landscapes on snowshoes at Red Lodge Mountain Resort and Beartooth Pass at 10,800 feet.

Wildlife and Nature Photography

Capture the beauty of the forest's flora and fauna through photography. Always practice responsible wildlife photography, respecting animals' natural behavior and habitats. Wildlife to spot here are bison, moose, elk, mule deer, bighorn sheep, mountain goats, elusive mountain lions, bobcats, wolves, and bears. The prominent bird species are peregrine falcons, merlins, and bald eagles.

Nearby Attractions and Activities

Visit the town of Red Lodge and explore its quaint shops, galleries, and restaurants. Or for more wildlife, venture out to the natural wonders of the Beartooth Mountains and the nearby Yellowstone National Park. For a last historic visit, explore the mining town of Cooke City and discover its unique charm and heritage.

Park Guidelines and Safety

Follow Leave No Trace principles to preserve the forest's natural environment for future generations. Be aware of the restrictions and guidelines during dry seasons, and stay up to date with weather and road conditions. Practice proper wildlife safety and be prepared for encounters with wildlife.

Let's continue our journey at Makoshika State Park, an impressive landscape with an unforgiving climate.

EXPLORING MAKOSHIKA
STATE PARK

66 Montana is a treasure. It's like a secret garden.

— ANONYMOUS

These rocky hills, deep gorges, and rock formations of over 100 feet were shaped by years of erosion. The hoodoos, gullies, and natural bridges make this a highly underrated spectacular park. Makoshika is named after the Lakota words *maco* and *sica* meaning "bad earth."

ITINERARY LOGISTICS

This is the largest state park in southeastern Montana—over 11,500 acres—and renowned for its badlands landscape laced with abundant fossil treasures. The park is open all year round but the visitor center hours do change seasonally. Campgrounds remain open 24/7. At Glendive, you can find interesting museums like the Makoshika Dinosaur & Fossil Museum and the Frontier Gateway Museum. The park has 22 miles of hiking trails and stunning scenery to be explored.

How to Get There

Makoshika Park is remote! The closest town is Glendive, on the other side of the Yellowstone River, a quarter mile away on I 94. The closest airport is Billings (Billings-Logan International), a three-hour drive (222 miles) away. The park is 40 miles north of the Dakota border.

Accommodation

Campgrounds or accommodations can be found in nearby Glendive, which is also the closest food and fuel point. Alternatively, search for lodgings in nearby Wibaux. In Glendive, I can make the following hotel recommendations: La Quinta Inn & Suites and Casino or Holiday Inn Express & Suites. These provide a reasonable base for exploring the outdoors.

VISITOR CENTER AND INTERPRETIVE EXHIBITS

Makoshika Park facilities include a visitor center, archery range, disc golf course, amphitheater, and campground. There are many park programs. Every Friday night, a campfire program discussing the ecological, cultural, and historical features of the area is hosted at the campground or amphitheater. Start your visit at the visitor center to gather educational and geographical information and maps plus facilities and updated trail information. Explore the interpretive exhibits showcasing the park's geological and paleontological features. Learn about the park's Native American history and cultural significance.

OUTDOOR RECREATION

Many outdoor activities abound—archery practice (for novices and experts), camping, hiking, biking, and discovering rock formations and natural rock bridges. Weather in summer brings highs of 90 degrees Fahrenheit while winter temperatures are between 5 and 45 degrees. The park has about one and a half months of rainfall (only about 15 inches a year) and snowfall is around 25 inches per year. Because of the climate, park programs are limited to shoulder and summer seasons, in winter, trails may still be accessible but hiking may be unbearable. This area was named the badlands for a reason!

Hiking and Nature Trails

Amateur and professional biking trails include the Vista Trail, Ponderosa Trail, and McCarty Trail. These can also be hiked. Discover the trails and observe the park's unique fauna and flora. Eleven hiking trails showcase the park's diverse landscapes:

- **Diane Gabriel Trail:** A 7-mile trek with 128 feet elevation for all skill levels. Here, you see rock formations, sinkhole caves, wildflowers, sunset overlooks, and end with a stunning Hadrosaur fossil on site!
- **Kinney Coulee trail:** It's a little less than a one-mile trek with 311 feet elevation, making this a moderate but rugged trail. You'll see lush green pine trees and badlands formations.
- **The Cap Rock Trail:** A more rugged and steep 92 feet elevation gain, but a short half-mile-long trek. It has panoramic views of the badlands and surrounding countryside and covers various formations and the natural bridge. It's a must-visit hike.
- **Bluebird:** A short half mile from the visitor center to a bird's-eye overlook with only 128 feet of elevation gain.
- **Gunner Ridge:** The longest hike and bike trail. After your 1.4-mile trek, you meet up with other trails and see lots of the park. It's a moderate hike.

- **Buccaneer:** You can drive or hike to the park boundary.
- **Switchback:** It connects to a variety of trails and a hike to see the Cains Coulee overlook.

Keep an eye out for wildlife, including deer, antelope, and various bird species. Take necessary hiking precautions: Watch out for rattlesnakes, wear closed shoes with firm traction soles, have water, sunscreen, hats, and a warm jacket, carry a map, stay on designated paths, don't hike alone, leave your info with someone at the starting point, and maintain safe distances from wild animals.

Scenic Drives and Overlooks

Take a scenic drive through the park and enjoy the breathtaking vistas. Stop at designated overlooks for photo opportunities and to appreciate the vastness of the badlands. Capture the changing colors of the landscape during sunrise or sunset, and turn your sights into memorable moments.

Camping and Picnicking

Set up camp at the park's campground (28 sites) and enjoy peaceful surroundings. These have to be prebooked. They include restrooms and fire rings. There are tent sites, yurts, or tipi sites. The park also offers first-come first-serve backcountry camping scattered throughout. With no hookups, you are truly wild and free. RV sites are at the Cains Coulee Campground, and here you will also find 14 campsites and one tipi. Experience stargazing and the tranquility of the night sky in the park's dark-sky setting. Take advantage of the picnic areas and enjoy a meal amidst the natural beauty.

With limited food and beverages in the park, the idea of bringing a picnic lunch sounds just right.

Fossil Hunting and Paleontology

Makoshika is part of the Hell Creek Formation—places abundantly rich in Dinosaur fossils. Over ten dinosaur species have been found here. Notable fossils include the 600-pound female triceratops skull and a fossilized rare thescelosaurus, the largest and most complete of its kind in the world. Both were discovered in the 1990s. The K-T Boundary line is also here. K for the cretaceous and T for the tertiary periods, indicating the time of the physical separation between these two periods: more than 65 million years ago! Participate in guided fossil tours or self-guided fossil hunts (following park regulations). Learn about the park's rich fossil history: discover ancient remnants and observe the unique geological formations and fossilized plant and animal life in the park.

Photography and Nature Observation

Capture stunning landscapes with the perfect backdrops and unique rock formations through photography. Set the artist in you free! The park's wildlife includes bighorn sheep, prairie dogs, rattlesnakes, sage lizards, coyotes, bobcats, mule deer, and various bird species. Practice responsible nature observation and maintain a safe distance from wildlife.

Special Events and Programs

Many events are hosted here. The Montana Shakespeare in the Park is a very popular event where you can watch Shakespeare's plays in an atypical setting. There are also Friday night campfires, full moon hikes, trivia in the park, National Fossil Day events, and the popular Buzzard Day Festival. This is an action-packed event with races, tournaments, kids' train rides, astronomy tutorials, guided hikes, disc golf, and paleontology presentations. Participate in the annual Makoshika Trail Run or other recreational events held in the park. Check the park's calendar for special events, guided hikes, educational programs, summer programs, paleontology events, and field excavating activities. Attend interpretive talks and demonstrations to deepen your understanding of the park's geology and history.

Nearby Attractions

Visit the Frontier Gateway Museum in Glendive. A nearby town, known for its dinosaur fossil discoveries. Experience the nearby Makoshika Dinosaur Museum for additional paleontological exhibits.

Park Guidelines and Safety

Follow park regulations and guidelines to preserve the park's natural cultural resources for future generations. Stay on designated trails and respect the fragile badlands formations. Be aware of potential wildlife encounters and practice proper safety measures. Most of all, enjoy the unique beauty of the badlands!

From the unforgiving hoodoos and badlands scenery, let's round off this incredible Montana journey at the tranquil Tongue River Reservoir.

THE TRANQUIL TONGUE RIVER RESERVOIR STATE PARK

> I read; I travel; I become.

— DEREK WALCOTT

To prove the robust climate of Montana, a record 15-inch diameter snowflake was seen at Fort Keogh—the largest snowflake ever. It seems that water comes in all shapes and sizes in Montana.

You were looking for open prairies—now you can find an oasis of life on the prairies at the Tongue River Reservoir: a 12-mile-long manmade reservoir among red shale and juniper canyons on a 642-acre state park, 3,468 feet above sea level. This is an anglers, campers, and boat lovers paradise. The lake is a vast palette for water-based activities to create memories on the "tongue" that starts in Wyoming and settles here in southeastern Montana.

ITINERARY LOGISTICS

This reservoir lies next to the Crow Reservation and just below the Northern Cheyenne Indian Reservation.

How to Get There

The lake is just north of the Montana-Wyoming State Line on I 90, six miles north of Decker. You'll discover meandering winding roads along the Tongue River to the lake, so be mindful when driving a camper and stop for some scenic photo shoots!

Accommodation

Choose from a wide range of accommodation options including campgrounds and RV parks within the park. Or consider nearby lodging options in Ashland or other towns in the region. Most adjacent towns are within a 20-mile range from the lake.

Outdoor Recreations

This is a rare water-based recreational fun area in the vast prairie landscape. You have abundant space for swimming and many picnic sites at Campers Point and Sand Point for day-trippers. Sand Point has a little beach for swimming, and there is a store at Campers Point with basic supplies. Here, you can also get your licenses and nonresident park pass. At the Marina store, you can rent boats. Winter activities create adventure, like ice skating (just make sure the ice depth is safe: four to six inches), ice fishing, hiking, photography, and wildlife viewing. Summer calls for boats and floats and all sorts of leisurely water activities. Camping is also allowed!

PARK ACTIVITIES

Boating

Enjoy boating on the reservoir's calm waters that are perfect for sailing, kayaking, motorized boating, water skiing, wind-surfing, kayaking, paddle boarding, and any kind of boating. Boat launches are at Peewee North Camp and Campers Point.

Fishing

Cast a line and try your luck at catching a variety of fish species, including crappie, walleye, bass, northern pike, and trout fishing below the dam in the river. State-record fish have been caught here! Remember to secure your fishing license. This is a very popular spot for ice fishing in winter, and the campsites cater to these with year-round electricity. Sites are then available on a first-come first-serve basis.

Swimming

Have a refreshing swim in the designated swimming areas within the park. Sand Point has a little beach area. There are no lifeguards on duty so be mindful of strong currents: water can be deceiving!

Beach combing

Relax on the sandy beaches and soak up the sun, read a book, and find some tranquility.

Wildlife Viewing

Diverse bird species and wildlife can be spotted here, like osprey, blue heron, bald eagles and wildlife like deer and antelope.

HIKING AND NATURE TRAILS

There are 12 miles of shoreline hiking. Explore the hiking trails that wind through the park's beautiful landscapes. Enjoy scenic views and nature observation opportunities along the trails while you keep an eye out for wildlife such as deer, antelope, and various bird species.

CAMPING AND PICNICKING

Outside the park, you'll find campgrounds in adjacent cities and towns if all the reservoir camps are booked up. There are various campgrounds in the park, some are non-reservable and some reservable. Set up camp at one of these well-equipped campgrounds around the water:

- **Campers Point South:** Offering 32 sites for tents and RVs (up to 65 feet) plus electrical hookups, campfire pits, and tables. Supervised pets are welcome. Reserve six months in advance!
- **Campers Point North:** Here are eight well-maintained sites on the waterfront for tents and RVs up to 65 feet. They have electrical hookups, a fire pit ring, a boat ramp, and a dump site. Make reservations up to six months in advance. Pets are welcome as long as they're supervised.

- **Peewee South:** The largest camp with a 146-foot length limit for RVs. Here, there are 54 sites for tents and RVs (27 double with electricity, 14 standard with RV hook-up, and 13 standard without RV hook-up and nonreservable). Pets leashed and supervised are welcome. There are five restrooms, water access, and fire rings.

- **Peewee North:** Eight sites on the waterfront and all sites have water views. There are potable water spigots, two restrooms, no hookups for RVs, and the RV limit is 79 feet. There are campfire rings, picnic tables, and a boat ramp. Reservations can be made one day in advance. Pets are welcome under supervision and quiet hours are enforced (so silence your generator).

- **Rattlesnake Point:** The camp is at the southern end of the park for long RV trailers. There are seven large campsites on the waterfront with electrical hook-ups, restrooms, a dumpsite, a fire pit, and a table. They can be reserved up to six months in advance. This site is popular because it's where the reservoir meets the river and it's great for swimming, tubing, rafting, floating, and fishing. As long as pets are leashed and supervised, they are welcome.

- **Riverside Campground:** Here are 14 sites for tents and short RVs at the most northern end of the lake, where there is access to the Tongue River. There are no electric hook-ups but you do have potable water spigots, a table and firepit, and restrooms nearby. Pets on a leash and supervised are allowed. These sites are reservable.

- **Sand Point Campground:** This campground offers 32 waterfront sites for tents and RVs with electrical hookups, campfire pits, and tables. Pets are welcome and this is a favorite camping spot at the lake.

Be aware that drinking water is only available between May and September. Boat ramps are at Campers Point and Pee Wee North. Enjoy the tranquility of the campgrounds and starry nights in the Montana wilderness.

DAY-USE AREAS AND RECREATIONAL FACILITIES

For day visitors, utilize the park's picnic areas for outdoor meals and gatherings. At Sand Point and Campers Point, you'll find covered picnic areas with barbeque pits. Take advantage of the park's day-use areas and utilize the park's amenities, such as playgrounds, volleyball courts, and horseshoe pits. Organize family gatherings or group outings in the designated areas. Find some peace and calm along the shorelines of the lake.

WILDLIFE OBSERVATION AND PHOTOGRAPHY

Observe the park's abundant wildlife including waterfowl, songbirds, and mammals in their natural habitats. Especially during winter months, this calls for epic photo shoots when crowds are gone and nature shows herself crisp and clear. This is the best time to capture the scenic beauty and wildlife on camera—day and night!

NEARBY ATTRACTIONS AND ACTIVITIES

Take scenic drives through the surrounding countryside and enjoy the views of rolling hills and prairies. Visit the nearby town of Ashland and explore its charming western atmosphere. Venture out to surrounding areas and engage in outdoor activities (hiking, fishing, and wildlife viewing) elsewhere before you return to base and watch the sunset on the waters.

PARK GUIDELINES AND SAFETY

Follow the park regulations and guidelines to ensure the preservation of the park's natural environment. Be aware of potential wildlife encounters and practice proper safety measures. Check for any updates or restrictions related to park usage before you visit. You don't want to turn around disappointed.

These tranquil waters soothe my soul. And they are away from the hustle and bustle of crowds; pristinely perfect.

If you enjoyed this book, please consider leaving a review.

AFTERWORD

We have been to the badlands, the battlefields, the bucking horses, the fossil finds, the rolling plains, rugged peaks, and footsteps of explorers, the sacred lands of Native Americans, and the glacial geology of a place that cannot be stifled in one book. Rocks and rivers introduced us to the old West of the cowboys, the discoveries of frontiersmen, the labor of miners and gold diggers, and the hopeful families who followed them in a land exposed to a relentless climate. And still, we see the smiling faces of local small-town hospitality.

Mining barons found their riches here. Iconic indigenous chiefs roared their victories on their plains as the bison listened and the wolves howled. Determined frontiersmen relinquished their pasts and faced their fears to find some hope in something new. Explorers searched and found and shared their luck with future generations. And now, these future generations hold this delicate ecosystem in their hands with loving admiration and respect, without leaving human traces as the landscape breathes and hums a silent history beneath their feet.

I was born and raised in this beautiful place, and I hope I introduced you to my heartspace of rugged beauty, wild adventures, and warm hospitality. Begin your journey today and let the spirit of Big Sky Country captivate your heart and soul. Get ready for an unforgettable experience in the Last Best Place.

It's time for you to embark on your own journey of exploration and discovery. This travel guide arms you with knowledge and provides an introduction to the endless horizons of my open skies. Pack your bags, plan your itinerary, and set out to Montana. Immerse yourself in the rich history and culture, marvel at the breathtaking landscapes, and engage with the friendly locals who call this place home.

I wish you my best wishes on your journey. Endless opportunities and memories await!

If you found this book useful, please share! I'd be delighted to see sincere reviews on Amazon that will encourage others to visit Montana.

BIBLIOGRAPHY

Alfano, M. (n.d.). *Eastern Montana*. AllTrails. https://www.alltrails.com/lists/eastern-montana--8

All Events. (n.d.). *Whitefish art & theater events tickets*. https://allevents.in/whitefish/art

AllTrails. (n.d.-a). *Best cross country skiing trails in Custer Gallatin National Forest*. https://www.alltrails.com/parks/us/montana/custer-gallatin-national-forest/cross-country-skiing

AllTrails. (n.d.-b). *Best wildlife trails in Glacier National Park*. https://www.alltrails.com/parks/us/montana/glacier-national-park/wildlife

AllTrails. (n.d.-c). *Big Hole National Battlefield*. https://www.alltrails.com/parks/us/montana/big-hole-national-battlefield

AllTrails. (n.d.-d). *Big Hole National Battlefield Trail*. https://www.alltrails.com/trail/us/montana/big-hole-national-battlefield-trail

AllTrails. (n.d.-e). *Custer Gallatin National Forest*. https://www.alltrails.com/parks/us/montana/custer-gallatin-national-forest

AllTrips. (n.d.-a). *Bitterroot valley history & museums: Marcus Daly mansion in Hamilton Montana*. https://www.explorethebitterroot.com/history_museums/daly_mansion.php

AllTrips. (n.d.-b). *Custer national forest in Montana*. AllTrips - Red Lodge Montana. https://www.allredlodge.com/nature/custer_national_forest.php

AllTrips. (2024a). *Flathead Lake Montana fishing, boating, activities*. AllTrips - Whitefish Montana. https://www.allwhitefish.com/flathead_lake/activities.php

AllTrips. (2024b). *Flathead Lake Montana fishing, camping, boating*. AllTrips - Glacier National Park. https://www.allglacier.com/lakes_rivers_falls/flathead_lake.php

Altschuler, W. (2020, December 14). *The weather and climate in Montana*. Trip-Savvy. https://www.tripsavvy.com/weather-and-climate-in-montana-4842743

American Prairie. (2011, April 27). *American prairie profiled by National Geographic* [Video]. YouTube. https://youtu.be/KitxeFuqOro

American Prairie. (2022, August 19). *This is American prairie* [Video]. YouTube. https://youtu.be/y5Gzm4w1MfI

Auma, Q. (2023, February 7). *14 things to do in Billings: Complete guide to the city on the Yellowstone*. TheTravel. https://www.thetravel.com/ultimate-travel-guide-to-billings-things-to-do/

Authentik. (n.d.). *Trip to Canada: online road trip planner*. Authentik Canada. https://www.authentikcanada.com/en/travel-guide/tourist-office-helena

Baber, F. (n.d.). *Great states - Montana culture*. PBS LearningMedia. https://www.pbslearningmedia.org/resource/great-states-montana-culture/video/

Banijay Documentaries. (2022, March 12). *Anthony Bourdain: Parts unknown - Montana - S07 E04 - all documentary* [Video]. YouTube. https://youtu.be/i0R_tYj9QTw

Barnett, M. (2021, September 23). *The 16 best dude ranches in Montana*. Discovering Montana. https://discoveringmontana.com/things-to-do/dude-ranches-montana/

Battle of the Little Bighorn Reenactment. (n.d.). *Battle of the Little Bighorn Reenactment: Home*. Little Bighorn Reenactment. http://www.littlebighornreenactment.com

Beck, W. (2021a, October 5). *10 amazing animals in Montana - including some unusual ones!*. Discovering Montana. https://discoveringmontana.com/montana/animals/

Beck, W. (2021b, October 5). *The 10 best campgrounds in Montana*. Discovering Montana. https://discoveringmontana.com/camping/best-campgrounds-montana/

Beck, W. (2021c, October 22). *6 scenic train rides in Montana you do not want to miss*. Discovering Montana. https://discoveringmontana.com/scenic-train-rides/

Best Places. (n.d.). *Helena valley northeast, MT climate*. https://www.bestplaces.net/climate/city/montana/helena_valley_northeast

Big Sky Fishing. (n.d.-a). *Billings, MT travel guide: The online guide to Billings, Montana*. https://www.bigskyfishing.com/Montana-Info/billings_mt.shtm

Big Sky Fishing. (n.d.-b). *Kalispell, MT travel guide: The online guide to Kalispell, Montana*. https://www.bigskyfishing.com/Montana-Info/kalispell_mt.shtm

Big Sky Montana. (n.d.). *Big Sky Resort visitors guide*. Big Sky Resort. https://bigskyresort.com/visitors-guide

Bilbrey Web Services. (2012). *Miles City saddlery*. Miles City Saddlery. http://www.milescitysaddlery.com/home.html

Billings Chamber of Commerce. (n.d.-a). *Visit*. https://www.billingschamber.com/visit/

Billings Chamber of Commerce. (n.d.-b). *Custer Battlefield Museum*. https://www.visitbillings.com/outdoor/custer-battlefield-museum

Booking.com. (n.d.-a). *Flathead Lake - 111 properties*. Booking.com. https://www.booking.com/searchresults.en-gb.html?aid=356980&label=gog235jc-1BCAUo7AFCDWZsYXRoZWFkLWxha2VIM1gDaHGIAQ GYAQm4AQfIAQ3YAQHoAQGIAgGoAgO4Arq2pK0GwAIB0gIkNzBj ZmYwODItNzU2Ny00NDNjLTk0MDMtNjdiZGQwNjZjNjAz2AIF4AIB& sid=f6a56a29ce12555fafa9c1f6be9bf989&landmark=67725&

Booking.com. (n.d.-b). *Hotels near Flathead Lake, USA*. Booking.com. https://www.booking.com/landmark/us/flathead-lake.html

Boughton, J. (n.d.). *Tour - Montana's historic forts and battlefields*. Historic Montana. https://historicmt.org/tours/show/105

Brown, C. (2022, June 24). *A local's guide to Whitefish, Montana*. Courtney Brown. https://www.bycourtneybrown.com/home/2022/5/23/a-locals-guide-to-whitefish-montana

Cedar Lake Ventures. (n.d.). *Helena valley southeast climate, weather by month, average temperature (Montana, United States)*. Weatherspark. https://weath erspark.com/y/2778/Average-Weather-in-Helena-Valley-Southeast-Montana-United-States-Year-Round

City of Billings. (n.d.). *Visitors*. https://www.billingsmt.gov/1781/Visitors

Conners, V. (n.d.). *An insider's guide to Little Bighorn Battlefield National Monument*. Visit the USA. https://www.gousa.in/experience/insiders-guide-little-bighorn-battlefield-national-monument

Cordingley, K. (n.d.). *7 things to love out here in southeast Montana*. Iexplore. https://www.iexplore.com/destinations/montana/reasons-to-love-south east-montana

Cybele, C. (2023, April 16). *Animals in Montana*. AZ Animals. https://a-z-animals.com/animals/location/north-america/united-states/montana/

Destimap. (n.d.). *The best attractions in Southwest Montana*. https://www.destimap.com/index.php?act=place&p=Southwest-Montana

Destination Paradise. (2021, July 25). *Montana 4K scenic relaxation film - Montana drone video - Glacier National Park* [Video]. YouTube. https://youtu.be/wwGN-rNZpV0

Dhaarna. (2023, July 1). *This US national park with 700 km of hiking trail is carved out of glaciers and lakes*. Travel Triangle. https://traveltriangle.com/blog/glacier-national-park/

Dilley, M., & Stanton, J. (n.d.). *Category: Montana forts - fortwiki historic U.S. and Canadian forts*. Fortwiki. http://www.fortwiki.com/Category:Montana_Forts

Discover Kalispell. (n.d.-a). *Events In Kalispell*. https://discoverkalispell.com/events/

Discover Kalispell. (n.d.-b). *Find your best sleep*. https://discoverkalispell.com/find-your-best-sleep/

Discover Kalispell. (n.d.-c). *Things to do*. https://discoverkalispell.com/things-to-do/

Discover Miles City. (n.d.-a). *Community profile*. https://milescitychamber.com/community-profile/

Discover Miles City. (n.d.-b). *Miles City area chamber of commerce getting here*. https://milescitychamber.com/getting-here/

Discover Miles City. (n.d.-c). *Recreation*. https://milescitychamber.com/recreation/

Discovering Montana. (2022a, February 25). *Kalispell, Montana*. https://discoveringmontana.com/towns/kalispell/

Discovering Montana. (2022b, March 7). *Makoshika State Park, Montana*. https://discoveringmontana.com/state-parks/makoshika/

Discovering Montana. (2022c, March 25). *Southwest Montana - forests, mountains & national parks*. https://discoveringmontana.com/southwest-montana/

Discovering Montana. (2022d, March 28). *Southeast Montana - discover the spirit of the old West*. https://discoveringmontana.com/southeast/

Discovering Montana. (2022e, April 1). *Fort Peck Summer Theater - A local theater with great charm*. https://discoveringmontana.com/theaters/fort-peck-summer/

Discovering Montana. (2022f, April 1). *Washoe Theater, Montana - amazing historic architecture*. https://discoveringmontana.com/theaters/washoe/

Discovering Montana. (2022g, December 9). *Montana public transport - travel by plane, train, bus and automobile*. https://discoveringmontana.com/transport/

Discovering Montana. (2022, April 1). *Rialto Bozeman - an unforgettable cultural hub in southwest Montana*. https://discoveringmontana.com/theaters/rialto-bozeman/

Downtown Kalispell. (n.d.). *Historic downtown Kalispell's self guided walking tour.* https://www.downtownkalispell.com/historical-walking-tour

Dude Ranchers Association. (n.d.). *Dude ranches in Montana.* https://duder anch.org/plan-your-visit/locations/states-provinces/montana/

Editorial Staff. (2019, January 9). *52 interesting facts about Montana, Montana state symbols.* The Fact File. https://thefactfile.org/montana-facts/

Expedia. (n.d.-a). *Big Hole National Battlefield Tours.* https://www.expedia.com/Big-Hole-National-Battlefield-Wisdom.d6115532.Vacation-Attraction

Expedia. (n.d.-b). *Big Hole National Battlefield, Wisdom, Montana.* https://www.expedia.com/Hotel-Search?startDate=2024-05-26&endDate=2024-05-27&selected=64995633&PinnedHotelID=64995633&HadPinnedHotel=true&regionId=6115532&adults=2&openPlayBack=true&destination=Big%20Hole%20National%20Battlefield%2C%20Wisdom%2C%20Mon tana%2C%20United%20States%20of%20America&theme=&userIntent=&semdtl=&useRewards=false&sort=RECOMMENDED

Expedia. (n.d.-c). *Big Sky travel guide.* https://www.expedia.co.in/Big-Sky.dx177831

Expedia. (n.d.-d). *Butte travel guide.* https://www.expedia.co.in/Butte.dx707

Expedia. (n.d.-e). *Helena travel guide - tourist guide.* https://www.expedia.co.in/Helena.dx1481

Expedia. (n.d.-f). *Miles City travel guide.* https://www.expedia.co.in/Miles-City.dx2351

Expedia. (n.d.-g). *Nez Perce stay and play cabins -unit #1.* https://www.expedia.com/Wisdom-Hotels-Nez-Perce-Stay-Play-Cabins.h64995633.Hotel-Information?chkin=1%2F1%2F2025&chkout=1%2F3%2F2025&x_pwa=1&pwa_ts=1715542927918&referrerUrl=aHR0cHM6Ly93d3cuZXhw ZWRpYS5jb20vSG90ZWwtU2VhcmNo&useRewards=false&rm1=a2&regionId=6115532&destination=Big%20Hole%20National%20Battle field%2C%20Wisdom%2C%20Montana%2C%20United%20States%20of%20America&destType=MARKET&selected=64995633&latLong=45.646827%2C-113.653548&sort=RECOMMENDED&userIntent=&proper tyName=Nez%20Perce%20Stay%20%26%20Play%20Cabins%20Unit%20%231&l10n=%5Bobject%20Object%5D&allowPreAppliedFilters=true&amenities=&chain=&daysInFuture=&origin=&group=&guestRating=&hotelName=&lodging=&paymentType=&bedType=&cleaningAndSafety Practices=&poi=&price=&neighborhood=&roomIndex=&star=&stay Length=&theme=&travelerType=&bedroomFilter=&deals=&

propertyStyle=&misId=&rewards=&pickUpTime=&dropOffTime=&
commissionTiers=&agencyBusinessModels=&mealPlan=&cabinClass=&
tripType=&airlineCode=&directFlights=&infantsInSeats=&driverAge=&
partialStay=false&vacationRentalsOnly=false&mapBounds=&stay
Type=&expediaPropertyId=&house_rules_group=&highlightedProper
tyId=&bed_type_group=&stay_options_group=&hotel_brand=&
multi_neighborhood_group=&logger=%5Bobject%20Object%5D&start
Date=1%2F1%2F2025&endDate=1%2F3%2F2025&petsIncluded=false&
bedroom_count_gt=&us_bathroom_count_gt=&pricing_group=

Expedia. (n.d.-h). *Southwest Montana travel guide - tourist guide*. https://www.expedia.co.in/Southwest-Montana.dx6056420

Exploring the Lewis and Clark trail. (2017, June 22). *Southwest Montana | Montana state parks, hiking, camping, Helena, Virginia City*. Lewis & Clark Trail. https://experiencelewisandclark.travel/southwest-montana/

Family Days Out. (2022a, March 22). *Top 5 ghost towns in the USA!* https://www.familydaysout.com/blog/top-5-ghost-towns-in-the-usa

Family Days Out. (2022b, May 24). *Living history in Virginia City!* https://www.familydaysout.com/blog/living-history-in-virginia-city#

Favre, L. (2019, August 15). *10 things to know about Montana*. U.S. News & World Report. https://www.usnews.com/news/best-states/articles/2019-08-15/10-things-to-know-about-montana

Finding Our Someday. (2022, December 12). *A Montana hidden gem - Always have a backup plan - RVing Lewis & Clark caverns S7 = ep 149* [Video]. YouTube. https://youtu.be/mqgUqyPhlCY

Flathead Indian Reservation. (2021, October 7). *Flathead Indian reservation*. Wikipedia. https://en.wikipedia.org/wiki/Flathead_Indian_Reservation

Flathead Lake Resort. (2023, July 10). *Flathead Lake Resort - private beach access on Flathead Lake*. https://www.flatheadlakeresort.com/

Fodor's travel. (n.d.). *Missoula, Kalispell, and northwest Montana travel guide - expert picks for your vacation*. Fodors. https://www.fodors.com/world/north-america/usa/montana/missoula-kalispell-and-northwest-montana

Forest Service. (2023). *Bitterroot National Forest - about the area*. https://www.fs.usda.gov/main/bitterroot/about-forest/about-area

Fort Peck Tribes. (n.d.). *Fort Peck tribes - tribal history*. Fort Peck Tribes. https://fortpecktribes.org/visitor-opportunities/tribal-history/

Fort Peck Tribes. (n.d.) *Visitor opportunities*. Fort Peck Tribes https://fortpecktribes.org/visitor-opportunties/

Foundation for Montana History. (2023). *Tours*. https://www.mthistory.org/tours

Frommers. (n.d.-a). *Things to do in Big Hole national battlefield*. https://www.frommers.com/destinations/big-hole-national-battlefield

Frommers. (n.d.-b). *Things to do in eastern Montana*. https://www.frommers.com/destinations/eastern-montana

Full Suitcase. (2015). *Yellowstone travel guide*. Full Suitcase Family Travel Blog. https://fullsuitcase.com/yellowstone-national-park/

Gass, J. (2022a, April 23). *The 13 best restaurants in Whitefish, Montana*. Discovering Montana. https://discoveringmontana.com/food-drink/restaurants-whitefish/

Gass, J. (2022b, May 18). *Little Bighorn battlefield - A complete guide*. Discovering Montana. https://discoveringmontana.com/little-bighorn-battlefield/

Glacier Country Montana. (2019). *Wildlife in western Montana + Glacier National Park*. https://glaciermt.com/wildlife-watching

Glacier Country Tourism. (n.d.-a). *Hockaday museum of art in Kalispell, MT*. https://glaciermt.com/listing/hockaday-museum-of-art

Glacier Country Tourism. (n.d.-b). *Transportation*. Western Mountain's Glacier County. https://touroperators.glaciermt.com/transportation

Glacier International Lodge. (2023). *Glacier International Lodge - hotels in Whitefish MT - Kalispell MT*. https://glacierinternationallodge.com/?utm_source=AllTrips&utm_campaign=AllTrips-AllWhitefish.com&utm_medium=referral&utm_content=/flathead_lake/activities

Glacier National Park. (n.d.-a). *Hiking the trails*. https://www.nps.gov/glac/planyourvisit/hikingthetrails.htm

Glacier National Park. (n.d.-b). *Leave no trace*. https://www.nps.gov/glac/planyourvisit/leavenotrace.htm

Glacier National Park. (2015, September 7). *Wilderness camping*. https://www.nps.gov/glac/planyourvisit/backcountry.htm

Go Northwest. (n.d.-a). *Bitterroot valley of Montana*. https://www.gonorthwest.com/Montana/northwest/Bitterroot_Valley.htm

Go Northwest. (n.d.-b). *Flathead Valley Montana*. https://www.gonorthwest.com/Montana/northwest/Flathead/flathead.htm

Go Northwest. (n.d.-c). *Glacier National Park*. https://www.gonorthwest.com/Montana/northwest/glaciernp/glacier_np.htm

Go Northwest. (n.d.-d). *Montana regions and cities*. https://www.gonorthwest.com/montana/Montana_Cities.htm

Go Northwest. (n.d.-e). *Northwest Montana.* https://www.gonorthwest.com/ Montana/northwest/mtnw.htm

Go Northwest. (n.d.-f). *Northwest Montana map.* https://www.gonorthwest. com/Montana/northwest/mtmapnw1.htm

Go Northwest. (2019, November 4). *Northeast Montana: Northeast.* https:// www.gonorthwest.com/Montana/northeast/mtne.htm

Go Traveler. (2013, January 7). *Glacier National Park* [Video]. YouTube. https://youtu.be/LNquUapZ_Sg

Goodreads. (n.d.). *Travel quotes (3201 quotes).* Goodreads. https://www. goodreads.com/quotes/tag/travel

Governor's Office of Indian Affairs. (n.d.). *Fort Peck Assiniboine and Sioux tribes - Fort Peck Assiniboine and Sioux tribes.* Tribalnations. https://tribalnations. mt.gov/Directory/FortPeckAssiniboineSiouxTribes

Graetz, R., & Graetz, S. (2013, February 27). *Northeast Montana... exploring new territory - Missouri River country.* Missouririvermt. https:// missouririvermt.com/article/exploring-new-territory

Guese, S. (2017). *Giddyup! How to have the ultimate Wild West experience in Montana.* Going Places. https://www.onetravel.com/going-places/ulti mate-wild-west-experience-in-
montana/#:~:text=The%2520Wild%2520West%2520is%2520alive

GuideAlong. (2022, April 13). *Don't miss a thing with guidealong audio tours app.* https://guidealong.com/yellowstone-national-park-travel-guide/

Hanlon, R. (2021, September 6). *The 10 best museums in Montana.* Discovering Montana. https://discoveringmontana.com/museums

Hanlon, R. (2022, April 30). *Big Hole National Battlefield, Montana.* Discovering Montana. https://discoveringmontana.com/big-hole-national-battlefield/

Harrison, M. (2020a, October 14). *Things to do in southeast Montana without the crowds.* TravelingMel. https://travelingmel.com/things-to-do-in-south east-montana-without-the-crowds/

Harrison, M. (2020b, October 21). *Visiting battlefields in Montana.* Traveling-Mel. https://travelingmel.com/visiting-battlefields-in-montana/

Hayes, M. (2021, November 15). *Geography of Montana.* Geography Realm. https://www.geographyrealm.com/geography-of-
montana/#:~:text=The%2520eastern%2520portion%2520of%2520-
Montana

Helena Montana. (n.d.). *Visit Helena - explore Helena attractions and plan your next trip.* Visit Helena, Montana. https://helenamt.com/

Henderson, C., & Hunter, M. (2020, July 22). *Complete guide to visiting Yellow-*

stone National Park. The Points Guy. https://thepointsguy.com/guide/yellowstone-national-park/

Hipcamp. (n.d.). *Camping in Montana: Best Montana campgrounds 2023*. https://www.hipcamp.com/en-US/d/united-states/montana/camping/all

Historic Downtown Kalispell. (n.d.). *Main Street and First Avenue East historic district*. Downtown Kalispell. https://www.downtownkalispell.com/_files/ugd/272254_5c25baa082d4431d8642eea1f2a49ff1.pdf

History.com Editors. (2020, May 19). *Montana*. History. https://www.history.com/topics/us-states/montana

Hockaday Museum of Art. (2019a, January 14). *Kalispell, Montana*. https://hockadaymuseum.com/

Hockaday Museum of Art. (2019b, January 31). *Glacier National Park mural restoration project*. https://hockadaymuseum.com/exhibition/mural-restoration/?back=ago

Holidify. (n.d.). *Helena tourism (2024) - USA > top places, travel guide*. Holidify. https://www.holidify.com/places/helena/

Holter Museum of Art. (2023). *About us*. The Holter. https://holtermuseum.org/about

Hopper, I. (2021, June 8). *Whitefish Montana travel guide 4K* [Video]. YouTube. https://youtu.be/QdAEFrHNdS8

Horton, C. (n.d.). *Virtual gallery visit*. C.M. Russell Museum. https://cmrussell.org/experience/virtual-museum/virtual-gallery-visit/

Hotels.com. (n.d.). *Where to stay in Virginia City?* https://it.hotels.com/de1413030/hotel-virginia-city-montana/?locale=it_IT&pos=HCOM_IT&siteid=300000007

I love Whitefish. (n.d.). *Top 5 hiking trails in Whitefish to explore*. I Love Whitefish Vacation Rentals. https://ilovewhitefish.com/top-5-in-whitefish/top-5-hiking-trails-in-whitefish/

iExplore. (n.d.). *Montana — history and culture*. https://www.iexplore.com/articles/travel-guides/north-america/united-states/montana/history-and-culture#:

Inbody, K. (n.d.). *Big Hole battle continues to resonate 140 years later*. Great Falls Tribune. https://eu.greatfallstribune.com/story/life/2017/08/03/big-hole-battle-continues-resonate-140-years-later/472407001/

Infoplease Staff. (n.d.). *Montana*. Infoplease. https://www.infoplease.com/us/states/montana

James, J. (2023, April 7). *12 amazingly unique things that Montana is known for*. My 103.5. https://my1035.com/12-things-montana-is-known-for/

Jelt. (2022, August 9). *What are the best campsites in Montana?* Jelt Belt. https://jeltbelt.com/blogs/jelt-blog/the-best-summer-campsites-in-southwest-montana-according-to-longtime-residents-and-native-montanans

Johnson, D. M., Crowley, J. M., & McNamee, G. L. (n.d.). *Montana - history*. In *Encyclopædia Britannica*. https://www.britannica.com/place/Montana-state/History

Johnson, D. M., Crowley, J. M., & McNamee, G. L. (2019). Montana - capital, population, climate, map, & facts. In *Encyclopædia Britannica*. https://www.britannica.com/place/Montana-state

Julie. (2019, September 24). *10 best things to do in Glacier National Park*. Earth Trekkers. https://www.earthtrekkers.com/best-things-to-do-in-glacier-national-park/

Jurga. (2017, May 4). *Best places to stay in & near Yellowstone National Park (complete lodging guide)*. Full Suitcase Travel Blog. https://fullsuitcase.com/yellowstone-best-places-to-stay/

Kalispell historic walking tour (self-guided). (n.d.). Crown of the Continent. https://crownofthecontinent.net/entries/kalispell-historic-walking-tour-self-guided-kalispell-montana/e4573c01-e382-4ab5-9b47-194497a5d187

KAYAK. (n.d.). *Kalispell travel guide - Kalispell tourism*.https://www.kayak.com/Kalispell.15351.guide

Kayak. (n.d.-a). *Butte travel guide - Butte tourism*. https://www.kayak.co.in/Butte.34566.guide

Kayak. (n.d.-b). *Helena travel guide - Helena tourism*. https://www.kayak.co.in/Helena.33905.guide

Kent, J. (2013, July 22). *Little Bighorn Tour Guide Brings Battle To Life*. NPR. https://www.npr.org/2013/07/22/203595888/little-bighorn-tour-guide-brings-battle-to-life

Keys, J. (2023, January 21). *Big Sky Montana travel guide*. Jesskeys. https://jesskeys.com/big-sky-montana-travel-guide/

Kiffel Alcheh, J. (2015, May 6). *Montana pictures and facts*. National Geographic. https://kids.nationalgeographic.com/geography/states/article/montana

Kilgore, G. (n.d.). *Dude Ranches in Montana*. Top50 Ranches. https://www.top50ranches.com/montana-ranch-vacations

Knapp, S. (2017, April 20). *A day trip to the ghost towns of Virginia and Nevada City Montana*. Destination Yellowstone. https://destinationyellowstone.com/day-trip-ghost-towns-virginia-nevada-city-montana/#:~:text=Madison%2520County%252C%2520Mon-tana%2520is%2520where

Komoot. (n.d.). *Attractions and places to see in Custer Gallatin National Forest - top 20.* https://www.komoot.com/guide/1895305/attractions-in-custer-gallatin-national-forest

Lane, B. (2023a, May 4). *16 best campgrounds in Montana.* Planetware. https://www.planetware.com/montana/best-campgrounds-in-montana-us-mt-50.htm

Lane, B. (2023b, May 10). *15 top-rated hiking trails in Glacier National Park, MT.* Planetware. https://www.planetware.com/montana/top-rated-hiking-trails-in-glacier-national-park-mt-us-mt-52.htm

Legends of America. (n.d.-a). *Montana forts of the old west.* https://www.legendsofamerica.com/mt-forts/

Legends of America. (n.d.-b). *More Montana forts.* https://www.legendsofamerica.com/more-montana-forts/#lewis-clark-fort

Legends of America. (n.d.-c). *More Montana forts.* https://www.legendsofamerica.com/more-montana-forts/#lewis-clark-fort

List of Parks. (2020, October 19). *Makoshika State Park Visitors Guide.* https://listofparks.com/blogs/state-park-visitors-guides/makoshika-state-park-visitors-guide

Little Bighorn Battlefield National Monument. (2020, April 24). *Triumph & tragedy along the Little Bighorn.* Youtube. https://youtu.be/yGLAAI7nYpk

Little Bighorn Tours. (n.d.). *Guided Little Bighorn tours.* https://www.littlebighorntours.com/little-bighorn-tours

Locampo, V. (2022, April 21). *The Missouri river - a complete guide.* Discovering Montana. https://discoveringmontana.com/missouri-river/

Lonely Planet. (n.d.). *Montana travel.* https://www.lonelyplanet.com/usa/rocky-mountains/montana

Marcie. (2022, June 20). *Exploring an underground city.* Just a Little Further. https://justalittlefurther.com/just-a-little-further/2022/6/18/sdodyuxs4p17tmrw0iwwj36vxofmr7

Maxwell, L. L. (2023, June 19). *Miles City.* Travel Safe - Abroad. https://www.travelsafe-abroad.com/united-states/miles-city/

McGowan, K. (2023, February 3). *Southeast Montana travel guide 2023.* Issuu. https://issuu.com/windfall/docs/semt_tg23_flipbook

McRae, B. (2022, September 2). *What does agritourism mean for producers in Montana?* Northern AG Network. https://northernag.net/what-does-agritourism-mean-for-producers-in-montana/

Michelle. (2022, September 14). *Where are the highest rated campgrounds in southwest Montana*. The Moose 94.7 FM. https://mooseradio.com/what-are-the-best-rated-campgrounds-in-southwest-montana/

Missouri River Country. (n.d.-a). *Community travel information*. https://missouririvermt.com/communities

Missouri River Country. (n.d.-b). *Getting here*. https://missouririvermt.com/getting-here

Missouri River Country. (n.d.-c). *Visit Eastern Montana*. https://missouririvermt.com/

Missouri River Country. (n.d.-a). *Plan your trip*. https://missouririvermt.com/plan-your-trip

Missouri River Country. (n.d.-b). *Top things to do*. https://missouririvermt.com/top-things-to-do-in-missouri-river-country

Missouri River Country Montana. (2019). *NE MT ag expo & night of honors*. https://missouririvermt.com/wildlife

Montana Agritourism. (n.d.). *Montana agritourism*. https://www.montanaagritourism.com/

Montana Arts and Home. (n.d.). *Montana arts & home - western art - rustic home decor- western jewelry*. https://montanaartsandhome.com/

Montana Department of Transportation. (n.d.). *511MT*. https://www.511mt.net/#zoom=5.8&lon=-109.64285858161821&lat=47.04112902986316&events&road-cond&rwis

Montana Fish, Wildlife and Parks. (n.d.-a). *Activities: culture and history*. https://fwp.mt.gov/activities/culture-and-history

Montana Fish, Wildlife, and Parks. (n.d.-b). *Lone Pine State Park*. https://fwp.mt.gov/stateparks/lone-pine

Montana Fish, Wildlife, and Parks. (n.d.-c). *Activities: Camping*. https://fwp.mt.gov/activities/camp

Montana Fish, Wildlife, and Parks. (n.d.-d). *Flathead Lake*. https://fwp.mt.gov/stateparks/flathead-lake

Montana Fish, Wildlife, and Parks. (n.d.-e). *FWP region 1 (northwest Montana)*. https://fwp.mt.gov/aboutfwp/regions/region1#:~:text=The%2520expansive%2520landscape%2520is%2520home

Montana Fish, Wildlife, and Parks. (n.d.-f). *Makoshika State Park*. https://fwp.mt.gov/stateparks/makoshika/

Montana Fish, Wildlife, and Parks. (n.d.-g). *Tongue River Reservoir State Park*. https://fwp.mt.gov/stateparks/tongue-river-reservoir/

Montana Fish, Wildlife, and Parks. (2013). *Lewis & Clark Caverns State Park.* https://fwp.mt.gov/stateparks/lewis-and-clark-caverns

Montana Historic Theaters. (2019, November 16). *Montana historic theaters.* Montana's Historic Landscapes. https://montanahistoriclandscape.com/tag/montana-historic-theaters/

Montana Historical Society. (n.d.). *History of our home.* https://mhs.mt.gov/education/Elementary/HistoryOfOurHome

Montana Office of Tourism. (n.d.-a). *Alder Gulch short line.* https://www.visitmt.com/listings/general/rail-tour/alder-gulch-short-line

Montana Office of Tourism. (n.d.-b). *Art galleries & installations.* https://www.visitmt.com/things-to-do/arts-and-culture/art-galleries-and-installations

Montana Office of Tourism. (n.d.-c). *Arts & culture.* https://www.visitmt.com/things-to-do/arts-and-culture

Montana Office of Tourism. (n.d.-d). *Big Hole National Battlefield.* https://www.visitmt.com/listings/general/national-historic-site/big-hole-national-battlefield

Montana Office of Tourism. (n.d.-e). *Boot Hill cemetery.* https://www.visitmt.com/listings/general/landmark/boot-hill-cemetery

Montana Office of Tourism. (n.d.-f). *Butte.* https://www.visitmt.com/places-to-go/cities-and-towns/butte

Montana Office of Tourism. (n.d.-g). *Craig.* https://www.visitmt.com/places-to-go/cities-and-towns/craig

Montana Office of Tourism. (n.d.-h). *Custer Gallatin National Forest.* https://www.visitmt.com/listings/general/national-forest/custer-gallatin-national-forest

Montana Office of Tourism. (n.d.-i). *Daniels county museum & pioneer town.* https://www.visitmt.com/listings/general/museum/daniels-county-museum-pioneer-town

Montana Office of Tourism. (n.d.-j). *Eastern Montana trips.* https://www.visitmt.com/plan-your-trip/trip-ideas/eastern-montana-trips

Montana Office of Tourism. (n.d.-k). *Flathead lake.* https://www.visitmt.com/listings/general/lake/flathead-lake

Montana Office of Tourism. (n.d.-l). *Food and drink.* https://www.visitmt.com/things-to-do/food-and-drink

Montana Office of Tourism. (n.d.-m). *Fort Peck.* https://www.visitmt.com/places-to-go/cities-and-towns/fort-peck

Montana Office of Tourism. (n.d.-n). *Ghost towns*. https://www.visitmt.com/things-to-do/history/ghost-towns

Montana Office of Tourism. (n.d.-o). *Havre beneath the streets*. https://www.visitmt.com/listings/general/specialty-tour/havre-beneath-the-streets

Montana Office of Tourism. (n.d.-p). *Historic sites & battlefields*. https://www.visitmt.com/things-to-do/history/historic-sites-and-battlefields

Montana Office of Tourism. (n.d.-q). *Lewis & Clark Caverns trail system*. https://www.visitmt.com/listings/general/state-park-trail/lewis-clark-caverns-trail-system

Montana Office of Tourism. (n.d.-r). *Miles City*. https://www.visitmt.com/places-to-go/cities-and-towns/miles-city

Montana Office of Tourism. (n.d.-s). *Missouri river country's top 10*. https://www.visitmt.com/places-to-go/regions/tourism-regions-top-10/missouri-river-countrys-top-10

Montana Office of Tourism. (n.d.-t). *Montana's official tourism, travel & vacation info site*. https://www.visitmt.com

Montana Office of Tourism. (n.d.-u). *Museums*. https://www.visitmt.com/things-to-do/arts-and-culture/museums

Montana Office of Tourism. (n.d.-v). *Nevada City*. https://www.visitmt.com/listings/general/ghost-town/nevada-city

Montana Office of Tourism. (n.d.-w). *Southeast Montana*. https://www.visitmt.com/listings/general/tourism-region/southeast-montana

Montana Office of Tourism. (n.d.-x). *Southwest Montana trips*. https://www.visitmt.com/plan-your-trip/trip-ideas/southwest-montana-trips

Montana Office of Tourism. (n.d.-y). *Southwest Montana's top 10*. https://www.visitmt.com/places-to-go/regions/tourism-regions-top-10/southwest-montanas-top-10

Montana Office of Tourism. (n.d.-z). *The buffalo*. https://www.visitmt.com/indian-country/additional-resources/the-buffalo

Montana Office of Tourism. (n.d.-aa). *Theaters & cinema*. https://www.visitmt.com/things-to-do/arts-and-culture/theaters

Montana Office of Tourism. (n.d.-ab). *Tongue river reservoir state park*. https://www.visitmt.com/listings/general/state-park/tongue-river-reservoir-state-park

Montana Office of Tourism. (n.d.-ac). *Washoe theater*. https://www.visitmt.com/listings/general/movie-theatre/washoe-theater

Montana State Parks. (n.d.-a). *Bannack State Park*. https://fwp.mt.gov/stateparks/bannack-state-park

Montana State Parks. (n.d.-b). *Lewis & Clark Caverns State Park*. https://montanastateparksfoundation.org/parks/lewis-clark-caverns-state-park/

Montana State Parks. (n.d.-c). *Lewis and Clark Caverns State Park, MT*. https://montanastateparks.reserveamerica.com/tourParkDetail.do?contract Code=MT&parkId=630315

Montana State Parks. (n.d.-d). *Lewis and Clark Caverns State Park, MT*. https://montanastateparks.reserveamerica.com/tourDetails.do?contractCode= MT&parkId=630315&tourId=62503&cat=1

Montana State Parks. (n.d.-e). *Tongue River Reservoir State Park*. https://montanastateparksfoundation.org/parks/tongue-river-reservoir-state-park/

Montana.Gov. (n.d.-a). *Agritourism*. https://agr.mt.gov/Topics/A-D/Agritourism

Montana.Gov. (n.d.-b). *Montana's Charlie Russell*. https://mhs.mt.gov/education/Educators/CMRussell

Montana.Gov. (n.d.-c). *Train rides and schedule - explore Virginia City and Nevada City, MT*. https://virginiacitymt.com/Experience-The-Old-West/Train-Rides-and-Schedule

Montana.Gov. (2012). *Montana's official state website - brief history of Montana*. https://mt.gov/discover/brief_history.aspx

Morgan, C. (2009). *Northwest history consortium Montana Indians and multiculturalism*. https://www.nwesd.org/wp-content/uploads/2013/10/9.4-MontanaIndians.Multiculturalism.Morgan.5.pdf

Nardelli, F. (2022, August 9). *Makoshika State Park Montana: Museum, trails, directions, hours and prices*. Travel in USA. https://www.travelinusa.us/makoshika-state-park-glendive/

National Forest Foundation. (n.d.). *Custer Gallatin national forest*. https://www.nationalforests.org/our-forests/find-a-forest/custer-gallatin-national-forest

National Geographic. (n.d.). *Montana travel guide*. https://www.nationalgeographic.com/travel/destination/montana

National Park Foundation. (2023, April 25). *Big Hole National Battlefield*. https://www.nationalparks.org/explore/parks/big-hole-national-battlefield

National Park Service. (n.d.-a). *Catch a fish - Yellowstone National Park*. https://www.nps.gov/yell/planyourvisit/fishing.htm

National Park Service. (n.d.-b). *Directions - Big Hole national battlefield*. https://www.nps.gov/biho/planyourvisit/directions.htm

National Park Service. (n.d.-c). *Fort Union Trading Post national historic site.* https://www.nps.gov/fous/index.htm

National Park Service. (n.d.-d). *Hike a trail.* https://www.nps.gov/yell/plany ourvisit/hiking.htm

National Park Service. (n.d.-e). *History & culture - Big Hole national battlefield.* https://www.nps.gov/biho/learn/historyculture/index.htm

National Park Service. (n.d.-f). *Montana.* https://www.nps.gov/state/mt/ index.htm

National Park Service. (n.d.-g). *Photography - Yellowstone National Park.* https://www.nps.gov/yell/planyourvisit/photography.htm

National Parks Service. (n.d.-h). *Plan your visit - Big Hole National Battlefield.* https://www.nps.gov/biho/planyourvisit/index.htm

National Park Service. (n.d.-i). *Ranger programs - Big Hole national battlefield.* https://www.nps.gov/biho/planyourvisit/rangerprograms.htm

National Park Service. (2016a). *Current conditions - Glacier National Park.* https://www.nps.gov/glac/planyourvisit/conditions.htm

National Park Service. (2016b). *Plan your visit - Glacier National Park.* https:// www.nps.gov/glac/planyourvisit/index.htm

National Park Service. (2016c). *Camping - glacier national park.* https://www. nps.gov/glac/planyourvisit/camping.htm

National Park Service. (2016d). *Plan your visit - Little Bighorn Battlefield National monument.* https://www.nps.gov/libi/planyourvisit/index.htm

National Park Service. (2017). *Plan your visit - Yellowstone National Park.* https://www.nps.gov/yell/planyourvisit/index.htm

National Park Service. (2023, March 3). *Custer national cemetery - Little Bighorn battlefield national monument.* https://www.nps.gov/libi/plany ourvisit/custer-national-cemetery.htm

National Park Service. (2023, July 19). *Ten essentials.* https://www.nps.gov/ articles/10essentials.htm

National Park Service. (2024, January 10). *Wilderness Camping - Glacier National Park.* https://www.nps.gov/glac/planyourvisit/backcountry.htm

Nations Online Project. (n.d.). *Map of the US state of Montana.* https://www. nationsonline.org/oneworld/map/USA/montana_map.htm

NG. (2016, December 15). *Transportation: Getting to Montana is easier than you think.* Glacier Country Montana. https://b2b.glaciermt.com/transporta tion-getting-to-montana-is-easier-than-you-think/

Nomads Unveiled. (2022, May 18). *15 things Montana is known and famous for.* https://nomadsunveiled.com/what-is-montana-known-and-famous-for/

NPS. (2020, October 14). *Summer Backcountry Camping Video*. https://www. nps.gov/media/video/view.htm?id=73A16C66-1DD8-B71B-0BDA3687A1AEC297

Office of the Governor. (n.d.). *Confederated Salish and Kootenai tribes*. https:// tribalnations.mt.gov/Directory/ConfederatedSalishKootenaiTribes

Otto, T. (2020, May 7). *13 best things to do in southeast Montana*. Rovology. https://rovology.com/united-states/montana/best-things-to-do-in-south east-montana/

Outdoorsy. (n.d.). *Tongue Reservoir State Park - RV guide*. https://www. outdoorsy.com/guide/tongue-river-reservoir-state-park-mt

Patterson, M., & Patterson, R. (2016, September 4). *Northeast Montana: A land of broad horizons and open sky*. The Gazette. https://www.thegazette.com/ travel/northeast-montana-a-land-of-broad-horizons-and-open-sky/

Peglar, T. (2023, February 24). *10 Montana gems between Yellowstone and Glacier*. Yellowstone National Park. https://www.yellowstonepark.com/ road-trips/road-trip-stops/visit-montana/southwest-montana/

Pilson, G. (n.d.). *Custer Gallatin National Forest*. PeakVisor. https://peakvisor. com/park/custer-gallatin-national-forest.html

Pursuit. (2019). *Lodging & activities in Glacier National Park: Montana specialists*. Glacier Park Collection. https://www.glacierparkcollection.com/

REI Coop. (2018, December 19). *The ten essentials for camping & hiking*. https://www.rei.com/learn/expert-advice/ten-essentials.html

Reimers, F. (2019, November 4). *The outside guide to Yellowstone National Park*. Outside Online. https://www.outsideonline.com/adventure-travel/ national-parks/yellowstone-national-park-travel-guide/

Resting_burtch_face. (2023, January 26). *June July road trip in Montana, tell me what's the best thing to see or do wherever you are in Montana*. Reddit. https:// www.reddit.com/r/Montana/comments/10ljc34/june_july_road _trip_in_montana_tell_me_whats_the/?+utm_source=share& utm_medium=web2x&context=3

Rialto Bozeman. (n.d.). *Bozeman concerts, Bozeman event space, live music, rialto Bozeman*. https://www.rialtobozeman.com/index.php#

Riddle in History. (2023, April 27). *What really happened at the Battle of Little Bighorn?* YouTube. https://youtu.be/mL88Hh9dXBQ

Riley. (2020, July 17). *Visiting Little Bighorn Battlefield National Monument: The parks expert travel guide*. The Parks Expert. https://parksexpert.com/visit ing-little-bighorn-battlefield/

Ryberg, K. (n.d.). *Capitol rock national natural landmark, Ekalaka, Montana*.

Hiking Project. https://www.hikingproject.com/gem/612/capitol-rock-national-natural-landmark

Samantha & Chris. (2023, March 9). *The top 6 Whitefish and Kalispell breweries to visit (map included)*. Boozing Abroad. https://boozingabroad.com/white-fish-and-kalispell-breweries-montana/

Sandy, J. (2020, April 7). *Billings > travel and vacation Montana*. Montana Traveler. https://www.montanatraveler.com/city-billings/

Sandy, J. (2023). *Travel north-central and northeast Montana*. Montana Traveler. https://www.montanatraveler.com/region-discoveryland/

Santenello, P. (2022, November 13). *First impressions on Native American Reservation - Flathead* [Video]. YouTube. https://youtu.be/tYTrPdLv634

Sara. (2021a, January 26). *Big Sky, Montana: Ultimate travel guide*. Travel À La Mer. https://travelalamer.com/big-sky-montana-travel-guide/

Sara. (2021b, June 21). *Big Sky, Montana: Summer guide*. Travel À La Mer. https://travelalamer.com/big-sky-montana-summer-guide/

Scenic Hunter. (2022, November 5). *10 best places to travel in Montana - Montana USA travel guide* [Video]. YouTube. https://youtu.be/M6gaaML6e6Q

Schatz, T. (2023, February 22). *10 outdoorsy things to do in Whitefish Montana*. Back Road Ramblers. https://backroadramblers.com/whitefish-montana-glacier-national-park/

Shelton, J. (2023, February 15). *Folklore and mystery: Underneath Montana's streets*. Distinctly Montana. https://www.distinctlymontana.com/folklore-and-mystery-underneath-montanas-streets

Smithsonian Magazine, & Fovenyessy, A. (2011, January). *Custer's last stand*. Smithsonian Magazine. https://photocontest.smithsonianmag.com/photocontest/detail/custers-last-stand-real-bird-reenactment-of-the-battle-of-the-little-bighor/

somewherelately. (2020, August 26). *Whitefish, Montana travel guide*. Somewhere, Lately. https://www.somewherelately.com/2020/08/whitefish-travel-guide/

Southwest Montana. (n.d.-a). *11 Things to do in Virginia City / Ennis area*. https://southwestmt.com/blog/things-to-do-near-virginia-city-and-ennis-montana/

Southwest Montana. (n.d.-b). *Montana hiking & backpacking*. https://southwestmt.com/thegreatoutdoors/hikingandbackpacking/

Southwest Montana. (n.d.-c). *Nevada City's music hall - Nevada City, MT*. https://southwestmt.com/listings/nevada-citys-music-hall/

State Symbols USA. (n.d.). *Montana state name origin.* https://statesymbolsusa. org/symbol-official-item/montana/state-name-origin/origin-montana

Stay Montana. (n.d.-a). *Big Sky Montana vacation guide start planning trip to Montana today.* https://www.staymontana.com/big-sky-montana/

Stay Montana. (n.d.-b). *Whitefish, Montana vacation guide.* https://www.stay montana.com/whitefish-montana-vacation-guide/

The Editors of Encyclopaedia Britannica. (2021, September 14). *Fort Peck Dam - description, history, & facts.* Encyclopaedia Britannica. https://www. britannica.com/topic/Fort-Peck-Dam

The Editors of Encyclopaedia Britannica (2012, January 6). *Flathead Lake.* Encyclopedia Britannica. https://www.britannica.com/place/Flathead-Lake

thehistorysquad. (2024, January 26). *Custer's last stand - journey through the battle of the Little Bighorn* [Video]. Youtube. https://youtu.be/ Ea6xve4U5QU

Thompson, S. (2024). *Tribal bison range - Montana.* Crown of the Continent. https://crownofthecontinent.net/entries/tribal-bison-range-montana/ d06a11c4-e3b7-4396-8fb3-5a74a40e7db1

Through My Lens. (2020, January 9). *15 things to do in Billings, Montana* [Video]. YouTube. https://youtu.be/3BI3NI54aAg

Tillison, J. (2023, January 17). *Big Hole National Battlefield - Montana.* Park Ranger John. https://www.parkrangerjohn.com/big-hole-national-battlefield/

Travelclast. (2023, March 24). *The big Big Sky Montana video guide - hiking, fishing and Yellowstone at your feet* [Video].YouTube. https://youtu.be/ NojLaFWeA-s

Trip.com. (n.d.-a). *Butte travel guide 2024 - things to do, what to eat & tips.* https://www.trip.com/travel-guide/destination/butte-38521/

Trip.com. (n.d.-b). *Helena travel guide 2024 - things to do, what to eat & tips.* https://www.trip.com/travel-guide/destination/helena-38574/

Trip.com. (n.d.-c). *Kalispell travel guide 2024 - things to do, what to eat & tips.* https://www.trip.com/travel-guide/destination/kalispell-38435/

Trip.com. (n.d.-d). *Miles City travel guide 2024 - things to do, what to eat & tips.* https://www.trip.com/travel-guide/destination/miles-city-38519/

Tripadvisor. (n.d.-a). *30 best places to visit in Kalispell - updated 2024 (with photos & reviews).* https://www.tripadvisor.in/Attractions-g45235-Activities-Kalispell_Montana.html

Tripadvisor. (n.d.-b). *Conrad mansion (Kalispell) - Top tips & reviews from trav-*

elers.   https://www.tripadvisor.in/Attraction_Review-g45235-d183831-Reviews-Conrad_Mansion-Kalispell_Montana.html

Tripadvisor. (n.d.-c). *Dumas Brothel Museum*. https://www.tripadvisor.in/Attraction_Review-g45106-d481535-Reviews-Dumas_Brothel_Museum-Butte_Montana.html

Tripadvisor. (n.d.-d). *Headframe Spirits*. https://www.tripadvisor.in/Attraction_Review-g45106-d3198609-Reviews-Headframe_Spirits-Butte_Montana.html

Tripadvisor. (n.d.-e). *Hockaday Museum of Art Alyssa Cordova - all you need to know before you go (with photos)*. https://www.tripadvisor.com/Attraction_Review-g45235-d183832-Reviews-Hockaday_Museum_of_Art_Alyssa_Cordova-Kalispell_Montana.html

Tripadvisor. (n.d.-f). *Hotels near Big Hole National Battlefield*. https://www.tripadvisor.com/HotelsNear-g60735-d264833-Big_Hole_National_Battlefield-Wisdom_Montana.html

Tripadvisor. (n.d.-g). *Montana forum, travel discussion for Montana*. https://www.tripadvisor.in/ShowForum-g28947-i982-Montana.html

Tripadvisor. (n.d.-h). *Nature & parks in Kalispell*. https://www.tripadvisor.com/Attractions-g45235-Activities-c57-Kalispell_Montana.html

Tripadvisor. (n.d.-i). *Northwest Montana History Museum (Kalispell) - your guide before you go (with reviews)*. https://www.tripadvisor.in/Attraction_Review-g45235-d4115451-Reviews-Northwest_Montana_History_Museum-Kalispell_Montana.html

Tripadvisor. (n.d.-j). *Plan your trip - Butte*. https://www.tripadvisor.in/Tourism-g45106-Butte_Montana-Vacations.html

Tripadvisor. (n.d.-k). *The 5 best Montana battlefields (updated 2023)*. https://www.tripadvisor.com/Attractions-g28947-Activities-c47-t4-Montana.html

Tripadvisor. (n.d.-l). *The 5 best resorts near Flathead Lake State Park, Kalispell*. https://www.tripadvisor.com/HotelsNear-g45235-d254964-zff8-Flathead_Lake_State_Park-Kalispell_Montana.html

Tripadvisor. (n.d.-m). *The 10 best Montana art galleries (updated 2023)*. https://www.tripadvisor.com/Attractions-g28947-Activities-c49-t1-Montana.html

Tripadvisor. (n.d.-n). *The 10 best Montana national parks (updated 2023)*. https://www.tripadvisor.com/Attractions-g28947-Activities-c57-t67-Montana.html

Tripadvisor. (n.d.-o). *The 10 best museums you'll want to visit in Montana (updated 2023)*. https://www.tripadvisor.com/Attractions-g28947-Activities-c49-Montana.html

Tripadvisor. (n.d.-p). *The 10 best parks & nature attractions in Whitefish.* https://www.tripadvisor.com/Attractions-g45402-Activities-c57-Whitefish_Montana.html

Tripadvisor. (n.d.-q). *The best resorts near Flathead Lake Alpine Coaster, Lakeside.* https://www.tripadvisor.in/HotelsNear-g45241-d25322400-zff8-Flathead_Lake_Alpine_Coaster-Lakeside_Montana.html

Tripadvisor. (n.d.-r). *Tips for wildlife viewing at Glacier - Glacier National Park forum.* https://www.tripadvisor.in/ShowTopic-g143026-i1168-k11036802-Tips_for_Wildlife_viewing_at_Glacier-Glacier_National_Park_Montana.html

Tripadvisor. (n.d.-s). *Traveling to Montana from VA beginning of March help! - Montana forum.* https://www.tripadvisor.in/ShowTopic-g28947-i982-k8136827-Traveling_to_Montana_from_VA_beginning_of_March_HELP-Montana.html

Tripadvisor. (n.d.-t). *Virginia City hotels and places to stay.* https://www.tripadvisor.com/Hotels-g45395-Virginia_City_Montana-Hotels.html

Tripadvisor. (n.d.-u). *Whitefish Mountain Resort - all you need to know before you go (with photos).* https://www.tripadvisor.com/Attraction_Review-g45402-d102476-Reviews-Whitefish_Mountain_Resort-Whitefish_Montana.html

Tripadvisor. (2022). *Little Bighorn Battlefield National Monument.* https://www.tripadvisor.in/Attraction_Review-g60888-d145853-Reviews-Little_Bighorn_Battlefield_National_Monument-Crow_Agency_Montana.html#/media-atf/145853/?albumid=-160&type=0&category=-160

Tripadvisor. (2023). *Woodland Water Park (Kalispell).* https://www.tripadvisor.in/Attraction_Review-g45235-d4360103-Reviews-Woodland_Water_Park-Kalispell_Montana.html

Tripadvisor. (2024). *Flathead Lake (Polson) - all you need to know before you go (with photos).* https://www.tripadvisor.in/Attraction_Review-g45310-d504495-Reviews-Flathead_Lake-Polson_Montana.html

Tripsavvy. (n.d.). *Makoshika State Park: The complete guide.* https://www.tripsavvy.com/makoshika-state-park-guide-5196683

Turner-Jamison, C. (2024). *Three Chiefs Culture Center (formerly the People's Center) - St. Ignatius, Montana.* Crown of the Continent. https://crownofthecontinent.net/entries/three-chiefs-culture-center-formerly-the-peoples-center-st-ignatius-montana/a2647872-c78f-4b5a-b8c1-2461cc69a252

Tyler, & Premier Travel Media. (2022, August 8). *Discover southeast Montana history and grandeur*. Leisure Group Travel. https://leisuregrouptravel.com/southeast-montana-is-your-trailhead-for-adventure/

U.S. Army Corps of Engineers. (n.d.). *Fort Peck Dam*. https://www.nwo.usace.army.mil/Missions/Dam-and-Lake-Projects/Missouri-River-Dams/Fort-Peck/

U.S. News & World Report. (2019, June 18). *9 best things to do in Yellowstone*. https://travel.usnews.com/Yellowstone_National_Park_WY/Things_To_Do/

University of Montana. (n.d.). *Montana museum of art and culture*. https://www.umt.edu/montana-museum/

US Climate Data. (n.d.). *Weather averages Billings, Montana*. https://www.usclimatedata.com/climate/billings/montana/united-states/usmt0031

US News. (n.d.). *Yellowstone National Park travel guide USA*. https://travel.usnews.com/Yellowstone_National_Park_WY/

USDA. (2024). *Custer Gallatin National Forest*National Forest - *about the forest*. https://www.fs.usda.gov/detail/custergallatin/about-forest/?cid=stelprdb5345849

USDA Forest Service. (2024). *Custer Gallatin National Forest - camping & cabins: campground camping*. https://www.fs.usda.gov/activity/custergallatin/recreation/camping-cabins/?recid=5566&actid=29

Vigilante Carriages. (n.d.). *Stagecoach*. https://www.vigilantecarriages.com/stagecoach-1

Virginia City Players. (n.d.). *Vaudeville - Virginia City players - United States*. https://www.virginiacityplayers.com/

Visit Big Sky. (n.d.). *Explore & discover Big Sky Montana*. https://www.visitbigsky.com/#:

Visit Southeast Montana. (n.d.-a). *History*. https://southeastmontana.com/history

Visit Southeast Montana. (n.d.-b). *Visit southeast Montana*. https://southeastmontana.com/

Visit Southeast Montana. (n.d.-c). *Stargazing*. https://southeastmontana.com/

Visit Southwest Montana. (n.d.-b). *Welcome to southwest Montana - southwest Montana tourism information*. https://southwestmt.com/

Visit Southwest Montana. (n.d.-c). *Welcome to southwest Montana - special features - wildlife viewing.* https://southwestmt.com/specialfeatures/ wildlife-viewing/#:~:text=Southwest%2520Montana

Visit the USA. (n.d.-a). *Southeast Montana: endless exploration.* https://www. visittheusa.com/experience/southeast-montana-endless-exploration

Visit the USA. (n.d.-b). *Southwest Montana: Big sky country and beyond.* https:// www.visittheusa.com/experience/southwest-montana-big-sky-country- and-beyond

Vujinovic, S. (2023, April 25). *Montana wild animals: Top 7 places to see stunning wildlife.* Southwest Journal. https://www.southwestjournal.com/us/ montana/montana-wild-animals/

Walker, N. (2023, July 21). *How deep is Flathead Lake? Discover Montana's deepest lakes.* AZ Animals. https://a-z-animals.com/blog/how-deep-is-flathead- lake-discover-montanas-deepest-lakes/

Wanderlog Staff. (n.d.). *The 35 best outdoor dining in Whitefish.* Wanderlog. https://wanderlog.com/list/geoCategory/273800/best-outdoor-dining- in-whitefish

Washoe Amusement Company. (n.d.). *About.* Washoe Theatre. http://www. washoetheatre.com/about.html

Waxman, O. B. (2023, June 25). *The true history of "Custer's Last Stand."* Time. https://time.com/6288437/custer-last-stand-history-education/

Weatherspark. (n.d.). *Miles City climate, weather by month, average temperature (Montana, United States).* https://weatherspark.com/y/3582/Average- Weather-in-Miles-City-Montana-United-States-Year-Round

Weiler, M. H. (2015, May 25). *Nat Geo staff picks: The best of Montana.* Travel. https://www.nationalgeographic.com/travel/article/nat-geo-staff-picks- the-best-of-montana

Western Regional Climate Center. (n.d.). *Western regional climate center.* https://wrcc.dri.edu/Climate/narrative_mt.php

Whitefish Chamber of Commerce. (n.d.). *Restaurants, food & beverages quick- link category.* https://www.whitefishchamber.org/list/ql/restaurants- food-beverages-22

Whitefish Gallery Nights. (2023). *Whitefish Gallery Nights.* https:// whitefishgallerynights.org/

Whitefish Montana. (n.d.). *Five winter adventures in Whitefish - Whitefish Montana lodging, dining, and official visitor information.* Explore Whitefish. https://explorewhitefish.com/entries/five-winter-adventures-in-white fish/910cd661-573f-46b2-aacd-e4202c0570c1

Whitefish Montana. (n.d.). *Whitefish travel guide - Whitefish Montana lodging, dining, and official visitor information.* https://explorewhitefish.com/guide

Wick, J. (2017, August 27). *10 amazing Montana secrets you never knew existed.* OnlyInYourState. https://www.onlyinyourstate.com/montana/amazing-secrets-mt/

Wick, J. (2018, March 2). *8 undeniable differences between the western and eastern parts of Montana.* OnlyInYourState. https://www.onlyinyourstate.com/montana/western-and-eastern-mt/

Wick, J. (2019, April 23). *Here are the best short and scenic hikes in all 50 states.* OnlyInYourState. https://www.onlyinyourstate.com/usa/usa-hikes-easy-scenic/

Wick, J. (2022, May 29). *Discover these eight charming old towns in Montana.* OnlyInYourState. https://www.onlyinyourstate.com/montana/old-towns-in-montana-mt/

Wick, J. (2023a, March 15). *The old railroad town in Montana with a sinister history that will terrify you.* OnlyInYourState. https://www.onlyinyourstate.com/montana/havre-sinister-history-mt/

Wick, J. (2023, August 7). *Here are the 15 absolute best places to visit in December across the United States.* OnlyInYourState. https://www.onlyinyourstate.com/usa/best-places-to-visit-usa-december/

Wikipedia. (2018, October 6). *Big Sky.* Wikipedia. https://en.wikipedia.org/wiki/Big_Sky

Wikipedia. (2020, April 12). *Fort Peck Indian reservation.* Wikipedia. https://en.wikipedia.org/wiki/Fort_Peck_Indian_Reservation

Wikipedia. (2023a, April 26). *List of battles fought in Montana.* Wikipedia. https://en.wikipedia.org/wiki/List_of_battles_fought_in_Montana

Wikipedia. (2023b, June 20). *Fort Union Trading Post national historic site.* Wikipedia. https://en.wikipedia.org/wiki/Fort_Union_Trading_Post_National_Historic_Site

Wikipedia. (2023c, June 22). *Battle of the Little Bighorn reenactment.* Wikipedia. https://en.wikipedia.org/wiki/Battle_of_the_Little_Bighorn_reenactment

Wikipedia. (2023d, July 27). *List of ghost towns in Montana.* Wikipedia. https://en.wikipedia.org/wiki/List_of_ghost_towns_in_Montana

Wikipedia. (2023e, August 6). *Fort Peck Theatre.* Wikipedia. https://en.wikipedia.org/wiki/Fort_Peck_Theatre

Wikipedia. (2023f, October 11). *List of museums in Montana.* Wikipedia. https://en.wikipedia.org/wiki/List_of_museums_in_Montana

Wikipedia. (2023g, October 16). *Fort Peck Lake*. Wikipedia. https://en.wiki
pedia.org/wiki/Fort_Peck_Lake

Wikipedia. (2023h, November 16). *Flathead lake*. Wikipedia. https://en.wiki
pedia.org/wiki/Flathead_Lake

Wikipedia Contributors. (2019a, April 4). *Glacier National Park (U.S.)*. Wikimedia Foundation. https://en.wikipedia.org/wiki/Glacier_National_
Park_(U.S.)

Wikipedia Contributors. (2019b, August 16). *Battle of the Big Hole*. Wikimedia
Foundation. https://en.wikipedia.org/wiki/Battle_of_the_Big_Hole

Wikipedia Contributors. (2019c, September 7). *Montana*. Wikimedia Foundation. https://en.wikipedia.org/wiki/Montana

Wikipedia Contributors. (2019d, December 18). *Charles Marion Russell*. Wikimedia Foundation. https://en.wikipedia.org/wiki/
Charles_Marion_Russell

Wikivoyage. (n.d.-a). *Billings – travel guide at wikivoyage*. Wikivoyage. https://
en.wikivoyage.org/wiki/Billings

Wikivoyage. (n.d.-b). *Butte – travel guide at wikivoyage*. Wikivoyage. https://en.
wikivoyage.org/wiki/Butte

Wikivoyage. (n.d.-c). *Miles City – travel guide at wikivoyage*. Wikivoyage.
https://en.wikivoyage.org/wiki/Miles_City

Wikivoyage. (n.d.-d). *Northwestern Montana – travel guide at wikivoyage*.
Wikivoyage. https://en.wikivoyage.org/wiki/Northwestern_Montana

Wikivoyage. (n.d.-e). *Southwest Montana – travel guide at wikivoyage*. Wikivoyage. https://en.wikivoyage.org/wiki/Southwest_Montana

World Travel Guide. (n.d.). *Montana history, language and culture*. World Travel
Guide. https://www.worldtravelguide.net/guides/north-america/united-
states-of-america/montana/history-language-culture/

Worlddata.info. (n.d.). *Climate: Montana in the United States*. Worlddata.info.
https://www.worlddata.info/america/usa/climate-montana.
php#:~:text=Montana%2520is%2520one%2520of%2520the

IMAGE REFERENCES

AAA Native Arts. (2015). Bison herd, Fort Peck Reservation [Photograph]. Internet Archive Wayback Machine. https://web.archive.org/web/20150330070214im_/http://www.aaanativearts.com/bison-herd-fort-peck-reservation.jpg

Big Sky Montana. (n.d.). *Lewis and Clark Caverns in Montana*. Retrieved June 16, 2024, from https://cdn.bigskymontananet.com/images/content/2535_Exi57_Lewis_and_Clark_Caverns_in_Montana_lg.jpg

Big Sky Montana. (n.d.). *Virginia City Ghost Town in Montana*. Retrieved June 16, 2024, from https://cdn.bigskymontananet.com/images/content/2543_k68Zk_Virginia_City_Ghost_Town_in_Montana_lg.jpg

Casey, C. (2019). *Train rails* [Image]. Pexels. https://www.pexels.com/photo/train-rails-2007135/

Ciulla, M. (2021). *A tent under the starry sky* [Image]. In *Pexels.com*. https://www.pexels.com/photo/a-tent-under-the-starry-sky-7897485/

Cristian, R. (2022). *Cowboy riding horse in village* [Image]. In *Pexels.com*. https://www.pexels.com/photo/cowboy-riding-horse-in-village-11259333/

D, V. (2019). *Bison standing on snow covered field* [Image]. In *Pexels.com*. https://www.pexels.com/photo/bison-standing-on-snow-covered-field-1752356/

Discovering Montana. (2022). Kalispell, Montana [Photograph]. Discovering Montana. https://discoveringmontana.com/wp-content/uploads/2022/02/kalispell-montana.jpg

Explore Big Sky. (n.d.). *Montage Big Sky opens doors to Montana's biggest building*. Retrieved June 16, 2024, from https://www.explorebigsky.com/montage-big-sky-opens-doors-to-montanas-biggest-building/42049

Flickr. (n.d.). Pompey's Pillar Eastern Montana [Photograph]. Retrieved June 16, 2024, from https://c1.staticflickr.com/3/2634/4185879057_a549db97f5_z.jpg

Fresh, D. (2017). Man in black jacket walking on snow [Image]. In *Pexels.com*. https://www.pexels.com/photo/man-on-black-jacket-walking-on-snow-744487/

Fruugo. (n.d.). Fort Peck Resevoir from the Pines near Fort Peck Montana

USA [Photograph]. Fruugo. Retrieved June 16, 2024, from https://img. fruugo.com/product/0/52/201253520_max.jpg

Gough, D. (2018). Water seizer [Image]. In *Pexels.com*. https://www.pexels. com/photo/water-geizer-1696474/

Gözel, B. (2022). Silhouettes of horse riders in sun [Image]. In *Pexels.com*. https://www.pexels.com/photo/silhouettes-of-horse-riders-in-sun-12513254/

Hagerman, D. (n.d.). Clark Copper King Mansion, Butte, Montana [Photograph]. Fine Art America. Retrieved June 16, 2024, from https://images. fineartamerica.com/images-medium-large-5/clark-copper-king-mansion-butte-montana-daniel-hagerman.jpg

Kudryashova, G. (2024). Rocky mountain behind wooden boat on lake [Image]. In *Pexels.com*. https://www.pexels.com/photo/rocky-mountain-behind-wooden-boat-on-lake-20291131/

Little Bighorn Reenactment Association. (n.d.). Fight in Camp. Retrieved from http://www.littlebighornreenactment.com/photos/ fight_in_camp.htm

Majchrowicz, A. (2019). *Big Hole National Battlefield, Montana*. Retrieved June 16, 2024, from https://alanmajchrowicz.com/wp-content/uploads/2019/ 01/big_hole_national_battlefield_montana_51789.jpg

Miles City Chamber of Commerce. (n.d.). Visitor Information. Retrieved from https://milescitychamber.com/visitor-information/

Montana Free Press. (2022). Bangtail Divide [Photograph]. Montana Free Press. https://montanafreepress.org/wp-content/uploads/2022/02/Bang tail_Divide_Eggert-scaled.jpeg

Montana Outdoor. (2012). Fishing at Fort Peck Reservoir [Photograph]. Montana Outdoor. https://www.montanaoutdoor.com/wp-content/ uploads/2012/05/101_0572.jpeg

Montana Survey Tool. (n.d.). *Dinosaur exhibit image*. Retrieved June 16, 2024, from http://montana-surveytoolimages.s3-website-us-west-2.amazon aws.com/general/full-size/635905468279528880.jpg

Montana Tourism. (2021). *Virginia City, Montana*. Retrieved June 16, 2024, from https://s22658.pcdn.co/wp-content/uploads/2021/07/MT-Virginia-City-Montana-Tourism-1_scaled-1.jpeg

National Park Service. (2009). *Bighorn Canyon National Recreation Area road sign*. Retrieved June 16, 2024, from https://www.nps.gov/biho/learn/ nature/images/BIHO_road_sign2_20090625.JPG

Only In Your State. (2018). Scenic view of mountains in Montana [Photograph]. Only In Your State. Retrieved June 16, 2024, from https://cdn. onlyinyourstate.com/wp-content/uploads/2018/11/ 25791201_1740805715951414_1382032745523331907_o.jpg

Outside Suburbia. (2019). Schott Whitefish Fall [Photograph]. Outside Suburbia. Retrieved June 16, 2024, from https://outsidesuburbia.com/wp-content/uploads/2019/10/Schott_Whitefish_Fall.jpg

Pinterest. (n.d.). *Depot, Nevada City Montana*. Retrieved June 16, 2024, from https://i.pinimg.com/originals/68/02/e8/ 6802e88f66909a131b013cf6b241fb34.jpg

Pininterest. (n.d.). *Helena, Montana*. Retrieved June 16, 2024, from https://i. pinimg.com/originals/b4/51/80/b45180b60cdbbd8739ee0d f84b5acb77.jpgPixabay. (2016). Wolves forest wintry [Image]. In *Pixabay.com*. https://pixabay.com/photos/wolves-forest-wintry-loneli ness-1341881/

Reflections, Gary. (2013, June 25). Battle of Little Bighorn: June 25th, 1876. Gary's Reflections. https://garysreflections.blogspot.com/2013/06/ battle-of-little-bighorn-june-25th-1876.html

Ride'm Cowboy - Miles City, MT Annual Bucking Horse Sale. (n.d.). [Pinterest pin]. Retrieved from https://www.pinterest.jp/pin/ride-m-cowboy-miles-city-mt-annual-bucking-horse-sale--82050024432635012/

State Symbols USA. (n.d.). *Montana Capitol Building in Helena*. Retrieved June 16, 2024, from https://www.statesymbolsusa.org/sites/statesymbolsusa. org/files/primary-images/MontanaCapitolHelena.jpg

Stuffed Suitcase. (2016). *Image of outdoor scenery*. Retrieved June 16, 2024, from https://stuffedsuitcase.com/wp-content/uploads/2016/09/ 13501774_837434773057819_3224520885661381624_n-1.jpg

TripAdvisor. (n.d.). *Billings, Montana Tourism*. Retrieved from https://www. tripadvisor.com/Tourism-g45086-Billings_Montana-Vacations.html

TripSavvy. (n.d.). Butte, Montana [Photograph]. Retrieved June 16, 2024, from https://www.tripsavvy.com/thmb/Ca1ITxRGUbmGmC1xL1f5g IAi0mA=/2145x1397/filters:fill(auto,1)/GettyImages-148728923- 565b7e82fbdb46c5ba1d3b96aafa07a0.jpg

TryTN. (2020). *Gates of the Mountains Canyon Photo Gallery*. Retrieved June 16, 2024, from https://media.trytn.press/gatesofthemountains/sites/13/ 2020/12/Gates-of-the-Mountains-Canyon-Photo-Gallery-5.jpg

Unusual Places. (2020). *Makoshika*. Retrieved June 16, 2024, from https:// unusualplaces.org/wp-content/uploads/2020/06/Makoshika.jpg

Wahlin, M. (2019). Photo of person skiing on snowfield [Image]. In *Pexels.com*.

https://www.pexels.com/photo/photo-of-person-skiing-on-snowfield-2433353/

Woroniecki, J. (2022). Lake McDonald MT United States [Image]. In *Pexels.com*.   https://www.pexels.com/photo/cobblestones-on-the-lakeshore-13578358/

Wyoming News. (n.d.). Montana's Crow Tribe Reenacts the Battle of the Little Bighorn. Rocket Miner. Https://www.wyomingnews.com/rocket-miner/news/national/montanas-crow-tribe-reenacts-the-battle-of-little-bighorn/article_45af996f-35f0-52d2-97b4-44452afa4946

Yahoo. (n.d.). *Helena Montana Mansion*. Retrieved June 16, 2024, from https://images.search.yahoo.com/search/images;_ylt=AwrO8KwMHW9m J6YMKXlXNyoA;_ylu=Y29sbwNncTEEcG9zAzEEdnRpZAMEc2Vj A3BpdnM-?p=helena+montana&fr2=piv-web&type=E210US1429G0& fr=mcafee#id=73&iurl=http%3A%2F%2Fww1.prweb.com%2Fprfiles% 2F2013%2F06%2F17%2F10843059%2FMansion27.jpg&action=click

Made in the USA
Columbia, SC
04 February 2025

53290788R00198